META-STATES

Mastering the Higher Levels

of Your Mind

L. Michael Hall, Ph.D.

Registered with the Register of Copyrights: United States of America
Number: **TX 4-085-549.**
ISBN: 978-189000133-9

ISBN 978-189000141-4

9 0 0 0 0

9 781890 001414

Publisher: ***NSP: Neuro-Semantic Publications***
               P.O. Box 8
               Clifton, CO. 81520 USA
               (970) 523-7877

Special thanks to:
        Cheryle Rayson (Australia):
                Meta-Coach, Real Estate Entrepreneur
        Pascal Gambardella, Ph.D. (United States)
                Neuro-Semantic NLP Trainer

        Brand Coetzee (South Africa)
                Neuro-Semantic NLP Trainer; Meta-Coach

        Steve Hodgson (Australia)
                Neuro-Semantic NLP Trainer; Meta-Coach

        Adrian Beardsley (Austrlia)
                Neuro-Semantic NLP Trainer; Meta-Coach

Neuro-Semantics® is the trademark for both the model and the International Society of Neuro-Semantics (ISNS).

www.neurosemantics.com   www.self-actualizing.org
www.meta-coaching.org   www.metacoachingfoundation.org
www.nlp-video.com

META-STATES
Mastering Your Mind's Higher Levels

PREFACE

TO THE SECOND EDITION

Bob Bodenhamer, M.Div.
November, 1999

If you would like to learn how to "run your own brain," you will love this volume. If *Neuro-Linguistic Programming* (NLP), General Semantics, and the Cognitive Sciences fascinate you, then *Meta-States* by L. Michael Hall will empower you. What I mean by this is that in *the Meta-States Model,* Dr. Hall synthesizes these and other models into a model of models—a model that describes what makes the other models work. And, he does this in such a way that you can understand it, try it on, experience it, and make it a part of your every day life.

I got involved in studying NLP in 1989. In 1990, I made it the major focus of my work and study. The model absolutely fascinated me. Over the next five or six years I found myself getting bored as I "thought" I knew everything that there was to know about NLP (of course, I didn't really). Then I met Michael Hall. And, what a difference he has made in my life. He ever so gently introduced me to his Meta-States Model as we worked together in developing new materials for our joint works.

As time progressed, I realized that we were on to something big, real big. The time required for me to get changes in my therapy clients was drastically reduced. Now, realizing that as a rule, NLP works quite fast already, this both amazed me and convinced me of the efficacy of Meta-States. I began to pour through the first edition of this book that Michael published in 1995, *Meta-States: A Domain of Logical Levels.* I did not waste my time. *Meta-States* has revolutionized my NLP training courses, my therapy work, my ministry, and my writing. I can't imagine teaching NLP without the Meta-States model. Why? Simple. *Meta-States explains what works in NLP, what doesn't work, and how to determine the meta-level or meta-state that makes the difference.*

Michael has now completely re-written the earlier editions. This edition has the accumulated knowledge and experiences of the last five years from his trainings, consultations, research, feedback, etc. And what a volume he has produced! This edition greatly expands the Meta-States Model. You will also find this volume much more readable as it has been prepared it for a much wider audience.

Enough singing the book's praises. I would run out of adjectives if I sought to do that. What can you expect to find within these pages? Lots of things, from theory to application.

If this has stirred up your interest, then take this volume, head off to a quiet place, and begin a journey such as you have never traveled before. You will visit places in that wonderful mind of yours that you did not even know existed. You will discover *powers* of choice that you never dreamed of. I believe that when you will finish this volume, you will be saying, "It has been good." And, I predict, that you will pick it up many times as you mine the treasures contained herein.

Recommendations

Wyatt Woodsmall, Ph.D.
"The *International NLP Trainers Association* (INLPTA) awards Michael Hall for his development of the Meta-States Model, for the most significant contribution to NLP, 1995."

Graham Dawes, Ph.D.
"The Meta-States Model could end up becoming known as the model that ate NLP." Review of *Dragon Slaying*, Rapport, 1997

Bobby G. Bodenhamer, D.Min.
"Michael has completely revised the original book to make this work most readable. I recommend two or more readings of this work to every serious student of NLP to *install* this model if you want to advance your neuro-linguistic and neuro-semantic and make them more elegant."

John Burton, Ed.D.
"*Meta-States* provides a clear and useful presentation of insights into human nature and how to promote change."

Dennis Chong, M.D.
"In the search for meaning, the study of semantics, and the field of Neuro-Semantics, Michael Hall's *Meta-States* is a most significant and critical contribution . . . In my view, *Meta-States* is a book that is best to be a standard for every medical student, student of psychology, philosophy student and their respective professional graduates."

Omar Salom, Psychologist, Executive Coach
"This is fantastic, well-grounded in research, and rich and coherent theoretically. I definitely think that *Meta-States* training represents a breakthrough in psychology."

Larry Dawalt, Sports Writer
"*Meta-States* helps a person to bring it all together. There's a difference between knowing *what* to do to make your life un-stoppable and knowing *how* to do it. Meta-States provides the skills to implement a strategy for becoming un-stoppable and helps you take steps immediately to get you moving."

PREFACE

The book you are now holding in your hands is a brand new and completely revised version of the original book, *Meta-States*. It was the original version of that book which launched a whole new approach to NLP and eventually gave birth to the field of Neuro-Semantics. In these pages I tell the story of finding and constructing the Meta-States model while simultaneously present the theoretical frameworks of the model.

I rushed to write the first version within a 6 weeks period excited by a wild rush of ideas that were popping and busting and exploding in my mind. In the five years that followed, research and experience enabled me to find four major mistakes in that book. So in the second edition I focused on correcting those errors to present a more consistent model of how our self-reflexive consciousness works to create states and states-about-states.

Another eight years have now passed and with it much more experience with the model and our expansion of its benefits. As *the Meta-States model* is now maturing, and as tens of thousands of people have now been trained and certified in using this model, it has become a tool for so many things:

- For *personal development*—as you access the prerequisite states of mind and emotion necessary to develop personal mastery and expertise in a given area.
- For *self-actualization*—as you set meta-states which enable you to step in and out of a state of "flow" and turn these on and off a "peak experience" at will.
- For *modeling expertise* and expert performances— as you identify the critical frames of mind that facilitate a specific excellence.
- For *accelerating learning and transformation*—as you can quickly get to the leverage frames that make the difference. As a result, this has led to all of *the frame game* books for winning

the inner game in numerous areas— being fit and slim, creating wealth, leadership, management, mastery fear, entrepreneurship, business mastery, etc.

If you are more interested in a simplified version of the Meta-States model, there are several books written precisely for that purpose. The easiest one to read is *Winning the Inner Game* (2006). This was formally published under the title of *Frame Games* (2000). In that book, states are presented as our "games"—the things we say and do to achieve our various objectives. And meta-states are our frames —our frames of mind which contain all of our rules for the game.

The next easiest to read is *The Secrets of Personal Mastery* (1999) which presents the Meta-States model using the language of personal development. After that is *Dragon Slaying* (1996, 2000) which uses meta-states for a therapeutic transformation.

My design in this third edition is to take you on a journey to the theoretical background, understandings, and constructions of the Meta-States model itself. My aim here is to more fully locate *Meta-States* in the field of the cognitive-behavioral sciences as it establishes the emergent field of *Neuro-Semantics*. Here we will probe the historical roots of *Meta-States* in the writings of Alfred Korzybski and Gregory Bateson and other pioneer thinkers in the field of cognitive and meta-cognitive psychology.

In most of what follows I assume that you have at least a basic understanding of Neuro-Linguistic Programming. If not, I recommend any of the following introductory books to NLP:

> *Introducing NLP* by Joseph O'Connor and John Seymour.
> *The Sourcebook of Magic*, Volume I by L. Michael Hall.
> *Using Your Brain—for A Change* by Richard Bandler.
> *MovieMind: Directing your Mental Cinemas* by Michael Hall

Meta-States is not just a model about how you think, feel, relate, act, and speak, it is also *a different way of thinking* about the way you function as a human being. Understanding your own meta-states within this model of self-reflexive consciousness is to enter into a non-linear way of thinking and feeling, and to go for a ride. That's because your self-reflexive consciousness goes round and round in circles, it spirals up and it spirals down. And often you can get lost in your own thoughts and hardly know which way is up.

If you find that happening as you read this book it is because you are using your reflexivity to understand your reflexivity. If so, then just raise your hands over your head, let out a good yell, and enjoy the ride as you go round and round and sometimes loop back upon yourself! I say *enjoy the ride* because if you stay with it, you will learn how to ride the energy of your own spiraling and when that happens, you'll be able to manage your own states and your own self-actualization in ways that you now consider unimaginable. And you will be able to more effectively communicate and work with others.

Learning the ins and outs of your meta-state reflexivity will make you a better leader, manager, coach, parent, and partner. It will enable you to be able to see into the very structure of experience and to model peak performances. It will enable you to more fully understand the higher levels of your mind that are typically outside of conscious awareness. And it will empower you to take charge of the higher functions of your creative mind to actualize your highest and best.

It's an exciting journey and I'm delighted that you have decided to begin your own exploration.

To your highest and best!

L. Michael Hall
Colorado Rocky Mountains
May, 2008

PART I

META-STATES

DISCOVERY

Chapter 1

THE AHA! MOMENT

"The self-reflexiveness of language
and the human nervous system makes possible
both our noblest and most destructive potentials."
Kenneth G. Johnson

I did not find meta-states, meta-states found me. In the adventure of discovering the levels of states-about-states that govern every facet of our lives, I did not set out to discover or create anything. Truth be told, I was minding my own business when the discovery grabbed me and sent me spinning up through a tornado of spiraling thoughts. It was not all that dissimilar to Dorothy's tornado that took her to Oz. I also landed in a place beyond the rainbow — in meta-land where I was surrounded by new and strange entities.

Does that mean the discovery happened quite by accident? Yes, definitely, by accident! It also happened at a time when I was fully engaged in finishing my doctorate in cognitive psychology. Yet it happened. And discovering the *Meta-States Model* felt as if I had stumbled upon a treasure of diamonds. It completely surprised and delighted me as I hope it will you.

What I realized is that that we humans not only experience mind-body states of consciousness, but that we also experience *states about our states,* and then states-about-those-states, and then additional states, and so on repeatedly. When I first discovered this, I felt a tremendous rush of excitement and an amazement of incredulity.

The *excitement* arose because by naming and describing the structure of our layered states of mind and emotion, I knew that this would allow us to more explicitly detect and manage the higher states that we experience. I immediately realized that those states which have always seemed far too abstract and complex, far too layered with dozens of thoughts-and-feelings for description, were suddenly open for description. And that would make them more manageable, easier to understand, simpler to explain, and perhaps most important, easier to replicate.

I knew that with *the Meta-States Model* I could now talk about them more clearly and succinctly. Meta-States would enable all of us to recognize and talk about our layered states when we feel—

- Impatient about our anger
- Frustrated with our hesitation
- Ashamed of fear
- Joyful about discovering new things
- Excited about developing confidence
- And many, many more.

I was also excited because the model provided a new and powerful format for bringing to the light of day some of the incredible discoveries in Alfred Korzybski's classic *Science and Sanity*, e.g., the Levels of Abstraction and his Theory of Multi-Ordinality. I knew that the powerful and incredible tools in General Semantics could now be stated in a much more accessible form.

The amazing incredulity that I felt arose because I wondered how was it possible that so many theorists, scholars, and psychologists had not developed a model of reflexivity even though they had alluded to it. Korzybski, Bateson, Viktor Frankl, and many others had danced around the edges of *reflexivity* which is at the heart of Meta-States. Yet while they danced around this mechanism they did not set forth the structure and mechanisms that govern *self-reflexivity in human consciousness,* and so were not able to access more of the secrets of the higher levels of our mind.

I found that strange and surprising. I also found it exciting. In many ways, it still surprises me. And yet I feel lucky that my research and experiences brought me to the place of that discovery. I don't think that it took any particular brilliance, just patience and patients, of which I had plenty of both as I launched my search into the layers of our states-about-states.

I had clients (patients) because at the time I had both a private psychotherapy practice as a LPC (Licensed Professional Counselor) in Colorado and a Communication Training Center. I also had patience because I was living in a small city on the western slopes of the Rocky Mountains where life moved slowly. So with a small business that moved at a rate much slower than what I'm used to these days, I had an abundance of time for experimenting with my clients, writing about my discoveries, making some hypotheses, and testing them.

As I had refined my skills in cognitive psychology (Rational Emotive Therapy, RET), Transactional Analysis (TA), and Neuro-Linguistic Programming (NLP) by testing patterns and processes with my clients, I began testing the meta-state principles and processes. And it was in the everyday application of *meta-stating* clients that they taught me what worked and what did not, how to make the model explicit as I tried to explain it to them in everyday language, and how to use these layered states as frames to solve life's everyday problems.

Many times during private consultations or in demonstrations before groups, the person with whom I was working would stop me and ask if they could try out a procedure. Or the person would want to change the process in a particular way.

> "Would it be alright if I just *blank out* my old belief about criticism being terrible? That would help me to feel that this new idea about 'criticism is just feedback' is more real."

Going along with their emergent ideas and creativity taught me a lot. I can't tell you how many times I thought, "That's a great idea! Why didn't I think of that?" And, encouraging their creativity led to more creativity in both of us.

> "Of course you can do that! You can do anything that empowers you in running your own brain and taking charge of your life."

Discovering *Meta-States* has completely changed my life both personally and professionally. Personally it has enabled me to take charge in meta-stating my own levels of awareness and texturing my states so that they enhance the quality of my everyday life. I have learned to dance with my own dragons to put a stop order to any and all of the negative meta-states that I had unwittingly created. I learned also how to manage the layers of states so that I can now step into a "flow" state at will. The state of being "in the zone" is now at my command, and I can tell you—it's a great resource.

Professionally it created a life revolution. Obviously, I certainly had no idea where *Meta-States* would lead me. If you had told me it would lead me to write book after book about it, more than an hundred patterns would emerge from it, and would give birth first to the *Meta-States Journal* and then to the field of *Neuro-Semantics*® itself, I would have said you're dreaming.

If you had told me there would be a website of more than 4,000 pages, some would mind-map the Meta-States books, others would incorporate Meta-States in their communications, modeling, therapy, sports psychology, etc., people would come together to create an association of the Society of Neuro-Semantics, others would set up Institutes of Neuro-Semantics, and we would create an international community, I would have probably dismissed all of that as wild exaggerations. If you had told me that I would close my private practice and begin training internationally, I would have dismissed it as being overly optimistic. Yet all of that happened, and that was just the beginning.

The NLP Connection
I developed the Meta-States Model as a certified NLP Trainer, running a NLP Training Center. Since then Meta-States has launched a movement and field of Neuro-Semantics. That means lots of people encounter and learn Meta-States without any knowledge or background in NLP. So today I am often asked, "How does Meta-States relate to NLP?" There are several answers to this.

First, *the Meta-States Model is a model of NLP.* Recognized as early as late 1994 by Dr. Wyatt Woodsmall of the International Association of NLP Trainers (IANLPT), Meta-States was designated the "most significant contribution to NLP in 1995." So on one level, it is a model of NLP. And as such, it is a model that subsumes all of the higher level human phenomena that we call "beliefs, values, understanding, frames-of-references, referential domains, paradigms, identity, mission, meaning, spirituality, core states," and much more.

Many people in NLP have discovered that *the Meta-States model* provides a way to more fully map the conceptual or neuro-semantic states which enables us to pull off the magic in NLP. This includes the concepts of time (e.g., time-lines), meaning (e.g., reframing), identity (e.g., re-imprinting), purpose, ecology, etc.

First and foremost *Meta-States represents a way to encode and describe the meta function in human cognition and emoting.* And because it does, it provides a fuller description of the entire NLP model. Since the first *Meta-States* book was published, the Meta-States model has become the fourth meta-domain in NLP. Prior to this, there were three meta-domains.

1) The first meta-domain—*The Meta-Model* of language.
> This is the domain and model which launched NLP in the first place as a meta-discipline. Using transformational grammar, Bandler and Grinder modeled the language patterns which Virginia Satir and Fritz Perls used to perform their "magic" in personality transformations.

2) The second meta-domain— *Meta-Programs.*
> This domain of perceptual filters and cognitive sorting arose when Leslie Cameron-Bandler discovered instances when various patterns broke down and failed to work. This allowed her to discover hidden higher "programs" that were interfering with the processes and preventing them from working.

3) The third meta-domain—Pragmagraphics or Sub-Modalities.
> This domain is a level above our sensory representations and serves as our editorial level. At this level we change, alter, and edit the cinematic features of our mental movies. This enables us to create a good deal of the magic of change that NLP is renown for.

The Meta-States model supplements these meta-domains and offers a fourth avenue to model and understand the structure of subjective experience. Each domain speaks about the same thing—*human experience* which we create via our thinking-and-emoting. When I fully recognized this, I put together what, at the time I called, *The Three Meta-Domains Model.* That was before I realized that the domain of "sub-modalities" were not "sub" at all, but *meta,* that is, higher to the representations.[1]

I recognized that the cinematic features of our sensory representations ("sub-modalities") actually operate at a higher level to our representations. That's because we have to step back from them to even recognize that we have these qualities and features in our representations. So putting them together, I created a systemic portrait of human personality using all of these meta-domains of NLP.

All of this then led to the creation of a new format for NLP—which Bob Bodenhamer and I decided to call *Meta-NLP.* Then, in trademarking that term, we used it to refer to Neuro-Semantic NLP. You can find a full description of this in the books that we co-wrote: *User's Manual of the Brain, Volumes I and II,* and *Sub-Modalities Going Meta.*

Beyond NLP
A second answer to the question about the relationship between NLP and Meta-States is that *Meta-States is not restrained by the boundaries of NLP.* During the 1990s, as it continued to grow and develop, Meta-States gave birth to a new field, Neuro-Semantics. What I discovered during that time was that Meta-States also describes the meaning-making and meaning-formatting processes of our mind-body. That led to the *frame games* approach which launched the whole games books and trainings.[2]

And that's how it began
After Meta-States found me, it has not left me alone. Having now lived with the idea of our self-reflexive consciousness and the layering of our mental-emotional states since 1994, every year sees new extensions and new applications of the model. Welcome to the adventure.

End Notes:

1. See the book, *Sub-Modalities Going Meta* (2005).

2. *Winning the Inner Game* was the first book. From that work came *Games Fit and Slim People Play, Games for Mastering Fear, Games Business Experts Play, Games Great Lovers Play, etc., In the Zone* (2007, Cooper and Goodenough).

Chapter 2

DISCOVERING

META-STATES

"Man is his own greatest mystery. . . .
He comprehends but little of his organic processes
and even less of his unique capacity
to perceive the world about him,
to reason, and to dream.
Least of all does he understand his nobles and most mysterious faculty:
the ability to transcend himself and perceive himself in the act of perception."
Lincoln Barnett
The Universe and Dr. Einstein (1950)

The discovery of Meta-States began with an exploration of resilience—*resilience,* the ability to bounce back when you are knocked down. I became interested in resilience for several reasons. My work at that time as a psychotherapist specifically involved empowering people who felt dis-empowered so that they could become more resilient. Week by week I would facilitate therapeutic conversations to help people develop the skill of bouncing back from set-backs. For some this involved bouncing back from significant distresses and major traumatic events. For others it involved bouncing back from a critical comment, a disapproving look, the loss of a sale— things that didn't seem to be that much of a setback, but which had somehow knocked the life and spirit out of a person.

At the same time I was conducting extensive trainings for practitioner certification in NLP. Here too resilience played a significant role, making or breaking a person's ability to develop competence as a professional communicator. I began to realize that people needed a significant amount of *bounce back power* to sustain them in the process of learning a discipline. Without resilience, many would start the training and then quickly throw up their hands and quit if the learning didn't come easy, if they felt awkward or stupid in the process, or if it didn't immediately create great success in their lives. Sometimes the smallest of set-backs would "blow them away." This seemed so unproductive to the results they would receive if they just stayed with the process.

"What gives? Do they have no strategy for coping?" I also became interested in those whom we can only describe as being *super resilient*. I'm speaking of those incredible "survivors" who came through war, rape, abuse, physical handicaps, etc. with a never-say-die spirit. They seemed to verge on the super-human in their ability to bounce back while others were completely stopped. These people seemed absolutely *unstoppable*. On a personal level, I wanted that kind of unstop-ability. This led to reflections about my own strategy of resilience. "How robust is my own resilience?" So I decided to enrich it with what I was finding so that I would give away less and less of my power to external events.

- What drives this spirit of resilience?
- How did the super-resilient build up this kind of attitude or program inside their minds-and-hearts?
- What is the structure of resilience?

As I researched resilience, I read multiple books and articles that addressed this special magical quality of resilience for endowing a person with the power to bounce back from defeats. I brought to my readings and explorations the tools and models of NLP to understand in greater depth how some people would not allow a disappointment or a rejection to take the wind out of their sails.

From this study I wrote a proposal to present a workshop at the NLP Conference in Denver on *The Resilience Strategy*. At the time I assumed that resilience was a simple state of consciousness. So naturally, I began gathering information about the components of that state. Then utilizing the two royal roads to state (mind and body), I focused first on all of the internal representations by which we encode information, and second, our use of body or physiology. With that I began exploring the component pieces making up the empowering resilience phenomenon.

Eventually, I had a general sense of what resilience involved in terms of thoughts, beliefs, values, understandings, attitudes, emotions, etc. With that I felt that I had enough to create a state of resilience. So I began looking around for people who had that quality. To confirm the research, I wanted to model those who had a robust resilience strategy. My intent was to then compare what they had to what the research showed.

- How do the highly resilient do it?
- What did they say to themselves? In what tonality?
- What kind of pictures do they create that put them into a state of mind where they can bounce back from a set-back?
- What cinematic qualities do they endow their pictures with?
- What do they believe about set-backs, upsets, and failures?
- How do they cope and master crises?
- What thinking patterns do they use?
- How do they think about, and use, their emotions?

To find such individuals I began making presentations on resilience around town and whenever possible I would do a demonstration. at the time I was conducting workshops on Communication Enrichment, NLP Introductions, Coaching, and Leadership. In demonstrations, I would elicit the referent experience that people used when they thought about resilience.

> Have you ever suffered a defeat or set-back, but then somehow found the required internal or external resources and bounced back from it? What was it like when you were un-resilient? What enabled you to bounce back? What stages did you go through as you moved back to a state of feeling resilient? What was the process of resilience like for you? What resource management did you use to support your resilience?

I would then contrast the person's memories or experiences of non-resilience with the factors that made them resilient. I then invited the rest of the participants to do the same.

> Think about a time when you experienced some defeat, some
> discouraging experience, something that knocked the wind out
> of your sail . . . but only temporarily. At a later time, you
> bounced back. You staged a come-back. You got up, dusted
> off your clothes, targeted your desired outcome again and *went
> for it—again!*

After modeling the resilience of numerous people and synthesizing
what I had learned, my next step was to see if I could transfer the
strategy. Could I help several clients replicate the resilience strategy
so that they could reproduce and experience it within their own lives?
That would be the test. Would the resilience strategy work in those
who needed it most? What shifts and changes would be required for
them to adopt the resilient strategy as their own? What change
processes would best enable someone to take it on?

By the spring of 1994 I wrote up a proposal for a workshop at the NLP
Conference. *Resilience: The Power to Go For It— Again!* Yet when
September came, I had actually become less and less sure in my
understanding of resilience. An apprehensiveness began to gnaw away
in the back of my mind.

> "There's something more here than just a linear strategy that
> creates this state of resilience. There's something very
> important that's missing. But what?"

To think through things, I sat down to diagram all the variant facets in
the resilience strategy that I had discovered from the research,
interviews, and experiences with clients. As I listened to the interviews
and to the therapeutic processes for installing the resilience strategy in
people, something kept nagging at me. It was like the tip-of-the-tongue
phenomenon when you know a name or term, and feel that its on the
tip of your tongue, but you still cannot articulate it.

With the feeling that something was missing I went to the Conference
in Denver to make a three-hour presentation. And that's when Meta-
States found me. After an introduction into the need for resilience, I
overviewed the steps and stages of the strategy. The strategy followed
how a person moves from suffering a set-back or being knocked down,
regains a sense of equilibrium, copes with the losses or challenges of
the set-back, comes to terms with the turbulent emotions, and then

regains enough vision, hope, courage, and boldness, etc., for returning to life with a vibrant and robust attitude.

I called for someone in the audience.

> "Who here has been to hell and back? Who here has been through a life-and-death challenging event, got knocked down, flat on your face, and yet today, you are back?"

Several raised their hands and after asking a little about each to get a sense of the experiences people were ready to share, I chose a gentleman who said that he had lost his business and his family, but was "now back into the magic that life holds for us all."

In the process of interviewing him to identify the natural steps and stages of resilience, he began speaking about shifting from one stage to another. So I asked him,

> "How did you know to move from that stage to this next one? What let you know you could do that?"

He looked up and thought about it for a moment and then said,

> "I knew I would come through it all, I knew it was just a stage that I had to go through."

So I again asked,

> "And how did you know that? What enabled you to have that conviction and realization?"

He said,

> "Well, it's like a larger state, a bigger awareness about the other states."

Then one of us, and to this day I don't know if it was him or me, but one of us said, "Like a meta-state."

While I do not know who used that terminology, I know that those words set my brain buzzing and whizzing away with ideas connecting so many of the things I had been reading. In those moments, months of contemplations came together, all rushing in at the same time. *"Aha! That's it!"* I said quietly inside my mind knowing that something was coming together for the first time. I was finding words for that inarticulate tip-of-the-mind phenomenon that had been torturing me. With that I began seeing meta-levels in my mind—states *about* states, meta-frames governing meta-functions, spiraling whirlwinds of states moving upward.

Now the Denver Conference was 300 miles to the east of my home in western Colorado. I had driven there with two friends. So as we drove home I talked their ears off as I rattled on and on about meta-states. They asked a great many challenging questions. All of this tremendously helped me to clarify the entangling thoughts and ideas that were still spinning around inside my head.

I then realized something critically important. *There is a meta-function within our brains that enable us to circle an idea, to buzz around it with other thoughts and feelings.* It is this circling, spiraling, and spinning around which builds up to more permanent thought structures that we experiences as our "beliefs" and "attitudes."

The very idea of a larger idea, a more comprehensive awareness, that has embedded inside it other thoughts means that the higher thought, the higher feeling *holds* the lower ones together, giving them structure, substance, and coherence. That means that the higher idea of "getting through it all" in the resilience strategy holds all of the thoughts and beliefs at each stage, and at the same time provides a higher level category of thought-and-feeling—what I would later identify as "an attractor frame."

And all of this explains why we can hold an idea in mind and carry it with us for years, for decades, even for a lifetime. It explains how that idea can operate as *a self-organizing frame of meaning* bringing order and coherence to every aspect of our lives. And all of this also witnesses to the systemic nature of mind, that is, mind operating at various levels and interacting with itself at those levels. This describes how we frequently loop back to a thought, a feeling, a memory, a fear, an imagination, etc. and then move above it, so to speak, and set a whole frame-of-reference of a larger concept or category about it.

> ** **Meta** **
>
> Higher
> above
> beyond
> about
>
> A meta-state is a state above a primary state, it is about that state.

Meta—Ah that was the magical word. Because we

can think *about* our thinking, think *about* our feelings, feel *about* our thoughts, use our physiology *in reference* to other thoughts or feelings— this whole maze of thoughts-feelings-and-physiology (the very components of our states) enable us to create all kinds and degrees of complexities in our states.

So in a *meta-state* we move up a level to our second conclusions, and then to our third generalizations, to our fourth classifications, to our fifth categorizing, and so on. With each *meta-move* of our self-reflexive consciousness, we build more complex and abstract concepts about our previous thoughts-and-feelings.

No wonder then, that in the resilience strategy, *there are meta-responses that a person makes to his or her own meta-responses.* In working with these spiraling thoughts and layers of feelings, I began wondering,

> "How can we chart this kind of a dynamic structure? How can we follow the line of reasoning, to the flow of our consciousness as it not only goes out linearly, but reflects back on itself and can do so repeatedly, layer upon layer?"

With these questions and explorations, it began to dawn on me ever so slowly that not only does resilience contain numerous pieces in a step by step linear fashion, it also involves ideas and feelings on top of each other. Some of the component elements of resilience operate as one state layered upon other state. And, of course, that initiated even more questions.

- Does a linear process of thinking-and-emoting accurately describe this or do I really need to develop a way to track the circular and systemic thinking that creates layers upon layers?

- Is the strategy made up of a series of states or are there states-upon-states involved? If so, what are these higher states? How do they work? How does a primary state differ from a meta-state?

- Is there a difference between a state and a strategy? Does resilience function more as a strategy or a state?

- Are these different? If so, how? Is there something that

transcends state and strategy?

That's how it all began. Years of reading and writing articles about the classic text of Korzybski (*Science and Sanity*, 1933), from doing the same with Bateson (*Steps to an Ecology of Mind*, 1972), from research into paradox, self-reference, meta-cognition, and systems suddenly came together in a rush of thoughts, images, and metaphors. This then enabled me to articulate a model about the self-reflexive nature of human consciousness—the Meta-States Model.

During the week after returning home from the Denver Conference, I crafted a 40-page document on "Meta-States as a New Model," a model about logical levels and self-reflexivity. Three weeks later I sent the manuscript to Dr. Wyatt Woodsmall for his evaluation. Little did I know at that time that some years later I would read his endnotes at the back of his monogram on Meta-Programs and see that he had lists of possible meta-programs, and that among them was "states: regular, meta."

Soon after sending the manuscript, Dr. Woodsmall contacted me to let me know that the manuscript on the Meta-States Model would be recognized by the International Association of NLP Trainers as "the most significant contribution to the field of NLP" in 1995.

And so the Discovery Began
Thomas Kunn in his classic work, *The Structure of Scientific Revolutions* (1962) notes that new models arise over a period of time because the current model cannot handle the incongruencies and other difficulties. As the current model becomes less and less capable of handling new details, questions, and problems, it gives way to a new paradigm.

So it was with Meta-States. As I spent three years on one problem (experiencing a set-back) and attempting to model the solution (the resilience strategy), I discovered that the state of resilience was much more complex than I ever imaged. I also discovered that the linear modeling process of NLP Strategies could not adequately map the process because the role of a person's self-reflexive consciousness had not been taken into account. This made possible the construction of the Meta-States Model.

Chapter 3

TRANSCENDING

STRATEGY AND STATE

"Man not only knows about his environment,
he knows that he knows; he is aware of his awareness;
he reacts not only to his environment, but to his own reactions.
His language is similarly self-reflexive. ..."
Kenneth G. Johnson

Having discovered *the idea of reflexivity in a state-upon-state structure* in the experience of resilience, I was on my way. Now I realized that in detailing the strategy of an experience, I would not only map its steps and stages, but I could also map its meta-levels, the layering of the mind with multiple thoughts-and-feelings occurring simultaneously. And with that I began an exciting exploration of defining and describing Meta-States as a model and how to use the model to map the structure of subjective experiences.

Is it a Strategy or State?
The very first question I felt I had to solve was whether a complex experience like resilience was a state or a strategy? Or perhaps it was both? Yet if so, how could it be both at the same time? And how could I map that simultaneality? In fact, at that point in my development, I felt torn about whether I should think and treat resilience as *a state* that a person could elicit, induce, amplify, and anchor or as *a strategy* that one could elicit, rehearse, streamline, install and use. Which model enables us to map out the experience more

effectively?

In some ways the subjective experience of resilience seemed like a holistic mind-body *state* rather than a linear strategy. Yet in other ways it seemed more like a linear step-by-step *strategy*. Which format best describes resilience? As I began to wonder about this dichotomy between state and strategy, I was forced back to explore yet another question:

- What is the difference between these two processes anyway?
- How does strategy and state relate to each other?

Given the number of component pieces which seemed essential to the structure of resilience and its power in human personality, I boiled the data I had found down to five key component pieces. I took these pieces as those "necessary and sufficient" for a person to experience *resilience*. For resilience, a person would have to have all of these:

1) Self-esteem:
> A sense of being centered in your own values and dignity, centered to such an extent that you would have nothing to prove, but everything to express.

2) Meaningful vision:
> A strong and compelling vision of an attractive future that you find highly meaningful and personally significant. The strength of the vision as a life-dream then shows up in the motivation it creates.

3) Robust meaning constructions:
> An explanatory style characterized by what Seligman called "optimism," so that when something unpleasant, challenging, or stressful happens, you explain it as "this, here, now" (or, "that there then"), rather than "me, everything, forever" (personal, pervasive, permanent).[1]

4) Masterful coping skills:
> A response style of bouncing back from defeats and set-backs, a refusal to stay down, a strong sense of self or ego-strength for handling the problems of life, resource management for handling emotions, the courage to face up to the challenges, problem-solving skills, etc.

5) Meta-perspective:
> A meta-awareness of the big picture giving you a sense of

perspective of where you are in the process, and a sense of direction.

With these as the essential elements of the strategy of resilience, I next sought to put them together in a strategy format. In NLP, this means putting them together using the TOTE model. Originally from George Miller, Eugene Gallanter, and Karl Pribram, the TOTE model stands for a structural format known as Test, Operate, Test, Exit.[2]

TOTE is a model that began the process of tracking consciousness in the "black box" of human mind. We process information by *testing* a goal against criteria, *operating* to change either, *testing* again to see if we have created a difference, *re-processing* by repeating the test-operate phrase if inadequate, and *exiting* if sufficient.

TOTE

Test
Operate
Test
Exit

TOTE as a model works like a flow chart of consciousness. When Dilts, Bandler, Cameron-Bandler, Grinder, and DeLozier (1980) enriched it with NLP representational systems, they created the NLP-enriched TOTE model which then became the fundamental strategy model in NLP for modeling expertise. It provides an excellent format for simple things like spelling and motivating oneself to get out of bed in the morning. However, for experiences involving multiple and complex states over a time frame beyond just a few second or minutes, it is quite inadequate and typically just does not work.

When I tried to force resilience into the strategy format, I attempted to get the resilience stages into representational steps that would sequentially elicit one state and then the next. This turned out to be very stilted. Resilience was suffering on the Procrustean strategy bed of NLP. There was something more dynamic, systemic, and circular at work in resilience.

What was it about the resilience strategy that didn't seem to fit? Clearly, at least two of the pieces involved a dynamic layering structure, a state-about-a-state. The meta-awareness of resilient people meant that they had, as a part of their strategy, the ability to continually track where they stood in the process in reference to their own unique big picture. In the bouncing-back process, their thinking-and-feeling did not just go out in a linear sequential way; first this, then that, etc. It simultaneously was looping back onto itself, and doing so about all five component pieces.

> "This is not going to defeat me. I may have to grieve this loss or deal with this other unpleasant thing for awhile, but this will not last. It's only a step in the process of recovery. And at the same time, this isn't about me as a person anyway, it's about the experience that I've been through, something external to my inner self, and it won't last forever, just for a certain time frame, and besides there are lots of other things of value and pleasure in life right now that I can focus on. And I'm excited about that, because it fits into the larger vision, this has just been one step back, now I'm ready for two steps forward . . ."

Within the consciousness of resilience, we are not only aware of what's happening in our world, we are also aware at higher levels. So we experience meta-cognition, meta-awareness, and meta-communication with ourselves. And this kind of reflexive awareness sends our brains upward to higher levels of beliefs, values, intentions, decisions, imaginations, hopes, dreams and back onto itself creating an ever-more robust sense of self. And all of this occurs simultaneously while we move through the stages of coping, problem-solving, developing and using resources, and mastering the set-back.

It was becoming obvious to me that what we call resilience involves much more than the linear strategy work that I had come to think about in NLP modeling. Now it is true that the original developers (1980) put a *meta-response* in the original strategy model. Yet they treated the "going meta" response in the diagrams and descriptions in the first volume of *Neuro-linguistic Programming* as just another linear step.

> "Now say these words about that feeling."
> "Next, feel this about that picture."

As I got a sense of the complex systemic richness of resilience, I felt that the old linear NLP strategy process was far too thin and shallow. It was not able to model the complexity of the experience of resilience. That's what got me questioning the state/strategy difference.

What Distinguishes Strategies and States Anyway?

The majority of strategies described in *NLP Volume I* describe linear, sequential, and horizontal processes. Far from being a negative thing, this is actually one of the strengths of strategies as a formula for mapping human subjectivity. The strategy approach greatly contributes to modeling subjective experiences by providing a language and format of experiences. In strategy analysis we use the representational language of the sensory systems (visual, auditory, kinesthetic) and the meta-representation system of language (A_d —auditory digital, that is, words and language). This greatly enriched the original test-operate-test-exit model by Miller, Gallanter, and Pribram.

In its time, the TOTE model was revolutionary. In the 1960s it helped to defeat classical Behaviorism and launch the Cognitive Psychology Movement. This test-operate-test-exit model provided a basic flow chart for tracking responses in the human system of mind and body. This was unheard of prior to its introduction. Miller *et al.* introduced it to track *the flow of information* through a system which Behaviorists had dismissed for decades as a "black box" preventing us from being able to peek inside. Consequently, TOTE greatly enriched the S—>R (Stimulus Response) model of Behaviorism.

NLP enriched that modeling further as it used the language of representations to serve as the "languages" of the mind. It then added a set of response sequences to assist a skilled modeler in tracking where a person's brain-neurology goes in responding to something and how it responds (e.g., congruently, incongruently, or as a polarity or meta response). And it structured all of this in a step-by-step manner. This kind of modeling enabled the co-founders of NLP to more fully replicate both expertise of geniuses and creative pathology of neurotics.

After several years of modeling with the Strategy Model, Bandler and Grinder commissioned Robert Dilts to put all of their distinctions together in what became the first official and formal work on modeling. We know this today as *the Strategy Model*—a model for eliciting and unpacking strategies, designing and installing strategies, and utilizing strategies (1980, *NLP Volume I,* pp. 26-38).

Now within strategy analysis, we sometimes find that a person may *loop around a set of distinctions* until he or she reaches a threshold.

This means the person is running a test-operate procedure over and over until something changes. At that point, the strategy propels the person into a place of reaching a decision point (success in achieving a change, no success) and then exiting the program.

Strategy analysis also enables us to take into account the synesthesias that run within the response-process. That is, we can identify where a see-feel (V-K) or hear-feel (A-K) or feel-hear (K-A), etc. circuit may occur in a strategy. Further, by practicing, rehearsing, anchoring, and using various technologies we can streamline a strategy so that its beginning point quickly elicits the whole process and puts one into the end experience (i.e., motivation, confidence, decisiveness, etc.) as if a single response to a single stimuli. When this happens we can quickly, automatically, and immediately go into a state.

> *A strategy is the step by step description of how we create a state.*

Ah, state. Is this the answer? Yes, of course! *A strategy is the step by step description of how we create a state.* What we call a *state*—a mind-body-emotion state, is the result of a particular strategy. It is the result of how we have "thought" and "felt" about something as we have responded to it. And that means there's always a strategy for accessing and eliciting a state. State follows strategy. State follows the NLP Representational Strategy.

Strategy's Left Brain Approach
Using this NLP model about strategies, we can now identify and unpack the structure of an experience and get, as it were, its recipe. Strategies identify how we take the component pieces of the sensory modalities or representations, various syntax orders, and varying amounts of sub-modality qualities to create an "experience." And then from this process, we get a holistic mind-body state.

Strategy describes the basic NLP model by which we can map, describe, conceptualize, and work with human experiences. It arises as part and parcel of the NLP Communication Model. As we use the "languages" of the mind—visual images for picturing, auditory sounds and sound-track for hearing, and kinesthetic sensations for internally and externally feeling, and language for classifying and categorizing meanings. Then as we communicate these things to ourselves, we create our experiences. We create our states of consciousness—our mind-body-emotional states.

This means that in the strategies model *we have a left-brain approach* to experience. It formats our experiences using a linear, sequential, and horizontal description. In this way strategies operate as a recipe or a blueprint whereby we can articulate a step-by-step procedure for modeling an experience. You can see that strategies presuppose a sequentially linear model in the following quotation:

> "A strategy is the basic unit of analysis of a particular TOTE, or set of TOTEs. Strategy analysis breaks a TOTE down into its representational components and describes the order of the particular representational activity that leads to specific behavioral outcome." (1980, Dilts, p. 38)

Strategies then operate as—

> ". . . formal descriptions of what a person does in his/her head and nervous system in terms of representations that generates specific behaviors, skills, responses, and states."

A strategy can be very simple. *See* item on shelf in grocery store and *feel* strong compulsion to buy. The visual representational activity of seeing (V) leads to or causes the kinesthetic representations or feelings (K) where one might say to him or herself, "I have to have that!" (words, A_d). This gives us the strategy for impulsive buying.

States' Right Brain Approach

By way of contrast, the language and conception of states is more right-brain. A mind-body state, which is an emotional state, refers to a dynamic and holistic experience. In a state, thoughts and feelings come together to create an overall gestalt which we experience as a mood or attitude. By *state* we refer to a larger phenomenon and do not deal with the small sensory bites of representations. So while *NLP Volume I* primarily deals with strategies, we can still discover a good bit of material about states in that volume because strategies contain states and meta-states.[3]

By developing a strategy, we can elicit and create a desired state. This means that a strategy gives us a way to get into a specific state. Yet when we repeatedly do so, the strategy will inevitably become streamlined through repetition so that we can then access a state within a second. As a strategy streamlines, we lose awareness of the internal steps and all of the thoughts-and-feelings that make up the strategy. It becomes automatic. As the strategy streamlines it often becomes anchored to a word, image, sound, or sensation so that a simple stimulus can now trigger it. And in this, the strategy operates as if it were a state.

The general process for accessing, eliciting, or evoking a state in NLP involves one of three basic inductions:
> 1) *Memory: Think about a time when . . .*
> 2) *Imagination: What would it be like if . . .*
> 3) *Modeling: Do you know anyone who . . .?*

> "Think of a situation in which you expressed yourself with what you regard as a fine representation of your full capabilities as an adult human being . . . " (Bandler and Grinder, 1979, p. 111).
> "Go back and recall a memory of something exquisitely pleasurable, exciting, and humorous from your past, and see what you saw at the time that it occurred. Now as you find that memory, turn up the brightness a little . . . "

Or to use another classification, we have *two royal roads to state*. First, *mind*. We can induce a state by accessing, remembering, or altering our sensory representations and words. We can also simply invent, create, or pretend to imagine what such an experience would look, sound, or feel like. Whether remembered or imagined, these comprise the human internal representations.

Second, *body*. We can induce a state by using the various facets of our physiology, namely our posture, breathing, muscles, facial expressions, etc. to act out and thereby demonstrate the movements of a state. Doing this is the essence of coaching the body to feel and express a mind-body-emotion state. That is, as we say in Meta-Coaching, *we can coach the body into the state.*
> "Show me the breath of calmness."
> "With your posture, show me what confidence looks like."

"Give me the eyes of compassion."
"Look around the room with the face and eyes of intentionality."

Upon accessing a state, we can then link a sensory or linguistic representation to it. Almost anything will do. Any sight, sound, or sensation, any image, word, or emblem. And when we do, the link to the state becomes a cue or anchor. And with the link, we can now re-cue or "anchor" the state. This enables us to step back into that state at the snap of a finger.

In NLP, anchoring is a central technology of Pavlovian conditioning that enables us to move an experience around in time and space. By anchoring a mind-body state, we can induce ourselves, or another, into an experience and then work with it as a state of consciousness. In contrast to strategy work, when we work with state inductions, we do not work with the subjective experience sequentially, but holistically.[4]

Transcending Strategies and States

Having sorted out that strategy describes the processes, formula, as well as the ingredients of states, and that states represent a different way to map experience than strategies, I was able to answer the original question, "What's the difference between strategies and states?"

Mapping things with the strategy model and with the mind-body state model cover a tremendous range of human experiences. Yet they do not cover everything. Some experiences demand yet another kind of analysis—one that combines and synergizes strategies and states, so that we can go beyond them , or perhaps I should say, *above* them.

We need a model that not only handles experiences sequentially and holistically, but one that handles complex experiences involving one or more levels. We need a model that takes into account *logical levels, reflexive consciousness, recursiveness, systemic thinking, the gestalting of experiences, and the layering of responses.*

This brought me to the place where I was ready to entertain some new and fascinating questions.
•   What is a meta-state?
•   What are the component elements within it?

- How does a primary state differ from a meta-state?
- How are strategies and meta-states related?
- How would a model that maps out the structure of meta-states operate?

Stepping Up to a Higher Level

When I began considering the need for a meta-level model, one way I challenged myself involved trying to write out the strategy formula sequentially for a complete state like the following.

> "Sometimes I get really upset when John doesn't come through with what he said he will do, and I feel like yelling at him. But then I feel really bad for my ugly angry thoughts about John. I feel like I'm a really bad mother. I wonder if I can parent at all. So I start to feel guilty. But with the counseling I've had, I feel ashamed that I've fallen back into the old guilt habit, and know that I'm going to be stuck in this dysfunctional way for the rest of my life. That makes me feel really depressed, so I go to the kitchen and eat."

Figure 3:1

$$A_d \text{-}^\rightarrow K^e_m - \text{}^\rightarrow K^- - \text{meta} - \text{}^\rightarrow K^- \text{-meta} - \text{}^\rightarrow A_d - K^- - A_d - \text{meta} - \text{}^\rightarrow K^- \longrightarrow$$
Exit

Words — External Emotions	Internal Emotions	Internal Emotions	Words about Feelings	Negative Words Feelings about	Negative Feelings
Feel upset & angry *at* John's failure to come through	Feel like yelling at and thoughts and behavior of John.	Feel bad @ ugly angry wonder if I can parent	Feel like a bad mother know I'm stuck & dysfunctional for rest of life.	Feel ashamed In old guilt habit	

[The at-sign (@) is here used to designate the meta-relationship, read it as standing for the word "about."]

Yet when I attempted to track all the representational steps as the strategy plays out in the state, I realized that it would be important to identify several things. First, to identify the states of mind and emotion involved. *It would also be important to map out the meta-relationship between various thoughts, feelings, and states.* This is precisely what makes the traditional NLP strategy analysis awkward and clumsy.

In this example, the speaker continuously jumps logical levels in her thinking and feeling as she creates layers of embedded thoughts-and-feelings (or states) about previous thoughts-and-feelings. Not only does she experience various states, *but she accesses states that reference other states.* And as she does, the overall experience or state becomes richer, fuller, and more textured.

Figure 3:Mapping the Meta-Levels in a Strategy
[P-S stands for primary state, M-S stands for meta-state, and the at-sign (@) stands for the word "about."]

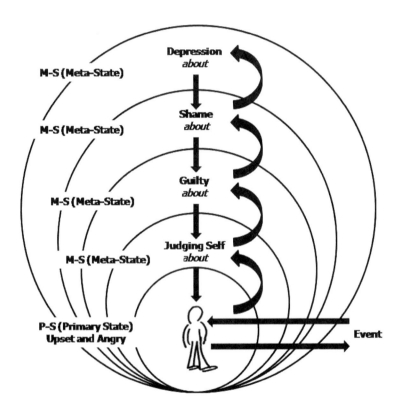

We can certainly track all the representations and put them into linear steps, and can even identify all the mind-body states elicited, as indicated in Figure 3:1. Yet this strategy analysis inadequately deals with the multiple logical levels involved, the reflexivity, and the mental-and-emotional looping that occurs.

In this example, the lady begins with *an anger state*. Then, in reference to that state, she went into *the state of self-judgment* ("bad" for ugly angry thoughts, "bad mother," questions parenting ability). About her self-judgment state, she then *felt guilty*. And about the guilt state about her self-judgment state about her anger state she accessed *a state of shame*. And about the shame state she went into a *depressed state*.

To track and analyze this multi-layered state of consciousness wherein her self-reflexive consciousness kept recursively looping back onto itself, we need a model that distinguishes levels and simultaneously provides an overview of the states-about-other states. This is what the Meta-States Model provides — it gives us a way to identify, distinguish, and separate levels. It enables us to recognize *the kind and quality of states* applied to other states. It also enables us to track the thoughts around the inner communication circuits over time as the mind-body system spins around.

Transcending to Include
This is the first Meta-State distinction— the difference between strategy and state. It is the difference that shifts us from linear, left-brain processing to a more holistic and right-brain process.

If the Strategy Model gives us the ability to track our sequential thinking, then *Meta-States as a model enables us to track all of the thinking in the back of the mind about our sequential thinking*. It enables us to take all of the higher levels of consciousness into account as our internal frames of reference. And because these are the thoughts that we "hold in mind," and have at ready access as we move through the world, these are the thoughts, emotions, beliefs, decisions, intentions and so on that make us who we are and give us our interpretative frames by which we make sense of reality.

We *transcend* each state to another state and then *include* it within the higher state. This is the *meta-function* that Bateson spoke about —the mental operator that creates a meta-relationship between the two states with one state operating as the *frame of reference*, or the mental context, for the other state. As one state is now in a position of being "about the other state, it operates as its mental context as its category or classification.

Summary

* As the distinction between strategy and state becomes clear in the Meta-States model where we combine left and right brain processing. Strategy provides description of experience from a left-brain point of view—of the stages and steps that enables us to create the experience. State describes the experience from a more right-brain perspective as it presents the experience as a whole.

* The Meta-States model transcends these two descriptions of experience and introduces a new distinction, that of meta-states which are states-about-states and hence the higher internal context for a state and for a strategy.

* In these ways, the Meta-States Model integrates and synthesizes *strategies* and *states* so that we have a more holistic, dynamic, and meta-level process for modeling the best and worst of human experiences.

End Notes

1. Martin Seligman, *Learned Helplessness* (1975), *Learning Optimism* (1990).

2. George Miller, Eugene Gallanter, Karl Pribram, *The Structure of Behavior* (1960).

3. *NLP Volume I,* 1980, pp. 129-133, 141 the relaxation state, pp. 138-9 the uptime and downtime state, p. 145 anchoring states.

4. Anchoring operates as a key factor in NLP, for more about anchoring see *Frogs Into Princes*, 1979: p. 84; *User's Manual for the Brain, Volume I,* and/or *Sourcebook of Magic*.

Chapter 4

INTRODUCING RESILIENCE

AS A META-STATE

The Meta-State that Began it All

G iven that I discovered the Meta-States model while modeling resilience, the next two chapters presents information about the structure of resilience. As you discover the inside story of this resourceful state, you will learn about the complexity of its structure. In this chapter we will explore resilience as a complex state regarding *its contents* (the specific thoughts and emotions that make up resilience) and in the next chapter *its structure* (the specific meta-state structure). In this way you will get an inside look at how resilience emerges through multiple layers of meta-states and how the meta-stating process gives rise to the gestalt experience of resilience. This requires two new distinctions—*meta-stating as a process and gestalt states.*

First, the meta-stating process is the process of applying one state to another. Meta-States are created by accessing a thought or feeling as a state of consciousness and applying it to another state. For example, if you access a state of joy or fun or playfulness and apply it to learning, you create the meta-state of *joyful learning*. You no longer have a primary state, you have a state of learning embedded within the higher frame of joy which powerfully influences the quality of your primary state.

Second, by meta-stating repeatedly something new emerges out of the systemic process, something that is "more than the sum of all of the parts"—which is what the term *gestalt* means. So, for example, suppose you meta-state the fear with a sense of care and love for your children (1). And what if you meta-state that state with a sense of responsibility for your children (2), and then meta-state that with moral accountability (3). If you do that and then discover your house on fire, you gather everyone and run out. Yet what if at that point you discover that one of your children is still in the house, the complex layers of your meta-states will give rise to something that cannot be explained by simply adding up all of the individual thoughts and feelings. Your layered states of love, responsibility, and moral accountability will drive you to run back into the house to save your child. From the outside, observers will call this "courage." But from the inside, you feel something other than courage. You will say, "I just had to, I had no other choice, my child was in that house."

In this example, *courage is a gestalt state*. It arises as an emergent state from the systemic nature of all of these states-upon-states. If we ask, "What makes up the content and structure of courage?" We can identify the various states, and yet when they all come together into the particular mix, they create a state that's "more than the sum of the parts." In Meta-States, we call this *a gestalt state*.

The Art of Staging a Come Back
• 	When a disappointment knocks you down, how much *bounce* do you have within you?
• 	How quickly can you bounce back?
• 	What does it feel like to stage a come back?
• 	Where in your body do you experience resilience?
• 	What resources do you use to evoke a resilient spirit?
• 	What higher frames of mind establish an even greater sense of resilience in you?

Resilience, as a high level state, is loaded with some of the most powerful, most robust, and profound frames of mind imaginable. Having resilience built into your higher mind empowers you to boldly seize opportunities and to go after your dreams. Without resilience, you cower, hesitate, vacillate, and give in to fear so you don't fully commit yourself to your dreams.

So what is resilience? It is the ability to keep bouncing back from set-backs. It is the ability to get back up when you've been knocked down, and "go for it" again. While this sounds simple enough, it actually comprises a complex layering of multiple meta-states. We engineer it into our mind-and-emotions by layering several states-about-states so that the gestalt of resilience emerges.

Because of this, there is no one right way to construct this executive program. As we here explore many of the facets commonly found in resilient people, you have the opportunity to custom design this vigorous state for yourself. To do that, keep asking yourself the following questions:
• What resources do I need to stage a come back?
• What linguistic frames best express resilience?
• What frames of mind will I need for resilience?
• What do I need to believe to believe in these resources?

When you meta-state yourself to unleash resilience, you build within yourself the ability to bounce back from falls, misfortunes, and set-backs. Key to your personalized development of resilience will be the specific resourceful states and frames that evoke this experience in you. As you identify those that you want and the syntax that activates the magic for you, then you will be able to apply the basic meta-state format for constructing your own individualized resilience strategy.

The Feel of Resilience
What does it feel like to bounce back after a fall, mistake, failure, rejection, divorce, firing, etc.? What is the feel of the state for bouncing back when life has tripped you? In resilience, you keep coming back to your dreams, hopes, decisions, commitments, etc. You refuse to be kept down.
• Are you quick in springing back from a set-back?
• How skillful are you in accessing a resilient attitude?
• What ingredients enable you to "jump back, recoil, sally, and withstand shock without permanent damage?"

In a world where things can go wrong, and do go wrong, where hurtful behaviors and experiences occur, and where mental and emotional shocks do occur, resilience is not only a tremendous resource, it is an absolutely necessary one.

Figure 4:1
Resilience

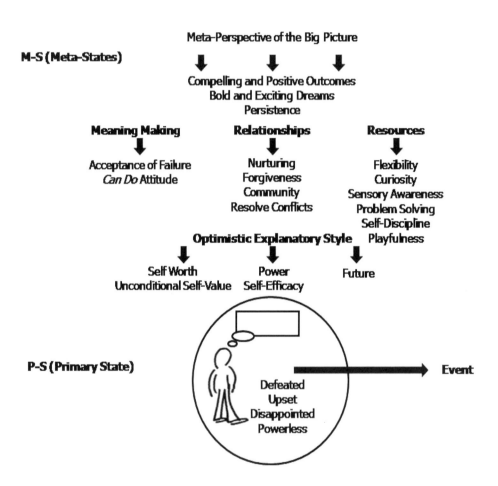

The Danger of Non-Resilience

Harry Overstreet (1954) equates the lack of resilience with the lack of resources in a context of danger.

> "A lack of resilience can best be understood as a lack of anything *to be resilient with* [a lack of resources]. Where there is no margin for error, error is total disaster; loss is total loss."

When you are resourceless, you are fragile. Without resilience you can easily get hurt, unnecessarily suffer defeat, and color the world as cold and brutal.

How does non-resilience manifest itself? It shows up in scores of unresourceful states—grudge-holding, non-forgiveness, a bitter attitude, a shame-based identity, the domination of negative emotions, etc. Yet the tragedy of the non-resilient is not only their lack of recovery power, it is also how they live. The non-resilient move through life defensively expecting hurt, retreating into self-pity, exploding in hostility, reacting with over-sensitivity, projecting onto others, being resentful and argumentative, etc. Defining themselves as victims, they expect bad things to happen, they feel insecure in themselves, and so they constantly make ploys for others to rescue them.

What must they be thinking? What ideas, beliefs, and notions generate those kind of responses? Among their thoughts are numerous limiting maps:
*   Getting hurt is the worst thing in the world.
*   Rejection is a terrible and horrible thing!
*   It would be the end of my world to be rejected, mocked, scorned, embarrassed, etc.
*   I want what I want *now*! Why should I have to wait?
*   Skills, knowledge, position, etc. should just naturally and spontaneously come to me. I should not have to work for it.
*   I'm damaged goods.
*   My past determines my future.

Precisely because the non-resilient give their personal power away by these limiting beliefs, they think of themselves as weak and incapable, as victims, broken, fragile, and lacking the innate strengths from which to forge courage. Of course, the real problem is these frames position them as choiceless as they play the victim game.

Resilience as a Multiple Layered Perspective
Resilience involves a higher state of mind about all of the ups-and-downs, demands, challenges, set-backs, struggles, learnings, etc. of everyday life. This resilience mind-set is a perspective of abundance; it is the attitude that you have the resources necessary to take on the

challenges of the day.   Again, Overstreet (1954):

> "Emotional resilience in a person is a sign of that person's having within himself *emotional resources* that are more than barely enough to get by with. Such an individual is like the man with talents to spare: he can afford to invest his interest, energy, and affection in the world around him; for even if he suffers a rebuff here and a loss there, he can still dig down into himself and find resources with which to stage a comeback. He has accordingly an access to the riches of human experience that is denied to the emotionally impoverished person. Being able to afford failure, he can constantly replenish his resources and add to them, as well as use them, so that life becomes richer and richer the longer he lives." (p. 97)

Physiological Resilience

Physically, our survival depends on the body's internal restorative powers. Life continues, not because we avoid all danger, but because of the resilience factor. *We have internal processes that are constantly righting what goes wrong.* This inner healing constantly propels the process of recuperation and ongoing renewal.

I became aware of this firsthand some years ago. It actually occurred during the time when I was first modeling resilience.   I was demolishing the inside walls of a room to create a much larger office space. While I was attempting to pull down some of the ceiling beams, I pulled a large two-by-six toward myself (yes, what was I thinking?) and, of course, it ended up smacking me in the face with tremendous force. *Pow!* The force of the blow was, in fact, severe. It crushed my glasses into my face, bruising my right eye and cutting into the skin. Literally within two minutes, the right side of my face began swelling.

I went to the bathroom to stop the bleeding and to examine the cut to see if I needed stitches. As I was cleaning the wound a realization smacked me in the mind. The insight was not that I should leave remodeling to the experts, although that might have been a good one! I realized that all I could actually do to heal myself was to provide the conditions to facilitate my body's natural restorative forces. As I saw the deep gash in my face, I realized, "My body knows how to heal itself." I only needed to stop the damage, prevent things from getting worse, and let the natural restorative forces do their job. In fact, those healing forces were already at work, and within a few weeks, it was replacing the old with new skin. My body has its own resilience forces. I can trust my body's resilience.

As a healthy body has this recuperative ability, so does a healthy personality, and so does a healthy mind and healthy emotions. *Resilience of the personality describes the ongoing ability of the mind and spirit to recover its health and well-being for a vitality of one's spirit.* We have recuperative powers within mind and spirit as well as within our body to recover our passion and vitality in living.

Given that you live in a world where hurtful things happen, you maintain mental and emotional health, not by avoiding dangers, but *by strengthening your recuperation powers*—your resilience. These recuperative powers give you both the freedom and the ability to become totally involved in the dangerous business of living fully and courageously. So in living, you don't need to seek to avoid getting hurt or risking at all costs; rather you only need to seek to take wise risks and trust your inner resilience if you fall down. Resilience frees you from living overly-cautious or fearfully timid. It frees you to take risks, and to sally out on adventures.

The Stages of Resilience
The strategy of becoming resilient with a great sense of *bounce* inside follows the following five stages.
1) The Set-Back
First something happens that knocks you down, that sets you back financially, physically, in a relationship, business, career, etc. You experience the triggering event that you evaluate as negative, hurtful, and undesired. It is an event that creates a sense of loss, disruption, stress, etc.

2) Hell: The Emotional Roller Coaster
If the set-back is a surprise, you will feel shock and may go through the five-stage grief process of shock, bargaining, anger, depression, and acceptance as detailed by Elizabeth Kubler-Ross. You will experience an emotional up and down about the set back, accepting/ rejecting.

3) Coping
This stage involves everything that's involved in trying to cope with

things. Here you begin to cope with the facts of life after the set-back. Here you focus of getting through it all, surviving, and putting your world back together. This stage may begin in the first hour of the set-back or it may wait for days, weeks, even months or years. Here you cope by the internal and external actions that you take to address the set-back. You begin gathering up resources–internal ones and external ones.

4) Mastering

If your coping works and you succeed in putting your world back together, getting your feet back on the ground, and dealing with the set-back or loss, then you move beyond merely surviving to mastering the events and situation of life. In the mastery stage you clean out the hurt, forgive, reclaim your vision or build a new one, renew your sense of power and energy, get back your passion to dream again, and forge ahead.

5) Recovery or Come-Back

The final stage is the stage of recovery. Here you are at the place where you can boldly say, "I'm back!" "I'm back in the game of life and am delighted to be back and to give myself to life and to love."

Summary

- Resilience is not a simple or primary state, it involves many layers of thoughts and feelings which make up beliefs, decisions, understanding, concepts, abstractions, etc. These make up the internal frames of mind that we typically call an attitude.

- To create the mental attitude of a resilient frame of mind we will have to meta-state many facets of self, our resources, our relationships to others, our sense of time, etc. When we do this sufficiently, a gestalt state of resilience will emerge as a complex meta-state.

Chapter 5

META-STATE STRUCTURE

OF RESILIENCE

It is higher-ordered awareness
that makes infinite change possible.

In the last chapter I introduced resilience as a meta-state by inviting
you into the process of examining it as a state and meta-state.
Resilience is simultaneously a state, a frame of mind, a disposition
of attitude, as well as a way of operating in the world. And for
resilience to emerge there has to be multiple belief frames within belief
frames.

Emerging as a gestalt meta-state from a set-back, defeat, or upset,
resilience starts with the primary experience of a disappointment,
frustration, or set-back. At the primary level there is an experience of
an event or situation as a set-back to your goals and hopes. You
experience a defeat of some sort and along with it appropriate negative
feelings of disappointment, upset, anger, frustraton, disillusionment,
sadness, etc.

From this initial experience you could go into many other states. If you
use a pessimistic explanatory style about the occurrence of "bad"

things, you would use your circumstances to feel defeated, frustrated, angry, fearful, self-contempt, guilt, and so on. And while you could go there, that would not support your resilience. So what does?

- What responses do lead to the state of resilience?
- What states do you need to access about the defeat so that you can bounce back effectively?
- What are the stages within the experience of resilience?

The Meta-Levels of Resilience

As a complex meta-state, *resilience has multiple levels.* There is first of all the primary level where you experience your first thoughts-feelings and reactions to some adversity, challenge, or painful event. Then there are the meta-levels of beliefs, understandings, feelings, meanings, etc. that qualify and texture the state you're in as you handle the ups-and-downs of life.

At the primary state of resilience, there is a set-back, defeat, upset, or some other undesirable outcome. In the primary state, some event has set you back from reaching your goals or dreams and you evaluate that situation as a defeat. You feel disappointed, frustrated, fearful, angry, confused, or other typical negative emotion and reactions.

The meta-levels of resilience involve all the ways that you respond to the primary experience of a set-back. If you use a pessimistic explanatory style you frame the circumstances in a way that leads to feeling defeated, even destroyed. You then engage in self-contempting and other diminishing states. Given that you don't want to go there, what are the meta-states that would enable you to be highly resilient in the face of challenges and adversities?

- *Optimistic explanatory style* to have a way of thinking and meaning-making that supports a life-enhancing style of life.
- *Unconditional self-esteem* to posit your value and worth as a human being as a given, and not as something outside of you. This empowers you to not personalize the hurt or bring the evil inside. The set-back has nothing to do with *you* as a valuable, lovable, and worthwhile human being.
- *Self-efficacy* to trust yourself to be able to live vibrantly in the future.
- *Meaning-making power* to create high quality and robust meanings for how to live with purpose and value.

- *Rapport* with others to get people on board as part of your support group to lift you up and to be there for you.
- *Ego-strength* as a resource to take the event as a problem to solve.
- *Self-discipline* to get yourself to do what's necessary as you face the challenges of getting up, coping with life, and rebuilding your vision.
- *Courage* to face the difficulties without giving in to fearfulness.
- *Self-confidence* to have the necessary resources and skills to cope with things.
- *Reflective mindfulness* to respond rather than merely react.
- Passion purpose to enable you to commit yourself to following your visions and values.
- *Playfulness* to not take yourself so seriously.
- *Relaxed alertness* to calmly face life and keep presence of mind.

Assuming that if these are the key meta-states required for a vital state of resilience, let's explore what they are and how to use them for creating the complex meta-states of resilience.

1) *An Optimistic Explanatory Style*

First and foremost, you will need an optimistic explanatory style. When bad things happen and you are knocked down—when you don't get the raise, your mate leaves, you suffer an accident, the business goes bankrupt, someone is raped, mugged, or shot, someone is taken hostage, someone in a car accident loses a leg, another goes to prison, etc. you definitely need a way to interpret things so that you can stay resilient in the face of such painful events.

In a nana-second after an unpleasant event occurs *you create or entertain an explanation regarding why those events occurred and what they mean to you and to your future.* This typically occurs so quickly that you are likely to assume that the negative interpretations are inherent in the event. In fact, you may actually believe that the event *makes* you think and feel as you do. Yet it does not.

What creates your thoughts and feelings is how you evaluate things —your style and way of explaining things. If you experience negative thought and feelings, it is your *explanatory style* that creates your experience. Your explanatory style determines whether you immediately access resilience or undermine and sabotage it. Given that, let's explore your explanatory style.

- How do you explain misfortunes, defeats, failures, and other bad things when they occur in your life?
- How do you mentally represent and frame set backs?
- What meaning do you set about the causation, nature, endurance and significance of these things?

How you explain things determines your resultant emotions, states, and responses. Your explanatory style determines how you feel, what you do, and the world that you live in. Your explanatory style is that crucial.

As a semantic-class of life, you inevitably seek to understand things, to search for causes, to grasp the nature of things, their significance, etc. Problems arise with this when you jump to conclusions; when you rashly create irrational, unrealistic, and distorted explanations. When these explanations become *your style of processing and framing* the events, you then use them as your perceptual prison for seeing the world.

Figure 5:1

Why did this happen?	Purpose / Design; Good / Bad
Why did this happen to me?	Bad / Inadequate / Test
What is the source of this?	Personal / External Interactional / Other contributing factors
How long will this last?	Permanent / Temporary
How significant is this?	Pervasive / Contextual
How do you **judge** this?	Horrible / Curable

The Contrast: A Pessimistic Explanatory Style

In his classic research, Martin Seligman (1975) described the *pessimistic explanatory style* as an interpretative style that ends in learned helplessness. Learned helplessness is why the set of meanings that you create frame the problem as *permanent* in time, *pervasive* in space, and *personal* in source. These three words begin with the letter "p" for a memorable format.

Three P-s	**How to P on Yourself**
The Set-Back is:	*This Means that the Problem is:*
Permanent in time—>	unchangeable, insurmountable, insoluble.
Pervasive in space—>	effects everything and undermines every facet of life.
Personal in source—>	internal, with my self, I'm inadequate, flawed, bad.

If you use the pessimistic style, you will feel inadequate, deficient, selfish, mean, criminal, etc. Add all of these together and you have an exquisite formula for dis-empowerment. This encoding creates a program for becoming depressed, passive, and suicidal. It is the inner framing for the Victim Game that will lock you into an unchangeable past.

Explaining Set-Backs Optimistically

Conversely, use *the optimistic explanatory style* and you will develop an entirely different focus. This will frame the experience in such a way as to shift from the Victim Game to the Resilience Game. What are the rules of this game? Interpret the event as *temporary* in time so that it is about a particular moment (then); *specific* in space as a particular referent event (that), and *external* in source (there). Explaining things in this way keeps the problem outside and prevents it from entering your inner world. This will give you distance from the problem, preventing you from personalizing it.   This frames the problem as in the environment and as a behavior or response, and not as an ontological problem of yourself.

Figure 5:2

The Set-Back is:	*This Means that the Problem is:*
External in source—>	*There:* It is in the environment, behavior, response, etc.
Specific in space —>	*That* particular person or event
Temporary in time—>	*Then:* at a particular moment or time-frame

Now you have three magical words to keep the evil away from you, three words to prevent it from entering inside you: *that there then*. Three **T**-s standing in contrast to the three **P**-s, formulates an optimistic attitude. And if the problem is current, then the three magic words become: *this here now*.

This optimistic explanatory style prevents the over-generalizing from negative events so that you do not darken your vision of the future. These framing distinctions enables you to recognize that what happened occurred (or is occuring) at a specific time, in a specific situation, involving specific people, etc. As a result, *this indexing* contains the "evil" so that it does not spill over onto other things or onto you. As a result, you can just perceive your situation and maintain your resources to cope with it. Then, with the presence of mind to stay objective and clear, you can take a proactive stance. You can think through the problem, discover what specifically went wrong, maintain a learning orientation**,** and use non-success as feedback for designing a smarter next response.

People who use the pessimistic explanatory style do not fare well. When misfortune happens, they send disastrous signals to their brain and their nervous system. The three P's message orders their neurology to treat the hurt as —

Personal	— I "am" the problem; it "is" me	Worthless
Permanent	— The problem will last forever	Hopeless
Pervasive	— The problem undermines everything	Helpless

2) Robust Meaning-Making

The principle here is that when adversity comes your way, take care how you language it and yourself. Your *explanations* will either empower or dis-empower you. It is not adversity that makes you angry, upset, or sad; it is *your explanation*. By staying mentally alert, positive, and objective during adversity you can mindfully avoid the pessimistic frames. That will save you from personalizing the adversity. Many, if not most, events do not revolve around you anyway. You're just not that important(!). You do not even have to read your behaviors as reflecting on you *as a person* as much as about your state, situation, body, history, culture, etc.

Personalizing adversity is what induces the states that prevent learning from it. Personalizing prevents you from using the experience as information. No wonder you lose "presence of mind" in times of stress and distress.

Conversely, thinking systemically in terms of the circles of causation and multiple contributing factors in explaining things enables you to think in terms of the interactive processes which feed-back recursively onto itself so that it influences itself. Every influence in a system operates as both cause and effect. In a feedback loop, linear causal attributions inevitably lead to inadequate explanations.

Because cause-effect processes within a system do not work directly or immediately, their connections are subtle and indirect. This makes the processes more difficult to detect. Short-term perceiving creates a blinding effect to the long-term processes which involve delay. Thinking systemically means looking for structures and patterns that work over time.

Suppose a person goes through some hell-of-an experience, some highly traumatic, unacceptable, and cruel experience (a war, a rape, a molestation, etc.). Suppose the person then constructs a map that explains the horror as personal, permanent, and pervasive. When this becomes that person's explanatory style, it traps him or her within an extremely limiting mental map for thinking about, explaining, and responding to defeats and problems. Over time this "terrible knowledge" then enters the person's neurology. Then the person will just "know" that the world is unsafe, lurks with evil, full of hurtful people, lacks predictability, and that he or she lacks any power to do anything.

And, of course, as this "terrible knowledge" becomes deeply installed in thinking, perceiving, feeling, and internal experiencing as pessimism, negativism, cynicism, etc., it makes both the idea of change as well as the experience of change much more difficult.

How does a person remap such a pessimistic state? The first step: *Recognize that the heart of the problem is the explanatory style itself.* The problem is not you as a map-maker, the problem is the mapping. As you do this, outframe the situation to separate person from behavior. "It's just a way of perceiving. It's just a map." What I say to clients is:

> "Given all of the trauma, disaster, evil, horror, etc. that you've been through, it makes perfect sense that you look for such, expect such, and interpret things in terms of such."

I say that because it is critical to recognize *maps as maps* or frames —*as constructs of the mind*. What you think about reality and how you represent it is only a neurological, psychological, and linguistic representation of the territory. It is a map of the territory, but not the territory. It is confusing the two that launches the damage of personalizing.

The second step: *Recognize that perceptions are fallible and changeable*. This recognition will free you to evaluate them more easily and objectively. Then if you find that they do not work for you in creating more enhancing experiences, you can change them. Your situation is now solvable. While you may not be able to change *what* happened to you, you can always change *how you think about it and how you remember it*.

This cognitive approach has been around for thousand of years. In the first century, the apostle Paul wrote, "Be transformed by the renewing of our mind." A little latter, Roman philosopher and emperor Marcus Aurelius wrote:

> "Men are not disturbed by things, but by their views and judgments of those things."

Resilience emerges when you remap your frames to build an optimistic explanatory style. Once you find these empowering meanings, you will be able to take effective action to make things different.

By contrast, the frames of the non-resilient create the suffering. They map themselves into corners with limiting ideas, beliefs, and decisions. To make things even worse, they then become wedded to these limiting mental maps. They suffer from mapping problems which leave them without hope, chance, or motivation.

> "I have lost all faith in . . . "
> "I just don't see any hope in . . . "
> "I can't get over . . . "
> "It's just too much, too hard, too . . . to deal with."

"It's just too shameful . . . "

There are many ways to frame yourself into a corner that prevents resilience. The cognitive distortions of Rational Emotive Therapy (RET) describe miserable ways to map yourself into a corner. Laura M. Markowitz (1991) describes one of these:

> "Resilience to trauma may also be traced to an inability to compartmentalize certain experiences that don't fit into our comfortable worldviews. Instead of saying, 'Airplanes are unsafe,' Most *over-generalizes* [a mapping distortion] and says, 'I'm not safe anywhere,' and decides the whole world is filled with danger." (p. 31)

If you can compartmentalize the experience, you can say, "Wow, that was a close call." When you do that you thereby limit the sense of danger to a particular flight.

> "Many people are unable to compartmentalize in this way. Unable to assimilate the memory of a trauma because it doesn't fit with what they need or want to believe, PTSD [Post Traumatic Stress Disorder] sufferers are plagued with thoughts about the experience endlessly swirling in their minds. Intrusive thoughts, nightmares, and flashbacks play over and over like a broken record; the mind is stuck on the trauma and can't play anything else."

The bottom line is this: *The way you map reality inevitably becomes your subjective reality.* Yet subjectively, you will seldom recognize your maps *as maps.* And it is no wonder that you feel them as real. They govern the operating of your mind-body functions, sending commands to the body. So, of course, they feel solid and real. If you then *believe* in these *feelings* or if you believe, "I have to be true to my feelings," you reflexively set that thought, and its inherent feelings, as a damaging meta-state. It becomes a frame that imprisons you. Freedom from that mess requires that you re-map and recognize it as just a map.

Creating Great Meanings for Internalized Values
If you have taken the first step, you've kept the evil out. You've contained it to a specific time, place, and event. You've accessed curiosity to explore the big picture of your life, now make sure you

keep your dream alive. To be resilient requires that you know *who* you are, *what* you passionately care about, and *where* you want to go. Together these will give you an unifying core of values and visions that will center you. It will prevent any set back from devastating or robbing you of value.

The three **P-**s of the pessimistic explanatory style robs people of *value*. It takes value away from your person, your life, and your future. As you keep the problem out, you create and maintain your personal sense of dignity. Now your core will not easily be shaken. Imagine living out of this center in your everyday activities. Feel yourself doing so with integrity and congruence as you express your principles with strength and compassion. How much bounce will this put into your soul?

Using this dignity state as your frame of mind in times of defeat and set-back will enable you to maintain your sense of self-integrity. As you center in your values and visions, you will have a stabilizing power within as a gyroscope. You will now be able to "live from within," rather than bouncing off external circumstance.

Being *centered* in your values and visions will not only establish strong and respectful boundaries between yourself and others, it will discern responsibilities and provide a filter against influences that does not fit. Your resilience will grow as you increasingly operate out of a clear vision of your direction and mission.

Creating Great Meanings about Failure
The next meta-state to explore is your attitude about failing. When something does not go the way you want it to, do you welcome and accept that fact? To what extent do you have a learning attitude in that moment? What frame would enable you to learn from what did not work, re-tool, and go for it again in a smarter way?

To develop a good realistic attitude toward "failing," interpret it as "just a step toward success." If you don't lose your step when you fail at something, you can step back and turn the mis-step into a dance. You will then keep developing, interacting with people who can assist, and discover more effective problem solving skills.

Lacking *the ability to learn from defeat* prevents us from coping well when things get tough. John Callender had a good relationship to failing. Callender served as an officer of the Massachuset's militia at the beginning of the American Revolution. But at the battle of Bunker Hill, he lost his nerve. Scared out of his wits, he ran. Later he was convicted of cowardice. In fact, one of George Washington's first duties in assuming command of the American forces at Cambridge was to give the order for the court-martial of Captain Callender.

In his official orders, Washington wrote:

> "It is with inexpressible concern that the General upon his first arrival in the army, should find an officer sentenced by a General Court Martial to be cashier'd for Cowardice. A crime of all others, most infamous in a soldier, the most injurious to an army, and the last to be forgiven."

Imagine coping with a defeat of that magnitude? Could you handle it with grace and dignity? Could you use it to learn from and turn it into a victory? Certainly one could crumble into embarrassment, deny and rationalize away the behavior, let the failure define oneself, quit, curse, and blame, or stage a comeback. Callender did the latter. No sooner had this tragedy befallen him, then he re-enlisted in the army—as a private. Shortly thereafter, at the Battle of Long Island, he exhibited tremendous courage. In fact, he showed such conspicuous courage that Washington publically revoked the sentence and restored him to his captaincy.

What a story! Callender learned from his blunder and used it positively by refusing to let it determine his future. He gave himself permission to try again, and again, and again, to use his past productively, to learn useful lessons from it. By persevering until he got it right, he went down in history as a courageous soldier with fortitude, rather than as a coward. He learned even in the school of defeat and so used it as feedback to learn how to be courageous.

What a powerful response style. By learning from defeats you can refuse to let a defeat crush your spirit. You can take it as information and fuel your motivation to "go for it again."

Creating Great Meanings about What *Is*

Using an optimistic explanatory style allows you to do the most paradoxical thing of all. *You can now meta-state your defeats and set-backs with acceptance.* It seems paradoxical, yet until you accept your situation, you will not be able to look at the set-back squarely in the face. So first, accept that you have landed flat on your face.

Outframing your experience with a basic attitude of acceptance empowers you so that you can gaze directly at reality without blinking. Simply accept the limitations, constraints, and the facts that you're up against. Although this seems counter-intuitive, it is the first step to bouncing back.

Acceptance simply welcomes what *is* as that which exists. It doesn't mean endorsement of the problem. It doesn't mean that you condone the problem. Nor does it mean resignation. *Acceptance means acknowledging your current reality for what it is.*
- What has happened?
- What do I have to deal with?
- What can be changed, what cannot be changed?

By recognizing that you have failed at something or suffer a limitation does not have to discourage you. Your feelings arise from the meanings that you attribute to your situation.
- How well do you tolerate imperfection?
- How persistent are you in working to progressively overcome the failure, the character flaw, the limitation?

How you accept, or fail to accept, the limitations of your humanity with all of your imperfections and fallibility determines the robustness of your resiliency. Perfectionism undermines resilience.
- Do you passively yield to problems?
- Do you lean on them as excuses?
- Can you look at them without self-contempt?
- How do you experience the emotional impact of your limitations, with hyper-criticalness, humiliation, dignity?

Learning to live graciously with fallibilities enables you to move forward with courage, commitment, and passion.
- So what do you believe about mistakes and limitations?

- What do you believe about making a fool of yourself in front of others?
- How did your parents model failing, receiving feedback, and coming back?
- Can you be what you are as a human being—a completely fallible, mistake-making human being—and maintain all of your dignity and grace?

Creating Great Meanings for a *Can Do* Attitude

As you cultivate your sense of personal power, you will develop a *can do* attitude. You will be able to consistently create rich and robust meanings that empower you in taking effective actions. Your *can do* attitude will enable you to give the best interpretation to events. Your optimistic explanatory style will frame "problems" as *solvable*. This attribution of solvability gives you a tough optimism so that difficulties, will activate your problem-solving energies. Then you will more easily flow with reality, handle limitations, and create solutions.

3) Healthy Nurturing Relationships

Resilient people do not go it alone. They draw on others for strength and support. They know that when they fall down, they need others to help them up, so they easily ask for help and receive help. Nor does this begin only on the day of the set-back. Resilient people also devote time and energy to building nurturing relationships. Then, when they get knocked down, others are there for them to draw strength from.

This ability to receive from others as well as to give is essential for resilience. Accepting that you will have times when you can't recharge your own batteries because some blow throws you for a loop, you have nurturing relationships that enable you to endure and recover.

What relationships have you nurtured for mutual support? *Nurturing relationships* come from self-disclosure, extending yourself for the benefit of others, validating, engaging in a mutual give and take, etc. Build such relationships by seeking first to understand, by sharing yourself, by nurturing, and by being supportive. In this way you create an interpersonal environment as a resource in times of storm.

Healthy nurturing relationships enable you to simply unload or download your mental and emotional stresses that sometimes rage within. This involves allowing others to unload their feelings of anger, stress, and frustration without taking it personal. Simply listen to understand and confirm, not to give advice or fix things. Hearing another out provides a chance for a catharsis. So does affirming and validating another's experiences.

Karen Horney described neurosis as the tendency to turn legitimate needs and wants into claims and demands. When you do that, you pound on others with orders to meet your needs. Yet this "entitlement" thinking that makes demands on others only sabotages relationships. The non-resilient use people, fail to extend themselves for others, and deplete others. As a result, they have few to whom they can turn to in a crisis.

Nurturing Forgiving Relationships

Resilient people show a high skill in the ability to forgive. Forgiveness facilitates resilience as you are able to bounce back in relationships. Given that, how are you at forgiving? How are you at forgiving yourself?

Forgiveness effects a comeback so that you can *give* as you did *before* ("for-give"). This speaks of a victory over your hurt feelings, upsets, or disappointments in relationships. Forgiveness enables you to get over hurts and to stop retaliation patterns. It helps you to tap into the interpersonal grace that provides others what they need— another chance.

What if you do not feel like forgiving? Good! You now have a state that really needs this grace. If you "felt" like forgiving, then "understanding" would be sufficient to shift you away from the suffered hurt. If you feel violated enough that the other person does not deserve your grace, then you have gotten into a position to truly experience the empowerment of forgiveness. Now you can be gracious to one who does not deserve it. And that speaks of your inner abundance.

Nurturing Relationships that Resolves Conflicts

Resilient people are also especially skilled at managing conflicts. This results in fewer of their conflicts getting out of control and ruining a relationship. They identify conflict when it is still small and manageable.   They confront problems gracefully, resolve them productively, and in the process create an atmosphere for resolving things in a win/win way.

What does conflict mean to you?   What significance does it hold? What state of mind-and-emotion do you need to outframe your primary states with so that you accept, even warmly welcome, conflict?   If conflict turns you off, what frame of mind do you bring to that experience? What if you thought of conflict as simply "life trying itself out?"

Sometimes bad habits get the best of us. Perhaps you have quarreled so long and persistently that disagreeing has become your communication style.   Of course, this will only work to your detriment.   Other bad interpersonal habits can do the same: keeping up your guard, telling, problem-solving and advice-giving rather than listening, interrupting, talking over others, failing to affirm, holding others at a distance, etc.

Improve your resilience by learning how to have really "good fights." Know when to leave things alone. Grapple with the issues in ways that guard everybody's dignity, listen thoroughly and compassionately, and stick in the process until you find acceptable resolutions.[1]

4) Resource Management
It takes power or energy to bounce back. Without the sense of personal power, we cave in and give up. We end up wallowing in self-pity, whining, adopting the spirit of a victim. Resilience involves an active orientation, the *ability to respond*. It is the spirit of:

> "I will not give up or give in. I refuse to think or feel as a victim to other people or events. I own and claim my full response-abilities as a human being. I play a determinative role in the directions I establish. I choose to take effective action as the architect of my future. If I dislike my situation, I will use my powers to think, speak, act, and generate new and better responses and to make a difference."

This empowering state starkly contrasts to the beliefs and language patterns that those who identify themselves as victims. Whining about misfortunes without taking effective action will only reinforce the Victim game.   It prevents taking pleasure in this day and the opportunities it affords. While there are many limiting and sabotaging beliefs that support the victim state, this state blows away most of them.

Resilience requires that you transform any and every meaning that creates limitations. So reframe "getting hurt" as the price for being alive, for caring. There is something worse than being hurt, it is failing to live. Thinking that every wound, hurt, disappointment, etc. is fatal, only frames you to act defensive, fearful, and timid.

Overstreet (1951) wrote about *self-efficacy* as the sense of personal power wherein you feel capable of handling the challenges of life:

> "When the person who is receiving psychological help begins to turn his attention from himself to the possibilities resident in the outer world—expressing however tentatively a wish for independence and a liking for other people—he shows that he is feeling resourceful enough to risk a few setbacks if these are the price of reaching toward life. He is beginning —though he may not realize this— to trust his own powers of self-healing. The enriching process thus started seems to have virtually no limits. To the extent that an individual trusts himself to survive failure, he can draw upon the resources of experience that are open to him. Making these his own—that is, converting them into inner resources, not mere possessions to be clutched and hidden away—he can give ever less anxious thought to the possibility of his being rebuffed or making a fool of himself, and can therefore enjoy all the more involving himself in experience." (p. 98)

Because personal efficacy enables you to be firm about your values and visions, it enables you to develop a toughness in handling the blows of fate so that you don't fall apart or give up. You develop a positive outlook and faith with yourself to act on and make real your values and visions.

Managing the Resource of Curiosity

If the problem is not *you,* or *everything,* or *forever* (the pessimistic explanatory style), and you have acknowledged that it is here to be dealt with, then you first need curiosity. Lots of curiosity. Curiosity about what the problem is, what resources are needed to access and manage, and what you may have missed.

Given that many set-backs are due to ignorance, how do you handle your own ignorance? What do you believe about ignorance? Can you skillfully handle your ignorance with honesty, gracefully and without embarrassment. Do you allow others to be okay with theirs? In many cultures people are taught to become phobic about ignorance. They are not allowed to be ignorant, to not know, and to acknowledge such. So they posture. They pretend. They don't ask those wonderful "dumb" questions.

Yet what has ignorance done to you that now creates such fear? How has "not knowing" something, lacking certain information, become a threat to you? What does it threaten?

Ah, perhaps it is not the state of not-knowing that's so threatening as it is *being viewed* as ignorant. Yet that fear only cons you out of being honest about your current understandings or confusions. Suppose you ask some different questions:
- What experiences have you had of others seeing your ignorance?
- Did you find those enjoyable or painful?
- What meanings do you give to being ignorant or imagining that others think that you are ignorant about something?

The taboo of ignorance undermines resilience. Fear of ignorance, as a frame, prevents you from asking questions, especially "dumb" questions. Yet that taboo undermines the ability to curiously explore what you do not yet know. This will shut down your creativity and exploration and makes your mind less alive, less vigorous, and less playful. To lose your curiosity, your sense of wonder, your sense of questioning, etc. eliminates a key facet in your ability to learn so that you can bounce back with energy.

Keeping your curiosity alive enables you to learn to live with problems without becoming negative. It motivates you to develop research skills for gathering more information, listening fairly even when you disagree, and discovering the key facets of success in a given area.

Conversely, you cultivate resiliency by accepting and recognizing the limits of your understandings without being emotionally stampeded by fear or embarrassment. Graciously accept that you will make mistakes. If you aren't making mistakes every day, you are probably not taking enough risks. Few mistakes probably means you're playing life too cautiously. By fully accepting your fallibility of mind, emotions, speech and behavior without distrusting yourself enables you to become more resilient. By all means, don't lose your power to venture. Reset your aim not to be flawless, but to be alive and passionate.

Managing Flexibility as a Resource

The bounce of resilience requires flexibility. It requires the ability to adapt, cope, and adjust as things change. The opposite is rigidity. Flexibility enables you to dance with life changes, learning new things, developing new skills, adjusting to experiences. When you are rigidly inflexible you keep repeating ways of thinking, emoting, and behaving. And that will create a stuckness in a way of life that no longer works.

Flexibility correlates to your ability to learn quickly, to be open to the moment, to be in sensory awareness, and to make changes that increase effectiveness. Contrast this with the lack of flexibility in rigid and dogmatic thinking. Without flexibility you are more likely to get stuck in negative emotions, caught up in grudges, unable to forgive or to shift your feelings. Then you'll hold on to your old patterns of speech and behavior and refuse to yield in the face of new information. You will have difficulty backing up, admitting error, or correcting your direction. Such fixation will then sabotage your creativity and resilience.

What frames create mental and emotional rigidity? The limiting beliefs will involve a sense of danger about change.

> Change is painful.
> If you make one change, you will never be able to stop it. Where will it lead to?
> You will lose your self. Who will you be if you change?

Managing the Resource of Sensory Awareness

Resilience requires sensory awareness so that you can be present in the here-and-now. Resilience is sabotaged by wasting time daydreaming instead of learning how to effectively deal with the immediate situation. Stepping into the present moment with full sensory awareness increases your capacity for receiving what *is*. Sensory awareness itself restores some of the bounce and vitality of being alive as you come into the moment and experience the pleasures of this day.

Sensory awareness brings you into the present thereby releasing you from the past. If you live "in the past" you lock yourself inside a hurt or set-back which prevents you from resiliently returning to life. If you continually rehearse an old past hurt you lock yourself up inside that old trauma. Do that and you make the past an emotional trap for yourself.

No wonder living in the past prevents resilience and reduces flexibility. With each replaying of the old trauma, you not only intensify the internal agony and strengthen your internal prison, you miss the present.

What belief frame do you need to come into the present with flexibility? You will need to recode the past event simply as "an experience I survived." Out of such experiences you constructed your mental maps, yet whatever you experienced was just that—*an experience you went through*. And that's all. And it may have been a poor, sick, and toxic one at that. Why make it the basis of your map-making? Why over-rate its importance? Does it serve you well? Does it enhance your life? What can you learn from it? Are you ready to dismiss it?

Managing Self-Discipline as a Resource

Who's in control— you or your circumstances? A person who has no self-discipline is a person who cannot control him or herself. Self-discipline involves bringing structure and discipline to your mind, emotions, speech, and behavior. This empowers you to master your states. Lacking self-discipline, you lack any real control over your life. This makes you dependent upon others, circumstances, and the happenchance of events.

Many people are unable to discipline themselves because they have a semantic block regarding the term "discipline." They frame it in terms of effort, work, and struggle. They interpret it as being controlled, losing freedom, etc. They recall the antagonism they once felt when dad (or someone else) "told" them what to do.

- What's a positive way to think about self-discipline?
- What meaning about self-discipline will enrich your experience of it?

Think of self-discipline as the internal mastery that enables you to get yourself to do what you want to do. It orders your thinking, emoting, speaking, and behaving to achieve your desired outcomes. It makes you *response-able* in the most positive way. It puts you in charge of your emotions so that you can keep your spirit up in spite of circumstances.

The resilience that Rocky showed in the *Rocky* movies grew primarily from his self-discipline. Disciplining his body and mind gave him his personal mastery that culminated in a *can do attitude* and an "eye of the tiger" motivation. Together these things empowered him to stage his comeback. Everything depended upon him getting himself in tip-top shape. His fitness level had to be awesome. He had to exercise the discipline that would not only recover his previous conditioning, but take him further.

5) Meta-Perspective

So where are you? Here's a set-back, it is not personal, pervasive, or permanent, so where are you regarding your highest intentions and most compelling goals? Resilience requires a meta-awareness so that you can think strategically about where you are today and where you want to go.

Resilience requires an ongoing sense of where you stand in respect to your long-term vision and values and day-by-day position toward that goal. If you can bring a sense of the big picture to your everyday life, you will be able to keep perspective during set-backs and defeats. To apply this larger perspective, step back from things. As you then transcend your current ups-and-downs of problems and challenges, you will be able to get a meta-level sense of the big picture of your life as a human adventure. This will prevent you from getting caught up in details of the problem and lose perspective.

Meta-stating yourself with perspective will help you to keep track of your frames about your primary state. You will be able to track where you are in the process. Otherwise, you could easily get caught up in the details of the defeat and begin to question yourself. Consciousness of where you are in the process enables you to take a long-term view and to build patience. It prevents discounting small significant steps. It prevents catastrophizing, awfulizing, and blowing things out of proportion.

Keeping perspective includes holding some negative thoughts and feelings in mind—so that you can stay aware of the terrible price you would pay if you don't stay resilient. This enables you to *attach massive pain to "sitting on your butt"* after something has knocked you down.[2]

•   What will happen if you do not develop resilience?
•   What consequences will you suffer in relationships, health, emotions, career, etc.?

Everything that weakens your resolve for your larger vision weakens your resilience. Every emotional state of feeling fragile, being "on the edge," "unable to take much more" sabotages your resilience. Use a higher executive level to catch these mental saboteurs and banish them from your mind.

Do the same with every *psychological "can't"* in thought or speech. Every "can't" sets a frame for becoming more limited (e.g., "I can't stand criticism," "I can't stand sarcasm," or the rejection and the embarrassment, "I can't get beyond her betrayal," "I can't endure the public exposure," etc.).

Psychological can'ts install limitations. They induce states of nervous reactions (feeling uncomfortable, worrisome, panicky, etc.). Stop. Refuse to tolerate this. It only programs an over-sensitivity that makes you less capable and less productive.

As you access a meta-level of awareness, you will know where you stand in the process of staging a comeback. Now you can *attach massive pleasure to every step of your resilience.* How much pleasure do you have connected to the idea of staging a comeback to defeats? List all of the wonderful things that will accrue to you if you keep bouncing back from set-backs and stay in the fray of life with an unconquerable spirit?

      Resilience gives me recovery power, it allows my powers of

mind, emotions, speech, behavior, etc. to keep rejuvenating me, it keeps these personal powers alive, it empowers me to have a courageous heart, it keep me going, strengthens my motivation, enables me to "live from within," gives me a "never-say-die" attitude, assists me in rolling with the punches, turns life into an adventure, enables me to become bigger than my circumstances, frees me from holding grudges, makes me more pleasant in company, etc."

Resilience gives me an emotional elasticity that allows me to make the most of any situation, to get along well with others, enjoy experiences, and keep learning and growing. With resilience I always win because I keep finding the power within to come back. It gives me true endurance and steadfastness. Resilience enables me to be centered and decisive.

The Meta-Perspective of a Strong Compelling Outcome

Once centered in your values, it becomes easier to feel powerfully propelled toward some compelling future vision. This vision may concern your relationships, career, business, health, hobby, or a combination of these.

Have you noticed the theme of resilience in the *Rocky* movies? What made Rocky so resilient in each movie so that he always staged a come back? Was it not his dream of becoming a champion? By Rocky IV and Rocky V, he could no longer bounce back due to youthful fitness. His resilience arose from how he set for himself some compelling outcomes. He set some compelling desired outcomes that enabled him to keep coming back.

To become truly resilient, use your meaning-making powers to *attribute significant value to your dreams.* Proactively reframe things with meanings that invigorate you. If you don't, you will default to meanings that put you into negative states. Take charge of your own motivation. What motivates you? What motives could you set at the highest levels of your mind? Set these as your frames to stabilize your vision. Increasingly add richer and more compelling motives to your perspective to give yourself more reasons for living your passion. Maslow described this as *sacrilizing*.

-       What highly desired outcomes will increase your resilience?

- What kind of a person do you want to become?
- What kind of experiences do you want to have?

Perhaps, "I want to become more loving, more caring, warmer to people, friendlier, more charismatic etc." This is a secret of vitality. Those who are resilient live purposefully. Use this to enrich the meanings of your everyday life. When you are short on vital meanings it reduces your resilience. Why live, why struggle, why work, why discipline yourself, why go through any effort if you don't have anything meaningful to live for? Here's something else—you don't have to know everything about your purpose, just enough to get started. You only need the beginning of a healthy and enhancing visions to activate the mind.

The Meta-Perspective of Persistence
With a *can do* attitude, persistence will be no problem. Of course, you will persist! Persisting in following your dreams and actualizing your dreams means you will keep coming back, time and again, to make your dreams real.
- What creates this consistency of perseverance?
- What do you need for more bounce within yourself?
- What will empower you to continually adapt to the ups-and-downs of life?
- What will eliminate becoming defeated and put bounce in your soul?

When you answer this question with a dozen or more resources, you will know the kinds of states that will create your own unique empowering response style.

Figure 5:3
Resilience

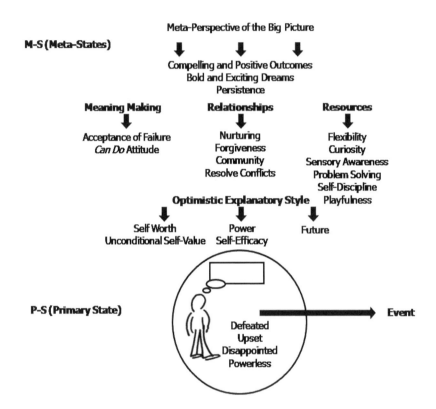

Summary

- Passionate life dreams are reached, not in one giant leap, but over time by distinguishing between what works and what does not work, by persistently returning to your outcomes, by learning from feedback, and by refining skills. As you create more accurate and enhancing beliefs, expectations, and commitments to your values and visions, *you develop the comeback power of resilience.*

- The gestalt of resilience emerges from the interaction of many meta-states outframing the primary state of defeat. To build this into your personality, add one resource after another until each becomes a quality in your overall frame of mind If you need yet another resource, add it to the mix. Keep exploring all your options until you have a strong and vigorous meta-state so that you can effectively bounce back.

- Ultimately your resilience will make you un-defeatable as you develop your own "eye of the tiger" motivation. Then you'll have and live a passionate commitment that will unleash your highest and best potentials.

- In all of this, learning from defeats is essential. It enables you to use information as important feedback so you can more effectively make your dreams come true. Developing a good relationship with fallibility, ignorance, failing, etc. enables you to not feel put off because you don't succeed on the first or the fortieth try. You keep learning and resiliently bouncing back.

End Notes:

1. See *Games Great Lovers Plays* (2003). Chapter is on how to have a good fight.

2. Two forces motivate us, attractions pull us forward *toward* what we want and aversions push us *away from* what we do not want. A healthy propulsion system requires both. See *Propulsion Systems* (2002).

PART II:

META-STATES

MODELING

SELF-REFLEXIVE

CONSCIOUSNESS

Chapter 6

DEFINING

META-STATES

"How do you feel about what is happening?
How do you feel about your feelings about what is happening?"
Virginia Satir

When I first discovered the presence of meta-states in human experiences, I not only had to define meta-states, but two other terms as well, *states* and *meta*. For the majority of people, these are not common words of their everyday vocabulary. I'm sure that for many they are still experienced as esoteric jargon.

My first way of defining meta-states was to literally define them: "meta-states are states-*about*-states." Yet since *meta* is not in the vocabulary of most people, I had to define it as well. The conversation would always begin and go in the same direction.

"You say 'meta-state,' I'm not familiar with that, what's a meta-state?"
A *meta-state* is simply one state of consciousness, a mental or emotional state, that's *above or beyond* another state and which is *about* that other state of awareness.

Often they would then give me a long stretched-out "Oookaaaay," which warned me that even if the definition was clear, it wasn't satisfying. "And so what does *meta* mean? Why do you call it *meta-states?*"

> "Oh yes, the word *meta* indicates a 'higher' level. It refers to something that's higher than another thing, something that's above, beyond, or about something else."

That's about the time that the eyes would glaze over and I could have easily said, "And as you understand each and every word I've just said fully and completely, letting it take you back to a time and place in your memory where you had lots of fun, how delightful does it feel to reach into your back pocket and pull out your billfold and joyfully hand over all your money because you have just *meta* me."

But I didn't. Caught up in trying to explain a term I would then desperately reach into my psychological toolbox and pull out my big guns to induce a negative spiraling meta-state.

> "Have you ever done something that you knew wasn't right and felt bad about it? But then to make things worse, you felt angry about feeling bad, and then felt ashamed of feeling angry at feeling bad, and then worried that maybe there was something wrong with you, and then felt confused about what you were feeling?"

By then they would be shaking their heads up and down in the affirmative, and saying, "Yeah! I hate it when I do that." Well, that's one state about another about another. And in that instance, those layers of meta-states creates a negative downward cycle. "Oh yeah, now I know what you mean."

Then, to not leave it there, I would follow up by asking, "Have you ever been on top of the world—in love, a moment of ecstasy, touched by a movie scene, extended yourself in an act of compassion and then felt delighted about that experience and then realized that life really is good? Well, that would be an example of layers of meta-states as a positive upward cycle.

Glad to Meta You
The word *meta* is a great word. Beginning with the idea of "above," it refers to *something at a higher level than something else*. So in meta-

communication we communicate about our communicating, how we are communicating. In a meta-feeling, we experience a feeling state about a feeling. In a meta-analysis, we step back from several analyses to look for patterns within those analysis.

Regarding the way we think and feel, *meta refers to a higher logical level.* And that means that when you bring one state to another, the higher state *classifies* the lower so that it becomes the *category* of the lower. The lower, in turn, becomes a member of the class set by the higher.

> If you bring joy and fun to your learning, then *joyful fun* becomes the classification or category of learning. Learning becomes a member of the class of things that gives you joy and with which you can have fun.

> If you bring judgment to your learning, then learning becomes a member of the class of things by which you make *judgments and evaluations.* Then the kind and quality of your learning is governed by judgment rather than joy and fun.

This illustrates how *a meta-level references the level below it.* It operates as a frame of meaning about the lower level. It takes a higher logical level position to the previous state. Then from that higher position, it influences and affects the lower levels. Higher levels do that, they drive or govern lower levels. They modulate and organize lower levels. And it is this that then has tremendous effects upon primary experiences as we shall see.

Levels of *About*-ness
Meta not only indicates a higher level, it shifts your focus. It shifts your attention and focus from the outside to the inside. In a regular state, you think about things "out there." You have thoughts-and-feelings about women, fire, dogs, ice cream cones, and fireworks. But when you experience a state about your state, the *about-ness* at this higher level refers to your own experience, to your state. And that changes everything. Now you have thoughts and feelings about your previous experience.

Figure 6:1

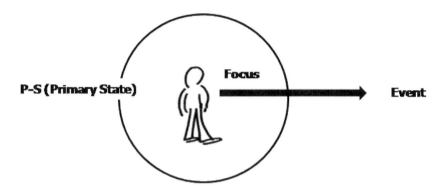

So it starts at the primary level where your regular states are *about* things "out there" in the world.

"I'm afraid *of* John. I don't want to get slugged."

"I like dogs; they are always so friendly."

"What do women really want? Who knows? Nobody!"

In a meta-state the *aboutness* shifts as you focus on your experience:

"I'm ashamed of my fear of John. Why do I have to be so timid. I need more courage?"

"I enjoy liking dogs, guess I'm a dog-lover at heart (identity)."

"I feel proud and clever that I've figured out that you can't figure out women. I'm really sharp!"

Figure 6:2

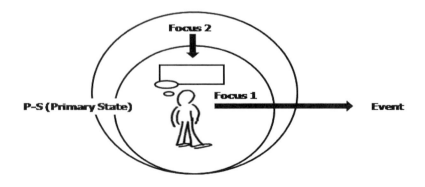

What are the Meta-Levels of your Anger?

Consider anger as an example. In the primary state of anger, you feel angry *about* something. It begins when you focus on some external object to which you then respond with angry thoughts and feelings. You say, "I hate that!" "Why does he have to be so stupid?" "Can't you get moving, you are so slow!" You feel irritated, upset, frustrated, blocked, and violated. The speed of your breathing increases, there's more tightness in your muscle tension, your throat muscles also tighten, your voice becomes harsh and perhaps more intense.

Okay, that was fun. Now imagine moving to a meta-level and bringing anger at this level to your primary state of anger. Suppose you get angry at yourself [second level] for getting angry [first level]! Have you ever done that? Now your thoughts-and-feelings relate to a different object and to an object in a different dimension. Now it relates to your own state. What is it like for you to be angry at yourself? What results? Self-contempt? Do you beat yourself up? Do you call all of your good intentions and highest values in question? Do you get depressed? Does your anger create rage?

Perhaps in getting angry at yourself for being angry, you focus on how bad and evil it is to be angry. Perhaps you focus on behaving like a hothead and saying something inappropriate and how it might hurt someone's feelings. Whatever you think, whatever you feel, at the meta-level of being angry at yourself for being in a state of anger, your state is no longer about the world out there, it is about you—your identity, your morality, your future, your well-being, or any other aspect of yourself. Now your anger shifts to the inner dimension of your inner world. And to that extent, it has nothing to do with the outer dimension of the external world.

Understanding Emotions to Understand Meta-States

Since a meta-state is a reflexive and layered state, a meta-state begins with the thoughts and emotions of a state, a primary state. To that state, you then layer one or multiple levels of more thoughts and emotions. Is a meta-state an emotion? Yes. Is it a thought? Yes, of course. Is it a somatic experience? Yes, definitely. It is a dynamic complex of your entire mind-body-emotion system.

I'll make this a bit more explicit by defining an emotion. An emotion

speaks about the *motions* that
arise in your body as a somatic
response to some awareness.
This means that *motion* is
occurring somatically within
your nervous systems,
neurology, and physiology. It is
motion that is seeking to move
you *out* from where you are,
hence the *e(x)* (e*x*-motion). A
technical definition of an
emotion says that it is an
"action tendency" generated in
the brain (thalamus,
hypocampus, amygdala) as a
response to some awareness.

That's the second part.
Emotions are *responses* from
your mind and body. These
responses do not have to be conscious, they can arise from an
awareness or experience outside of your conscious awareness. Bodily
sensations prior to that awareness are your kinesthetic and
proprioceptive sensations— "feelings." When you add an awareness
of threat, danger, overload, safety, attraction, etc. then you have an
"emotion."

An emotion is *the difference* that you *register in your body* between
your mental and conceptual maps about the world and your felt
experience of the world. It is the difference between your map and the
territory. As a scale measures the difference between two things, when
the difference shifts downward on the *experience* side, you feel the
"negative" emotions and when the difference shifts upward on the
experience side, you feel the "positive" emotions.

Emotions are relative to thinking and experiencing. The relativity of
your emotions arise because they weigh the difference between
expectation and experience. You map your sense of things (your model
of the world) and then use it to navigate the territory. How you go in
the world *compared* to your map of the world creates your up and

down (positive and negative) emotions. As the difference between these two phenomena, your model of the world and your experience of the world, emotions somatically registers this difference.

If you think about your inner map on one side of a scale and your outer experience in the territory as the other side, then when the scales tip downward on the *experience* side, then you feel that the world isn't living up to all that you had mapped and expected about it. So you feel bad. You were expecting, wanting, believing, and hoping for a lot more than you received. As this doesn't feel good, it elicits "negative" emotions (anger, fear, discontent, frustration, stress, upsetness).

When the scales tip upward on the *experience* side, then your experience of the world is higher than your *inner maps*. So you feel great. You receive more from the world than you expected. This elicits the "positive" emotions (joy, happiness, pleasure, delight, playfulness, contentment).

This relativity of your emotions does not tell you what is real, what exists "out there," or what is right or wrong. You can't trust your emotions to provide you that kind of information. All that you can trust them to tell you is about *the relationship* between your mental mapping and sensory experiencing.

In the experience of "positive" emotions, you value and attribute significance to the comparative relationship between your map and your experience, and so you set a valued frame of importance. "This is good." This elicits an internal expectation of desire and hope and if you receive it, then joy, happiness, excitement, contentment, fulfillment, etc. Your nervous system then reflects this "sense" of valued significance. In the experience of "negative" emotions, you are doing the opposite. You are *dis-valuing* something, viewing it as hurtful, ugly, distasteful, undesirable, etc. "This is not good."

A state is always an *emotional* state and so never static or non-moving as the term "state" (static) may suggest. Your states are dynamically alive and forever changing. In your "e-motions" the *motion* that you feel is somatic energy, an urge to *move* (motion) *out* (ex-) to change things. In a so-called "dissociated" state, you are still in your body and feeling things, but your feelings are of a certain quality. Typically you feel numb, weird, incongruent, and disoriented and so you conceptualize yourself as being out-of-your-body.

The accuracy of your emotions can go astray in two ways. First, you can have an ill-formed, mis-informed, and distorted model of the world so that your inner frames of expectations, understandings, beliefs, etc. are erroneous. Second, you may lack the skills to translate into action what you have mapped so that your experience of the territory fails to achieve your objectives.

Layering the Complexity
If you think the anger-about-anger was complex, you haven't seen anything yet. After all, meta-states typically involve several pieces, or even multiple pieces, of thoughts and feelings. They often involve multiple layers of consciousness about consciousness. In this way you have an incredible ability to build *complex* meta-states.

> "I feel bad about feeling so petty about my embarrassment and getting upset over being caught off-guard about the surprise party the other day."

Ookkaaaay! So, what exactly do you feel? It's kind of hard to say, isn't it? There's a mixture of different emotions relating to several different things.

The core of that experience involves feelings of surprise and shock. Then comes a self-conscious sense of embarrassment about that state along with feeling upset—perhaps uncomfortable or out of the person's comfort zone. Then petty thoughts and feelings occur which made a big deal, thus complicating matters. Then later as the person processes through it all, more thoughts and feelings occur that evaluates and judge his/her response in a negative or "bad" way.

All this arises from your human ability to go meta and to abstract about whatever abstraction you have created (Korzybski, 1933/1994). In other words, it is the exercise of the very special kind of consciousness that you have which separates you from every other creature—*your self-reflexive consciousness*. It is this very capacity which enables you to create and experience meta-states. After all, you can always think about your thinking (meta-cognition), talk about your talk (meta-communication), feel about your feelings (meta-feelings), model your models (meta-model), analyze your analyses (meta-analysis), etc. You are a meta-class of life and you spend most of your life at meta-levels.

This meta-cognizing enables you to layer your states not just once, but multiple times.   And with multiple layers, you set one frame of thoughts-and-feelings upon another, and so on up the levels. In the end you create *a matrix of frames* around something and that endows you with the framework for a belief system.[1]

Are you surprised by this?   As your meta-states involve your self-reflexive consciousness, layering back onto itself multiple layers, no wonder you are able to create complex states of consciousness. No wonder you can create immensely complex states about the simplest of things.

What do you think about sports? If that's too broad, then soccer. Rugby. Tennis. Marathon running. Baseball. Use any of these or any other sport that evokes a lot of meaning and emotion from you, and take a moment to *explore the layering that you live inside of.* You have thoughts about whether you like or dislike the given sport. You have thoughts about whether you enjoy playing it, watching it, and supporting it. You have feelings about key people in that sport., the amount of money they make, the celebrity status they may have, and their use of that fame, and so on.

Figure 6:3

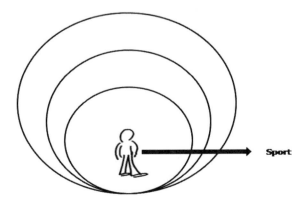

Take almost any subject and you, like all of us, have dozens, scores, perhaps a hundred frames of beliefs, understandings, memories, perceptions, etc. about it. And together these make up your *matrix* [1] *of meaning frames* within you. And that's yet another consequence of your meta-states. *By your meta-states you build up a construct of meanings* as you map things in multiple ways so that in the end you create an entire system of embedded frames—this is what we call the *Matrix.* [1]

Rising up with Meta-States to Transcend
This unique human ability of reflexivity by which you think-and-feel about your thinking, feeling, choosing, behaving, etc. facilitates yet something else. It enables you to *transcend* your immediate time, space, being, values, experiences, etc. Yet you do not only transcend, you *include* your first state inside of your first additional layers of awareness.

As you rise up in the meta-response, you transcend yourself. This transcending capacity, in turn, makes possible those experiences that we call "transcendence, spiritual, and existential." When you go meta, you move into a dimension that uniquely characterizes the human kind of consciousness. As your awareness now reflects back onto itself, you transcend your first experience. You can then transcend that experience and so on all the way up.

Figure 6:4

New gestalts and configurations emerge from this process. In this emergence you experience even more complex states of *ontology* (existence and being-ness), *teleology* (the study and awareness of where things are going, the last things), and *theology* (our questions, beliefs, and wonderings about whether there is a higher intelligence directing things).

Your meta-states takes you to those "realities," experiences, and states of consciousness that enable you to transcend time, space, body, person, etc. And by transcending the dimensions that help ground and locate your experience, you are taken into less frequented states—existential and conceptual states that relate to purpose, destiny, self, mission, existence, etc.

In this, however, you do not only transcend in the meta-move, you *transcend and include*. That is, as you rise above an experience by transcending and relating new thoughts-and-feelings to it, *you include the former inside it*. This has the effect of texturing the primary experience with the meta-state and creating a holoarchy of states.[2]

Because of this wondrous human ability of always going meta and abstracting another level to your current state, *you can create many levels and kinds of meta-states*. We can now distinguish between simple meta-states, complex meta-states, congruent and incongruent meta-states, gestalt states, etc.

The Reflexivity of Meta-States

What I find exciting about Meta-States is that now I can not only track how an experience moves sequentially and horizontally from one response to another, I could also track how a person moves vertically to generate his or her internal response about a previous response. *This introduces vertical modeling*. Because meta-stating shifts logical levels, so we can transcend one state and include it within another, via meta-stating we create matrices of states. We construct layers of states that reference its own internal representations and physiology in a holistic and dynamic way.

Self-reflexive consciousness makes all of this possible. As your consciousness reflects back onto itself you generate meta-cognitions and meta-emotions. This reflexivity of mind-and-emotion involves a recursive process that is endlessly iterative and initiates systemic functions. As consciousness and experience becomes *recursive,* it takes on many of the qualities of a system—interactive parts, emergent properties, simultaneality, non-linearity, embeddness, etc. This recursiveness of mind-and-emotion also creates some really strange human phenomena as you'll discover.

Fearing Fear

I'll illustrate with another primary state—fear. Suppose we begin by accessing a basic and primary state of fear. In this state of fear we entertain internal representations of our fear object which evokes fear's corresponding neurology and physiology. Actually, this process provides a tremendous resource because it activates our fight/flight survival response patterns. If the content of the fear is a true physical danger—the state energizes, activates, and mobilizes us. If the content does not represent a true danger, it still energizes, activates, and mobilizes us and it does something else. Without an actual external referent to relate the energy to, we experience a lot of unnecessary mobilization. Typically this plays havoc with our mind and body. We then experience the fear we can't respond to as an unrealistic fear, as worry, panic, and anxiety, and all of this puts us into a stew with nowhere to go.

If that isn't destructive enough, consider what happens when we shift to a meta-level and *fear our fear.* What does this create? It generates a dis-empowering meta-state of self-fear or paranoia. In this meta-state, the object of fear does not involve something outside (i.e., a wolf, a dangerous place, an angry spouse, getting hurt in a sport, etc.). At this level, *you now fear your own state*—your thoughts, emotions, sensations, neurological processes, etc. You fear your experience of fear. You fear what it means to experience fear.

Suppose, to make all of this even worse, that you now get angry at your fear? To your feared fear, now apply anger. Now you have self-anger, or anger turned inward against yourself. Sigmund Freud said that this will typically manifest as self-contempt, self-judgment, and clinical depression. The state of anger, as it reflexively turns against you, takes on new complications through the complexity of the layering of frames.

The Negative Layering of Meta-States

A state that is problematic to many people is the state of failing. Most people label this experience as "failure." So, how do you respond to yourself when you're in a state of failure? When you fail to achieve a desired goal, what's your next response? Do you resourcefully gather more information, discover what did not work, adjust your behaviors, and give it another try? Or do you go into a judgment state against yourself? Do you engage in self-contempt. Do you become depressed? How do you respond to that first response of failure?

In these meta-states responses, the second state, and then the third state, progressively intensifies the original experience. And what if you judged yourself, then felt guilty for judging yourself, then felt anger at feeling guilty for judging yourself? And, as if that's not negative enough, you could reflexively keep turning more and more painful and negative emotions against yourself to create a whole matrix of a "dragon" state of self-sabotage and self-abuse.

It is in these ways that we humans turn our energies against ourselves. This puts us in self-conflict and self-abuse. And as we send negative thoughts-and-feelings against ourselves, our body will then attempt to do what our nervous systems are designed to do—to actualize those messages. Yet that energy has nowhere to go except against our mind and body. This self-attack is the very structure of psychosomatic illness, disease, neurosis, and all forms of psychopathology.

Rediscovering Korzybski and Second-Order Abstractions

After Korzybski (1933/ 1994) founded the field of General Semantics, he conducted neuro-linguistic trainings in the 1930s and 1940s. He coined the terms "neuro-linguistic" and "neuro-semantic" in his classic work, *Science and Sanity* as well as "human engineering" (1921).

He also played around with the process of transforming what he called "first order effects" into "second order effects."

> ". . . ["W]e then have curiosity of curiosity, attention of attention, analysis of analysis, reasoning about reasoning (which represents science, psycho-logics, epistemology, etc.); choice of choice (which represents freedom, lack of psycho-logical blockages, and shows, also the semantic mechanism of eliminating those blocks); consideration of

> consideration gives an important cultural achievement; knowing of knowing involves abstracting and structure, becomes 'consciousness', at least in its limited aspects, take as consciousness of abstracting; evaluation of evaluation becomes a theory of sanity, etc." (1933, p. 440)

Korzybski warned about other meta-states that "represents *morbid* semantic reactions." In Meta-States, I interpret *morbid* using the metaphor of "dragons," as dragon states as described in the book, *Dragon Slaying: Dragons to Princes* (1996).

> "Thus the first order worry, nervousness, fear, pity, etc. may be quite legitimate and comparatively harmless. But when these are of a higher order and identified with the first order as in worry about worry, fear of fear, they become morbid."

These dis-empowering meta-states or "dragon" states are the complex meta-states that create negative downward spiraling.

> "Pity of pity is dangerously near to self-pity. Second order effects, such as belief in belief, makes fanaticism. To know that we know, to have conviction of conviction, ignorance of ignorance, etc. shows the mechanism of dogmatism; while such effects as free will of free will, or cause of cause, etc. often become delusions and illusions."

Layering your state in these ways create gross distortions because these negative meta-level states amplify and exaggerate the primary states. As you can see, this meta-state analysis points to the complexity that arises in human experience, nature, and consciousness. But we are not yet finished. Korzybski speaks of another group.

> "A third group is represented by such first order effects as inhibition, hate, doubt, contempt, disgust, anger, and similar semantic states; the second order reverses and annuls the first order effects. Thus an inhibition of an inhibition becomes a positive excitation or release; hate of hate is close to 'love'; doubt of doubt becomes scientific criticism and imparts the scientific tendency; the others obviously reverse or annul the first order undesirable semantic reaction."

Korzybski's genius here recognized that some meta-states will *negate,* and even *reverse,* the content level emotions and thoughts at the primary level. Other meta-states create *paradox* as they shift our thinking-and-emoting, and experiencing, to a higher level. This offers lots of possibilities for transformation. It provides a way of analyzing such powerful techniques as the "paradoxical intention" intervention in Logotherapy.[3]

In Logotherapy, Viktor Frankl (1953) developed "paradoxical intention" to address the subject of "anxiety about anxiety," "fear about fear." The most typical reaction to fear of fear stands as flight from fear.

> "'Flight from fear' as a reaction to 'fear of fear' constitutes the phobic pattern, the first of three pathogenic patterns that are distinguished in logotherapy. The second is the obsessive-compulsive pattern: whereas in phobic cases the patient displays 'fear of fear,' the obsessive-compulsive neurotic exhibits 'fear of himself,' being neither caught by the idea that he might commit suicide — or even homicide — or afraid that the strange thoughts that haunt him might be signs of imminent, if not present, psychosis. How should he know that the obsessive-compulsive character structure rather is immunizing him against real psychosis." (pp. 131-132)

When we take the primary state of procrastination, and reflexively apply procrastination to itself, we create a seeming contradiction. As we feed it back onto itself, we shift levels and the meta-procrastination results in negating the primary procrastination. If you have ever procrastinated, recall the experience for a moment. At the primary level you experienced it as an immediate and intense mind-body state of putting off something. You know it needs to be done, but you hesitate. You excuse yourself. You don't feel that you're ready. You have lots of inhibiting thoughts and feelings holding you back. That's the state of procrastination.

Now imagine meta-stating the procrastination with procrastination. As you bring a "putting off" state to eventually getting around to the task of procrastinating, you know that one of these days you'll get around to procrastinating. But just not now. Today you procrastinate on your procrastination. And when you put off your procrastination, you get busy with things. Ah, the seeming contradiction!

In this case, the meta-level procrastinating negates the procrastination state. This structure creates paradox. The result *seems* like a contradiction, the solution to procrastination is to procrastinate on your procrastination? Who would have thought? Yet actually you are creating a second response to the first one at a different level.

Figure 6:5

         curiosity of curiosity (intense curiosity)
         attention of attention (attending attention)
         analysis of analysis (study of analysis)
         reasoning about reasoning (science, epistemology, etc.)
         choice of choice (freedom, lack of blockages)
         consideration of consideration (cultural achievement)
         knowing of knowing (abstracting, consciousness)
         evaluation of evaluation (a theory of sanity)
         worry about worry (morbid state of worrisomeness)
         fear of fear (paranoia)
         pity of pity (self-pity)
         belief in belief (fanaticism)
         conviction of conviction (dogmatism)
         ignorance of ignorance (innocence)
         free will of free will (an empowering sense of choice)
         anger at fear (self-anger)
         joyful about anger (celebrative about the freedom to feel anger)
         sad about anger (awareness of misusing anger)
         angry about sadness (inappropriate sadness)
         fearful about sadness (self-paranoia)
         guilty about feeling angry (self-judgment for anger)
         inhibition of an inhibition (positive excitation, release)
         hate of hate (love)
         doubt of doubt (scientific criticism)
         procrastination of procrastination (action)
         interruption of interruption (confusion)
         prohibition of . . . anger, fear, joy, etc. (stuck!)

So, What have we Learned?

•   *Meta-states* as a model formulates an entirely new domain of NLP. By mining resources from the field of General Semantics Meta-States now offers new distinctions about the very structure of mind, consciousness, and human states.

•   Because of the layering effect, Meta-States as a model gives us a way to work with more complex pieces of subjective experiences which takes us beyond the analysis available by the strategies and simple state models.

•   Because the Meta-States Model uses the process of logical levels and self-reflexive consciousness, this model allows us to tease out the embedded layers inside of complex states. It allows us to deconstruct and then construct new state-about-state constructions that increases our resourcefulness.

End Notes:

1. *The Matrix Model* (2003) provides a full description of how meta-states and meta-stating creates our constructs of meaning.

2. A holoarchy is a structure of holons. Holons literally mean wholes-in-parts. In a holoarchy each whole is a part of a larger whole and each part is a whole within itself.

3. In chapter 19 we will explore the many systemic interfaces that occur when we meta-state layer upon layer.

Chapter 7

DIAGRAMING

META-STATES

"The ultimate of abstract, analytical thinking
is the greatest simplification possible,
i.e., the formula, the diagram, the map, the blueprint,
the schema, the cartoon . . ."
Abraham Maslow (1968, p. 209)

In developing Meta-States as a model and seeking to present it in many different forums over the years, I discovered that anything as conceptual and abstract as "consciousness" or as a model of "mind" needs a way so that people can see it. And I mean this literally. Most of us need some way to *see* and *imagine* a concept so that the propositional language explaining the model and how it works makes sense at the perceptual level.

Yet this is the problem. *How do we see concepts*? By definition, a concept is an abstraction of the mind. We create it by abstracting from our experiences as we create understandings, principles, meanings, categories, etc. about things. It is precisely because concepts are mental abstractions that they are not empirical which, in turn, explains why we cannot see, hear or feel them.

However, there is one way to see a concept. We can use symbols or metaphors of concept and in that way develop a way to *see* a concept and how it operates. We can see concepts through diagrams, flow charts, decision trees, formulas, cartoons, symbols, metaphors, stories, and checklists. Often we are able to employ the visual arts when we develop a workable metaphor that conveys the conceptual ideas of the model.

As NLP began, the developers called the meta-representational system of words and language *auditory-digital* (A_d). Playing off of that, Richard Bolstad of New Zealand describes diagrams and other visual representations as the *visual-digital* representational system (V_d). So, for example, we often think of the concept of "justice" by using the symbol of scales.[1]

For me this explains why Transactional Analysis (T.A.) became so popular in the 1970s. TA gained tremendous acceptance because it utilized simple visual representations to present its complex ideas of human psychology. In the best seller, *I'm Okay; You're Okay,* Thomas Harris created a way to *see* the concepts of "ego states" and "transactions." He did that with three circles one on top of the other which stood for the three ego-states (Parent, Adult and Child). He then used simple lines showing straight and crossed transactions to the three vertical circles standing for another's Parent, Adult, and Child states. As a result, people were able to understand and readily use the model.

Diagrams for *seeing* Meta-States
When I first began using the model of Meta-States I did so with clients in therapy. That was my profession at that time. And I did so using a clipboard. On the clipboard I would sketch a stick person and then circles for states and reflexive lines and arrows indicating the reflexive processes of the person while he or she was speaking. This would provide in real-time a way for the person to track his or her own processes of reflecting back onto him or herself, creating the higher level frames of meanings and meta-states.

I did this originally as much for myself as for the person with whom I was working. By sketching out a circle for the primary state experience I would put the stimulus outside of that circle as an X to indicate that the person was responding to something in the world "out there." As a visual diagram this separated stimulus and response and began to create a difference between them at the experiencing level of the person. From there I would ask simple questions about the person's first level state:

> "Given that this happened, what do you think about that? What do you believe about that? What state does that elicit in you?"

After identifying the primary state and putting the person's words about the state in the circle, I could hold that diagram on the clipboard before the person, and again ask:

> "Okay, given that, so what? What do you think or feel about being in that state? What does that mean to you?"

Doing this allowed me to hold the person's first response in place and begin to separate out the higher frames. Then as the person spoke I would sketch out the higher states as frames of mind reflecting the internal mapping creating the person's overall experiences and inner game.

Then, almost without exception, when the session ended people would ask for my sketches. At first I felt embarrassed and even hesitant. The reason was simple. By the time I finished with the diagrams, they were usually quite a mess with lines and words hastily sketched out. But they insisted—they really wanted the diagrams. Eventually I realized that the sketches, by enabling people to *see* their own processes, were empowering them to sort out their experiences. And as it enabled them to *visualize* the structure of their own processes, they became aware of precisely how they were creating their experiences. Catching the processes on paper enabled people to stop spinning round and round all of their different thoughts and feelings. They now had a way of seeing how they were creating their meta-level frames and that put them at choice point.

So in the context of a private psychotherapy practice I slowly developed various ways of diagraming the features of the Meta-States model. It was my laboratory for working out the visual-digital images that enable people to conceptually see their own meta-stating processes and the matrix of frames they created and lived inside.

Similarly, throughout the pages of this book, I have diagramed the meta-state processes. By *diagraming* the meta-level structures of our self-reflexive experiences we combine the state and the strategy models and picture the layering of thoughts and feelings of our neuro-semantic system. These visuals enable us to begin to see the reflective structures, the self-organizing processes, and many other concepts. And the time has now come to explain the symbols and the notational processes of the diagrams.

Notational Symbols in the Diagraming

The following provides an overview of the meta-state diagraming and the notational symbols used in the diagrams.

A Person. The diagrams always begins with a person, a stick figure of a person or a more elaborate diagram of a man or woman. This signifies that the experience always grows out of how a person uses his or her mind-body-emotion system.

Person

Circles. Around the person, a circle or elipse designates the primary state as an experience. Additional circles or eclipses above the first circle designates a state-about-a-state or meta-state and the *place* that our thinking-and-emoting creates. The circle designates *a space* or *energy field* which holds all of our mind-body or neuro-linguistic energies. The circle also conveys the idea of a person's boundaries—what's within our space and what's without.

Person inside of a circle

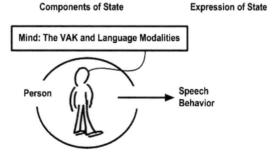

Lines for Intensity. When the state within the circle is very intense, we have *state-dependency.* The neuro-sciences have confirmed that all learning, memory, perception, communication, behavior, etc. is state-dependent. *The behaviors, emotions, thoughts, responses, etc. that emerge from our states depend upon our state.* Liked or disliked, these productions indicate the state out of which we live, the model of the world that drives that state, and the intended outcome of that experience.

Movie strip. In cartoons we see a person thinking with the series of little tiny circles coming out of the head and into a message cloud above the person's head. Here we use this to indicate the movie that's playing in a person's mind. What's on the screen of his mind? What movie is she playing in the theater of her consciousness? The movie strip stands for that movie, all of the sensory representational systems of the VAK (visual, auditory, kinesthetic).

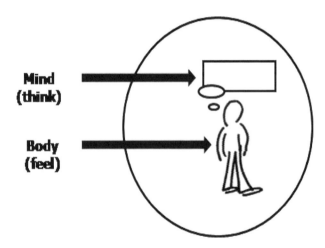

Pathways of entrance. At the primary state level, we can draw lines as roads or pathways into the sate. This enables us to visually represent the two "royal roads" to state—our internal representations (IR) and physiology. Within our internal representations are all of the things that are on our mind. This enables us to designate all of the sensory modalities of our mind as well as all of our beliefs, values, paradigms, decisions, etc. (the meta-states).

For the second pathway in we can use *body* to stand for all of the inherent physiological-neurological factors involved in our state. And because thinking-and-emoting always occurs as a holistic system, *T-F* stands for our state (or sometimes the letters *M-B* for mind-body).

Lines with arrows. These represent the feed back and feed forward loops of communication, the lines with arrows going out of the state to an object "out there" (X) identifies what we are in reference to — some person, event, situation, words, etc. We are thinking about and experiencing emotions about some event or situation. The lines with arrows pointing from the stimulus (X) to the state refer to the triggering of the stimulus. When we use arrowed-lines that point upward, we are referring to our meta-states as our responses to our responses.

Lines above the circle. Sometimes instead of a circle, *a line* will represent the higher *frames* of thought and emotion above a state as it refers back to the previous state. This indicates that the higher level conceptual state operates as the higher *frame-of-reference* and so it brackets within itself the lower levels. The line represents the higher frame as a category or classification of the experience which the person has set over him or herself.

*Person
inside of
layers of
frames*

Layers of Lines or Circles. By using one or more layers of lines or multiple circles we convey the idea of multiple layers of reflexivity. This creates the *matrix* of meanings that we live within and from which we operate. This maps out the fuller layers of beliefs upon beliefs that multiple meta-questions can flush out.

*Layers
of
circles*

Positive Intentions. As we move up the levels, setting another state or frame, we can explore our higher intentions, "What's my positive intention of thinking that, feeling that, or believing that?" Doing this repeatedly eventually enables us to discover our own or another's *positive intention* (PI). This fits the NLP premise, "Behind every behavior is a positive intention." Behind or above all of our actions is an attempt to do something of value for ourselves, to make things better, and to improve the quality of life.

This premise originated from the Human Potential Movement that Maslow launched from his studies of psychologically healthy people. He said that human nature is good or at least neural and not "evil," and that all of us seek to do the best we can for ourselves (even if the consequences are sometimes bad for others). It is our nature as human beings to expend our energy in seeking benefits and values.[2]

In diagraming a PI in the background of any state, we now have a visual picture of this presupposition that "Behind every behavior is a positive intention." It also incorporates the basic reframing principle that distinguishes person from his or her intention and behavior.

Dashes across as a frame line. Conceptually while we accept that we do things for positive and valued reasons, which arise from how we map things, the dashes as lines indicate that we are not always conscious of our positive intentions. Our first level intention may be negative—to get revenge, to get back at someone, to hurt someone, etc. So the dash lines indicate the line that separates what's in our conscious awareness and what is outside of consciousness.

Above the dashes are *our beyond-conscious-awareness-frames and understandings.* Here we are not aware of our positive intentions, our ultimate aims or values. Often we don't know what we feel or believe. So when we are asked, "What are you trying to do that's positive?" we are invited into a position where we are then able to either find or create positive intentions. In either case, it enables and empowers ourselves or another to be more and do more than before.

Before and Beyond. In the following diagram, the terms "before words" and "beyond words" incorporates Korzybski's distinctions about the "unspeakable" realms of reality. *Before words* refers to the energy manifestations beyond our skin "out there" which our sense receptors pick up on, but which do not register consciously in any way that we can talk about. This "before words" area (pre-verbal) involves the sensory-based awareness within our body and also the pre-sensory based awareness.

Going up the scale of abstraction, as we say words about words, and then evaluative words about those words, we finally get to the place *beyond words.* Here our ideas, conceptualizations, and abstractions race past our ability to articulate the experience. Here we don't have the words to describe our thoughts. As we move into higher and higher levels of meta-states, our mind-body experiences change as we transcend our languaging capabilities. Here we experience our highest transcendental or "spiritual" meta-states which operate as our executive states and self-organizing attractor states.

Figure 7:1

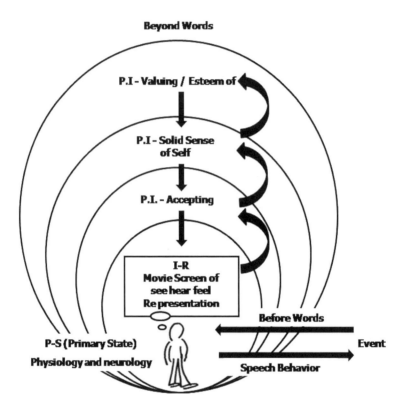

Summary

- The Meta-States model involves numerous concepts that are pretty abstract, however the model offers a way to see these concepts.

- You now know some of the ways we can diagram the processes of being in a state, going meta, reflexively abstracting, jumping logical levels, setting higher level frames, feedbacking to ourselves, feed forwarding out into the world, etc.

- Diagraming the meta-stating process of transcending and including level upon level of our thoughts and feelings and tracing the communication loops of feedback and feed-forward enable us to have a visual representation which simplifies the concepts.

End Notes:

1. Richard Bolstad and Margott Hamblett wrote about the visual digital system in an article by the title, "Visual Digital: Modality of the Future?" *NLP World,* Volume 6, No. 1, March 1999.

2. See *Self-Actualization Psychology,* pp. 266-269 under the section on Social conflict about "evil" in human personality.

Chapter 8

STATE #101

The Foundation for our Higher States

If *you* don't manage your state of mind-and-emotion,
your mind-body *state* will manage you.

I never leave home without my states.

When I teach, train, or present *Meta-States* as a model, I always begin with states — with primary states. There's a reason for that. The reason is that *to understand meta-states, you have to understand states.* There is also a second reason — meta-states grow out of primary states. This means that a regular or primary state serves as the foundational experience of a meta-state.

This shouldn't be a big surprise. After all, I found meta-states in the first place through exploring states. In the process of modeling the structure of resilience, I first identified the primary states of mind — states of emotion and body which made up the variables within resilience. From there, it was a simple meta-question that allowed the meta-state structures and frames to emerge. It was the simple meta-question:

"How did you know to go from this state in this stage of the resilience process to the next stage?"

That first meta-question invited the person being interviewed to step back from his experience and consider the higher state which he was operating from. As it did, it gave him the larger perspective that we would get through it all.

> "Oh, I'm here in this state right now, but I won't always be here. I'll move on. I have a larger perspective that I will get through this. In fact, I know that I'll get through this."

These thoughts and feelings were *about* the experience of working through things. They indicate a higher state about the person's current state. I didn't know it then, but now I realize that I called forth that meta-state in him by asking a meta-question. And because at that moment, with the three years of research in Korzybski and Bateson behind me, I just so happened to have the eyes and ears to see and hear the higher state, the meta-state.

The State of a State
*   What is a state?
*   How do states work?
*   What are the elements of a state?
*   What principles govern the experience of our states?
*   How do we work with our states for high level state management?

While *states* are part and parcel of the field of psychology and common language since the father of American Psychology, William James, wrote extensively about states, I really didn't learn much about states until I started studying NLP. That's when I learned that our states are *neuro-linguistic states,* states of mind-and-body which we experience primarily as emotional states. Outside the field of psychology, in business and everyday life, we refer to them as attitudes, moods, or emotions.

What then is the state of a state? Well, in spite of the term "state," which sounds like something static, unmoving, and stable, *a state is a dynamic, ever-changing, and always in flux experience.* And no wonder. As a mental state, it involves what's on your mind at any given moment. As an emotional state, it involves what you're feeling in the here-and-now. And as a physiological state, it involves the condition and state of your body. And because a state involves all of these components simultaneously, states are dynamic, full of energy, holistic, and non-linear (systemic).

A state is an energy field. When you are in a state, you experience mental energy, emotional energy, and even physiological energy. They encompass the energy you expend in thinking, emoting, acting, behaving, relating, valuing, symbolizing, anticipating, and so on and they create *the energies that make up your experiential state.* This is true whether you are in a state of fear or confidence, whether you are in a state of lust or love, in a state of self-esteem, forgiveness, bitterness, hatefulness, or justice seeking.

Because states involve your physical energy fields, you feel them. That's also why you can pick up the feel of the states of other people. You can sense and feel another's sadness, excitement, tension, calmness, and so on. You can feel the energy of the state in the person's breath, movement, gestures, voice, posture, etc.

The Communication Mapping of a State

When I began studying NLP, I discovered that it presents the structure of a subjective state from the standpoint of communication. That is, *a state results from what and how you communicate to yourself about the things happening to you.* Starting from the events "out there" in the world, NLP models inner subjective experiences in terms of your mental mapping. What, and how, you map what you see, hear, and feel and how you map the meanings you attribute about such becomes your inner reality—all of this *mapping* operates as your model of the world.

This means that your experience or reality is not a function of the world "out there" as much as it is a function of what and how you map that reality. This is reflected in Korzybski's famous statement, "The map is not the territory." A map, as a representation or fascimile of the territory, is useful to the extent that you can use it to go places. If you can use the map to navigate your way in and around the experiences that you want, then the map enhances the quality of your life.

This means that the crux of the matter of your life is not your DNA, parents, talents, etc., it is *what and how you map* the territory.

- How do you represent the outside world?
- What representations do you use?
- In which representational system—visual, auditory, kinesthetic, etc.?
- What is the quality of the sensory map that you use?
- What is the quality of your linguistic maps?
- What is the quality of your symbolic and metaphorical maps?

Whatever it is, *it is your mapping that creates your sense of reality.* Your mapping also puts you in various mind-body states—states that you experience. That is, as goes your internal self-communications about the world and events in the world, so goes your mental-and-emotional state. That's why when you're in a joyful state, it is inevitable that you are thinking joyful thoughts. When you're angry, you are entertaining angry thoughts. Think thoughts of anticipating a hopeful future, and presto! You will be feeling a hopeful anticipation. As goes your thoughts, so go your states. Or to express this biblically, "As you think in your heart, so you are."

"This Way to State" — The Royal Roads
Given this relationship between inner mapping and state, and as you will see in a minute between physiology and state, we have two royal roads to state. I use the phrase "royal roads" to play off of Sigmund Freud's phrase about dreams being the "royal road" to the unconscious. As mentioned earlier, both *mind* and *body* create the royal roads by which you can access and step into a mind-body state. As such, this gives you the ability to work more precisely with a state.

- *Mind:* What are you *thinking* right now that creates the confidence that you're feeling?
- *Body:* What's the most effective way for you to use your *body* to go into a deep and comfortable relaxation?

These "royal roads" also allow you to construct a desired state and even to work with its quality so that it is just right for you. How? Simply ask, "At its best what does this state look like, sound like, and feel like?" Ask that, and then all you need to do is to feed your mind great internal representations for your inner mental movie, step into that movie, and be there fully so that all of your physiology—your posture, breathing, behavior, movement, tone of voice, etc. begins to actualize it. Accessing a state is that easy.

And guess what? When you can do this, you are using the cognitive-behavioral discipline of NLP and its basic model and patterns to manage the contents and structure of consciousness. *You are running your own brain.* And, of course, when you take charge of running the content and processes of your brain, you are then able to manage your own states. Now you can call forth highly resourceful states at will. You can use your most resourceful states for taking your performance to new levels and even unleashing more of your unique potentials.

The first royal road of *internal representations* includes all the sensory-based information that you use. It includes the sights, sounds, sensations, smells and tastes of immediate sensory experience. It also includes the words and language forms that make up your beliefs, values, understandings, interpretations, explanations, etc. It includes your perceptual filters or meta-programs.[1] These are those outside of consciousness factors that govern what you pay attention to. Do you perceive things globally or specifically, by matching or mismatching, by stepping into your pictures or watching them.

As you internally re-present ideas, understandings, beliefs, etc. in the sensory and linguistic modes, you supply the contents of your mind-body state—your information. Yet *information* isn't neutral, it *forms* on the *inside,* that's the meaning of the word *in-form* and *in-form-ation.* You become inwardly formed and shaped by your sights, sounds, sensations, smells and language.

The second royal road to state of *physiology* includes all of your inner and outer behaviors, all of your neurology which activates motor programs, glands, neurology, emotions, etc. Physiology also includes such external factors as what and how you eat, sleep patterns, exercise and health behaviors, your biochemistry, intake of psychoactive drugs, disease and illness, etc.

State Management
NLP focuses on state management in terms of "running your own brain." Co-founder Richard Bandler uses the metaphor of driving your own bus. "Who's driving the bus?" If you are not, then someone else is![2] Today, we are more apt to talk about state management in terms of *emotional intelligence.*[3]

As a communication model about human functioning, NLP focuses attention on your mapping and how you are bringing into your inner mental theater the landscape of events out there inside yourself. You do that by using sensory representations and language as you make sense of things and create your reality constructions. And because these are the processes that create your states, all you have to do to manage your states is to monitor and control the content of your thoughts, how you think, and your physiology. If you do that, you will be able to manage your states and experience the emotional intelligence of self-awareness and self-discipline.

Self-Awareness
The first requirement for becoming aware of the presence, nature, and functioning of your state is to *identify your states*.
- What is your present state?
- How did you get into that state?
- What are the contributing factors in this state?
- How can you effectively interrupt a state or spin-out a state?
- How do you quality control the state to determine if it is productive or limiting?
- Is it empowering or dis-empowering?

Three Kinds of States
NLP has historically only distinguished between *the quality* of states (i.e., limiting or enhancing) and "core" states (Andreas and Andreas, 1991). With the discovery of Meta-States, we distinguish three kinds of states. First, *primary states* at the first level of experience, then *meta-states* at multiple higher logical levels. And as a system of interactive parts, multiple meta-states gives rise to new emergent properties that gives us even richer and more complex states, *gestalt states*.[4]

Primary States
Every human experience begins with a primary state. Like the primary colors from which come all of the other states, the primary states give rise to all of the higher meta-states. There are probably twelve to twenty or thirty such states.[5]

Tense / Stress	— — — — —	Relaxed / Calm
Love	— — — — —	Apathy/ Indifference
Anger	— — — — —	Fear

Approach	— — — — —	Avoidance
Like /Attraction	— — — — —	Disgust / Hate
Glad	— — — — —	Sad
Strong	— — — — —	Weak
Surprise	— — — — —	Familiarity

Because states are comprised of many component elements within our mind-body system, *states are systemic*. This means that the interacting parts of a state influence the whole of the state. As a system of interacting parts, every component affects the overall gestalt. This requires a degree of systems thinking to understand and work with your states. Your states emerge from a total effect of many parts—your learning history, health and well-being, relationships, career, friendships, purpose, pain—pleasure conditioning, thoughts, beliefs, values, etc.

One indicator of a primary mind-body state is that it has direct reference to the world "out there." Primary states represent a kind of primordial experience—direct and undiluted. Typically, we find these more pure experiences characterized also by intensity, directness, and simplicity.

A prototype primary state is the state of fear. In the state of fear your thoughts-and-feelings represent an awareness of danger or threat and so send messages to your nervous systems to prepare for danger. The messages signals your old brain (the deeper parts of the brain and brain stem) to activate your physiology of retreat and avoidance—of flight. In fear, everything in your thinking-feeling state seeks to *move away from* the feared object. The feeling of avoidance activates our motor programs with adrenalin that quickly, automatically, and powerfully moves us away from fear's object.

Anger also fits this prototype of a primary state. Anger activates the same total physiological arousal as does fear with one exception. The anger state propels us in the opposite direction—to *go at* the threatening object. In anger, our entire neurology becomes aroused along with our thinking, evaluating, and believing so that we seek to take on, defeat, conquer, win over, and do away with the threat.

The primary state of *sadness* involves the perception of loss and so triggers feelings of loss. When we feel sad, we engage in a reality adjustment as we "come to terms with a loss." Here our physiology and cognitions enable us to adjust to a loss as we grieve that loss. This enables us to adjust ourselves to the new reality of life apart from the valued person, thing, event, situation, or idea. The tears of grief, along with the de-pressing (pushing down) of energies, hopes, desires, actions, etc., assist us in withdrawing interest and attachment. This frees us so that we can redefine ourselves, our reality, and the loss. It enables us to recognize what we do not have (perhaps cannot have), and moves us to create a new direction into which we can invest our emotions, energies, time, and self.

How do you experience the primary state of *joy*? As you think about some simple pleasure to which you respond with a pleasant delightful happiness—a sunset, biting into a delicious apple, a sense of health, laughing with some friends, where do you experience "joy" in your body? How does it feel in terms of muscle tension, breathing, and posture?

In primary states, your immediate thoughts (internal representations) elicit corresponding emotions so you can easily specify where in your body you experience that *specific set of corresponding kinesthetic sensations*. Sometimes you may discover that you do not have to have any specific words or sentences in your mind. We often experience primary states as a set of sensations without any words. We experience the state prior to bringing words to define or describe it. We may simply have a visual image or internal movie, or some sounds, tones, music, or words represented in a specific way, or just sensations of breathing, muscle tone, posture.

Precisely because you experience these pure or primary states so directly, simply, and intensely, *you can easily anchor them*. You can link them to some other stimuli (a sight, sound, word, smell, etc.). By *linking* the state with another stimuli whenever you trigger ("fire off") the linked stimuli, you re-trigger the state. You bring it back into your mental-neurological experience.

State Dependency
You are always in a state. You never leave home without being in some state. You always operate out of some state. Recognizing this

enables you to learn to calibrate to your states and the states of others. This develops your emotional intelligence and self-awareness.

Stop for a moment and think about your current state. Describe your state. As you read this material, are you in a *learning state?* Are you feeling curious and receptive? If so, then you undoubtedly have easily followed along with this discussion. If not, then you may experience some difficulty following, remembering, and processing these ideas. You may find your thoughts sliding off to other concerns.

You experience life as we do via your states. Your life, like my life, is a composite of your mental and emotional states. This becomes true with a vengeance in "state dependency." As states are holistic mind-body phenomena, all of your learning, memory, perception, communication, and behavior are state-dependent.

So when you get into a silly state, you can laugh at almost anything. The lamp stand. Your shoe. His ear. Later, when you get into a more sober state, you may scratch your head and wonder. "What in the world was so funny about that?"

State-dependency explains why everything looks so dark and gloomy when you access a depressed state. You then easily remember depressing things, seeing depressing things, talking and acting in depressive ways. So with the angry state. From that state, anything can be taken as a threat or insult. You see the world through red lens. If you stay in that state for long, you may eventually carry around a "chip on your shoulder" which enables you to quickly "fly into a rage" at any moment.

State dependency does a trip on all of us. When it happens to you, the problems you suffer which seem to be about something out there are actually a problem of your state. Then with habituation, you streamline the state allow you to quickly fly into that state. And once there, you see the world through the eyes, ears, and skin of that state. The state becomes your *frame* for how you perceive things. For this reason, you need to have some excellent ways to break or interrupt state. Then you can *have* our states rather than them *having* you.

The Daily Flow and Ebb of States

States come and go; we are constantly shifting our states. How many states do you go in and out of throughout a day? There are days when I visit a dozen or so states, there are days when I will experience thirty or more states. How do I know that? Because I have kept a journal of my daily states for weeks at a time.[5]

This constant shifting of state arises from numerous factors. It arises, in part, from the very structure of our biorhythms. Merely waking up in the morning involves a shifting of state, from the sleep state to the waking state.

How *pleasant or unpleasant* do you experience the states you visit during your days? What would you say represent your favorite states? Describe your most disliked states? You can evaluate states in this way —quality control them using various criteria. You can run an ecology check on your states to see if they serve you well or not, whether they increase your resourcefulness or not, whether they bring out your best or not. After all, who has control—you or the state? State management involves awareness, monitoring, and effectively managing your states.

Speed State Shifting

How quickly can you shift state? Can you "fly into a rage?" What a high level skill of state shifting. You have all the neurological equipment necessary to fly into anger, fear, self-pity, stubbornness, and other negative states. And you do. You fly into those kinds of states with greater facility than you fly into more positive states of calmness, joy, thoughtfulness, assertiveness, contentment, etc. What explains this perversity?

Habit. You have repeatedly practiced getting moving into a state of negative thinking and emoting and so the shift has streamlined. Now you can do it with incredible speed.

Yet, do you have a telephone voice that you can access with great speed? Can you be yelling at your kids or spouse one minute, then when you hear the phone ring, answer it with a calm and pleasant "phone voice." "Hello?" You can shift gears and all of a sudden answer the phone with a pleasant voice. If you can do that, then you have all the neurological equipment you need to fly into a different state. You may only need the training with any given specific state.

States solidify. By habituating a response you streamline the accessing process (i.e., the strategy). Then you can quickly get back to it and do so on cue. Simply sending your brain continually to certain internal representations and putting your body into the corresponding physiology reinforces and streamlines the state. As the signals become habituated, the neuro-pathways become well-conditioned as an automatic response. You can then fly into a state without even thinking about it.

Some people show remarkable powers at shifting states. A person who grows up in an unsafe environment, where they had to learn to respond in a hyper-alert state, may habituate *shifting* all the time so that it becomes their style. Later a doctor may label them as A.D.D. or "hyperactive." If a person lives constantly in a hyper-vigilant state, and the vigilance becomes chronic, he or she will probably undermine the inherent skill at focusing consciousness on one thing. "Attention deficit," in a great many cases, simply describes someone who has made such learnings and over-does vigilance. Consequently, they under-practice the states of focus and concentration.

The Nature of Primary States
Primary states are primarily governed by the sensory-based representations—what you see, hear, smell, sense, etc., yielding primary awareness for primary states. And as you will see in the next chapter, what we call "sub-modalities," (i.e., the distinctions of our sights, sounds, sensations, smells, etc.), actually operate at meta-levels to these sensory systems which means they are not really *sub* at all, but *meta*.

What drives your states? Often it is the specific pictures, sounds, words, and sensations. A person phobic about flying may have a picture of a airplane in mind and see it flying in mid-air and then exploding. The person will almost always see this short movie in color, 3-D, filling the screen of the mind, and with appropriate sounds of explosion. And because this movie drives the fearful state, changing the movie changes the state.

Suppose, however, that the person sits back and edits the movie so that a new script is played out: the plane takes off and lands safely without incident. The person sees himself onboard, enjoying the trip, and then de-planing by walking off in a relaxed manner. That movie induces a different state.

Instantaneous Learnings

There are times when the emotions of a state are so strong that you experience what's called a one-time learning. This associative learning leaves so strong a first impression that almost any of the sights, sounds, smells, or sensations thereafter re-trigger the state. A strong emotional-laden experience can then become so linked with a primary emotion like fear, anger, aversion, attraction, stress, relaxation, etc. that the experience, or a part of it, can re-trigger or anchor that state. Thereafter, every time a guy sees an elevator, for example, he goes into panic state. Every time a gal hears, "You idiot!" in a particular tonality, she feels the aversion and fear state of being profoundly insulted. Every shaking of an index finger elicits a sense of being scolded.

In primary states, you see, hear, and feel things from out of your own eyes, ears, and skin. You are in "first person." You see, hear, and feel the information *as if you are inside the movie.*

Your States — Your Life

As you are undoubtedly picking up, states are important. Mostly they are critical to the quality of your life. That leads me to a critical principle:

> *The quality of your states determines the quality of your life.*

And since you "never leave home without your states," and since they govern the quality and nature of your everyday experience, and since state-dependency governs your thinking, perceiving, remembering, languaging, and behaving—then *the quality of your states determines the quality of your life.* Your ability to implement what you know, and to live out of your wisdom, depends entirely upon getting yourself into the right kind of state.

Given all that, what prevents you from putting your knowledge into practice more consistently? Think about the last time that you did not put something you know into action. What stopped you? What held you back? Did you just not feel like it?

Isn't this why and how self-sabotage occurs? How often do you use, *"I don't feel like it!"* as an excuse? And doesn't that, in turn, undermine your implementation power? As a mind-body state, it does prevent you from activating your highest insights and skills, and works against you taking effective action.

Given that states can undermine your effectiveness and crucially govern the quality of your experiences, what can you do to take charge of your states? How can you learn to manage your states more effectively? How can you access the right kind of resourceful states?

> *The quality of your states determines the quality of your life.*

Managing Consciousness and Meaning

Because of the correlation between thoughts and state, *consciousness inescapably plays a crucial and determining role regarding your states.* As goes your mind—so goes your states. Your state inevitably reflects your consciousness.

Consciousness is crucial because it induces, creates, and generates states. You can count on this psychological principle as the causative factor driving how you experience your states. It will not always *seem* this way. External stimuli in the form of people, events, words, situations, etc. *seem* to cause the state. But they do not.

Meaning causes and determines your states as consciousness reflects your states. This explains why different stimuli evokes different responses in different people. What evokes fear in one, evokes anger in another, humor in another, and depression in another. Jumping out of an airplane triggers one to panic, one to attack, one to faint, and one to jump for joy!

Losing a job triggers one person to depress:

       "I'll never succeed; I never get any breaks!"

It leads another to guilt:

       "I should have worked harder! What's wrong with me?"

Another will blame:
        "That rotten, good-for-nothing boss!"
Yet another will anger and rage:
        "Take this job and shove it!"
It will lead another to use it as a stepping stone for learning:
        "What can I learn from that experience?"
        "I feel excited about the possibilities that I can now explore!"

One trigger, yet so many responses. What explains the range of these different responses? *Each person's unique and individual consciousness of attributed meanings creates these responses.* As goes your thinking, valuing, believing, perceiving, understanding, attributing of

> Meaning causes and determines your states as consciousness reflects your states.

meaning, deciding, judging, evaluating, etc.—so goes your state, out of which flows your thinking, emoting, communicating, behaving, and responding.

States have the property of being semantic in nature. Your states involve your cognitive processes which generate the meanings that you experience. Your states function as expressions of the meanings (semantics) you attribute to your experiences. Some of these represent sane, unsane, and even insane semantic states.

State Governs Consciousness

Now for a twist. Not only does your consciousness create your states, but once you are in a state—*the state itself determines, or at least strongly influences, consciousness.* This brings us back to state-dependency. At the experiential level, your state colors your perception, memory, learning, communicating, feeling, and behaving. Or you could say that your states operates as your frames—your frames of mind.

This explains why you think, perceive, feel, etc. in ways that *accord to your state.* In a learning state you feel curious and experience your mind open and alert. State-dependency explains this. *You experience life via your states.* Often this comes true with a vengeance as when you access a state characterized by depression, jealousy, fearfulness, timidity, pessimism, etc.

Upon entering into a state, the state influences your psychological functioning. It governs your thinking, remembering, learning, perceptions, communicating, emoting, and behaving. And the more you experience state-dependent learning, perceiving, and emoting, the more you can kiss goodbye your "objectivity." Your world becomes increasingly colored by your states.

Recall the last time you experienced a *ludicrous* state? You could perceive just about everything from a viewpoint of ludicrousness. Suddenly, the whole world seemed like a Bugs Bunny cartoon. You took nothing serious. You perceived things in a light-hearted way; it all looked ridiculous.

Compare that to the last time you experienced a *sad* state. How did you feel then? Probably down, blue, and unmotivated. You probably thought in terms of your loss and the diminishment of your world. You saw grief wherever you looked. Everything reminded you of your sadness.

Figure 8: 1
A State of Consciousness

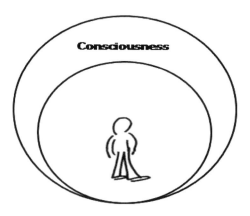

Compare that to the last time you felt "as mad as hell" about something. How did you experience your body, breathing, muscle tension, energy level, and motivation? When you experienced that state, how did your thoughts order themselves? Where did your mind go? Did you speak differently?

So as you go into various states, your whole experience changes. Your perceiving, feeling, thinking, remembering, learning, communicating, and behaving changes to correspond to the state. And all of this functions as a loop. Your consciousness creates your states and your states determine your consciousness. Together these phenomena systemically work together to affect and influence each other. They feed each other.

The more you get into a stressed-out state, the more things stress you out. The more you access an anger state, the more things anger you. The more you access the fear state, the more fearful, scared and paranoid you become. In this, *states often operate as a self-reinforcing loop.* On the negative side, this can create vicious cycles of responses amplifying and intensifying the original state and blowing things all out of proportion.

This aspect of states explains how you experience your states cycling around and around on themselves, feeding and amplifying your experience until they become bigger, wilder and more out-of-control. This describes one of the ongoing challenges of living. *It also underscores that either you take charge of your states or they will control you.* And, on the positive side, it can lead you from strength to strength, amplifying your resources and creating more resources.

The Streamlining of States
Due to this holistic mind-body phenomenon of habituation and state dependency, your mental and emotional states often take on a life of their own. This happens, in part, because by repeatedly experiencing a state of thought, emotion, or physiology, it habituates.

Everything perpetuated over time-space becomes a habit. And so you create habits of mind, habits of emotion, speech, and behavior. Eventually, the process by which you create and generate the state drops out of consciousness and becomes increasingly unconscious. When it operates rapidly and automatically, that's when you can "fly into a state."

As you perpetuate states, the habituation process installs them so that they define your personality. They solidify to become your attitude. Experiencing and re-experiencing a state also streamlines the accessing process. You develop the ability to move quickly into the state. Your mental and physical cues enables you to now get into those states almost instantaneously and without thinking about it. It becomes one of your unconscious competences. It becomes a frame-of-reference so you have an internal context by which you stay cued up to quickly access that state. And because you live out of it, we say it has become your character.

The chief disadvantage of this occurs when you forget. You forget that *you* created this entire process. As the habituation process takes the process out of conscious effort, it leaves you with the feeling that you don't *have* your states, but *your states have you*. It contributes to your sense that external stimuli causes your states. The consciousness that you used to create the state simply becomes un-conscious in you. Then you lose awareness of the thoughts, beliefs, understandings, etc. by which you create your states.

Interrupting a Run-Away State

To manage your mind in accessing productive and empowering states, you need the ability to interrupt dis-empowering and unresourceful states. You can do this because you interrupt states all the time.

It happens anytime you engage yourself deeply in some activity, and suddenly the phone rings. You then become engrossed in a conversation about a completely different matter. When you eventually hang up, you can't seem to remember where you had left off. You say, "Now where was I?"

Or, you suddenly remember that you need something from another room. You get up to go get it. Then about halfway across the room, the thought slips away. You can't remember what you got up to get. "Now what did I get up for?" That's a state interrupt.

Sometimes you can recover that thought if you retrace your steps and sit in the chair where you first conceived the thought. State-dependent memory is at work here. The memory has become anchored to place, events, and situations.

State interruptions occur all the time. Do you only experience it in undesirable ways rather than manage it so it works *for* you? State interrupts happen to you when you least expect it or want it. You simply do not intentionally and consciously use it as a tool for managing your lives.

When you really need it, as when you continue to toss and turn on your bed, and suffer the agonies of insomnia, you don't seem able to interrupt the rush and flow and intensity of your thoughts. Yet let a person drive hour after hour on a desolate freeway, when they could really use a good case of insomnia, and insomnia evades them. Or when you really want to interrupt some unresourceful state that a loved one has gotten in, but you can't think of any way to do a pattern interrupt except for some very inelegant method (and ineffective) like yelling, "Will you shut up!?"

Because there will be many times when you'll really need to interrupt your own states as well as those of others, be sure to develop a number of pattern interrupts. Then you can manage your consciousness and prevent your states from cycling around un-usefully.

Quality Control
One of your powers of consciousness is to use your mind as an evaluator. You can step back from whatever level of your consciousness, step up to the next level and evaluate it in terms of its quality. Now you can evaluate your states. Now you can quality control your mind-body system. To quality control states, simply ask yourself a variety of ecology questions:
* Is my current state productive or unproductive?
* Do I find my current state useful or unuseful?
* Enhancing or unenhancing?
* Empowering or dis-empowering?
* Does my state feel resourceful or unresourceful?
* Does it make things better or make them worse?
* Does it put me more in charge of my life or less?
* Does it move me in the direction of my values and principles or away from them?

Summary
* States are ubiquitous because you never leave home without them. Yet these states are dynamic, ever-changing, holistic, neuro-linguistic, and semantic. They govern the very fabric and

quality of your lives.

- *State* describes a way to think about the nature and quality of your everyday experiences. The quality of your states determines the quality of your life. No wonder state management is so important.
- Knowing that you have two *royal roads* to state—mind (internal representations) and body (physiology) gives you two pathways into state.

- *State dependency* can be a horrendous problem or a fabulous resource. In both cases, when a state becomes intense, your learning, perception, communication, behavior, memory, etc. becomes dependent on the state. This indicates the systemic influence and power of your states.

- In every domain of life, your competency in managing your state management plays an essential role in mastery and responsibility.

End Notes

1. In the final analysis, meta-programs are solidified meta-states. See *Figuring Out People* (2005).

2. See *Using Your Brain—For a Change* (1985).

3. For a book about NLP applied to emotional intelligence, see *Seven Steps to Emotional Intelligence* (1997) by Denis Bridoux, Patrick Merlevede, and Rudy Vandamme. Also see Daniel Goleman, *Emotional Intelligence*.

4. For more about primary states, see *Emotional Mastery* training manual. Also Robert Plutchik (1962) work, *The Emotions: Facts, Theories, and a New Model.*

5. Robert Plutchik (1962, 1991) introduced a model based upon primary emotions, secondary emotions, triary emotions, etc., *The Emotions: Facts, Theories, and a New Model.*

6. See Appendix A, Journaling States for a full description of how to use bubble journaling to raise awareness of the states we are always experiencing.

Chapter 9

THE HIGHER STATES

Up the Levels of Your Mind

If *primary states* are your first-level sensory-based experiences and correspond to your primary emotions (sad, mad, glad, and fear), *you enter an entirely new domain of existence and experience when you make the meta-jump into meta-states.*

At the higher levels *meta* to your primary states, you experience second-level, third-level, etc. phenomena of mind and emotion. These states involve complex and multi-layered emotions like self-esteem or self-contempt, resilience or "feeling like a failure," etc. When you experience these, you experience conceptual or semantic states. This is the next stop on our discovery. Now we move beyond the primary states to the higher states of mind and emotion, to the executive states that involve greater complexity and layeredness of consciousness, and to the states-*about*-states.

Moving Up the Levels of States
It always begins with state as the combination of thinking (mind), emoting (emotions), and physiological experiencing (body). This dynamic experience is a holistic expression of attitude and orientation and emerges as a gestalt from thinking (representing, valuing, believing, etc.) and physiology—your royal roads to state.

In a *primary state*, you use your thinking, emoting, and somatic responses to relate to the outside world. In the primary state of anger, you feel angry *about* something external to yourself—to a threat or danger. Some external object evokes your attention and triggers your emotions of anger.

> "It angers me that I have to work on the weekend."
> "I get really mad when a reckless driver tailgates me."
> "It pisses me off when John talks down to me at work."

All of this changes radically when you move up. In meta-states your thoughts-and-emotions relate to something *internal*, rather than to something "out there." Now your thoughts-emotions *reflect back onto yourself* —to previous thoughts-and-emotions, to a prior state, or to the products of another state (how you have talked or acted).

> " . . . the human nervous system has become so complex that it is now able to affect its own states, making it to a certain extent functionally independent on its genetic blueprint and of the objective environment. A person can make himself happy, or miserable, regardless of what is actually happening 'outside,' just by changing the contents of consciousness."
> Mihalyi Csikszentmihalyi
> (*Flow*, p. 24)

> "I hate it when I feel so uptight about the way John talks down to me."
> "I feel guilty about feeling angry and bitter about what happens at work."

Figure 9:1

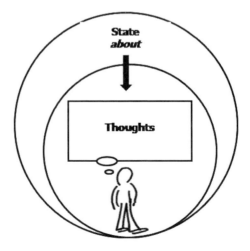

From the primary experience of interacting with the world at large and experiencing thoughts-and-emotions about that world, you move to a meta-level of experiencing so that *now you are interacting with your own states of consciousness.* You are responding to your responses.

In self-contempt, you relate a state of contemptful thoughts to your primary state of self. You now experience, and live out of, a higher level state that references a previous state. Let's start with the state of feeling anger, or behaving like an irrational hothead, or being fearful and timid in speaking up. Now let's ask a meta-question, "How do you feel *about* that experience?"

Whatever thoughts-and-feelings arise to that point, those thoughts-and-feelings reference your *first level* thoughts-and-feelings. Doing this moves you into a position *meta* to your first level. You move to a meta-level of awareness, feeling, and experiencing.

Figure 9:2

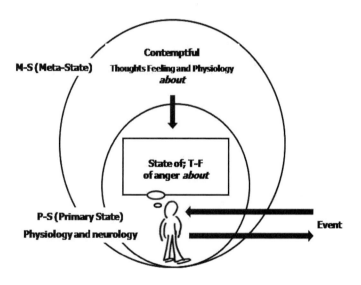

Meta-Levels

What is a meta-level? It is a level that is above another level, it has reference to a level below it. As this meta-relationship emerges, the higher level inevitably affects the lower levels as it organizes and drives it. It serves as the higher frame-of-reference for the lower level. From this, meta-states can generate a wide range of interfacing effects from amplifying the primary state, reversing it, negating it, transforming it, etc. From the meta-level, the state can create a more intensified experience and it can also create paradoxical experiences.

Meta-states involves several pieces, or even multiple pieces, of awareness and emotion. Such states may even involve many layers of consciousness about consciousness.

> "I feel bad about feeling so petty about my embarrassment and upsetness over being caught off-guard about the surprise party the other day."

A state of mind-emotion like that is not only a meta-state, it is a *complex* meta-state—one comprised of several layers of embedded states within states.

Figure 9:3

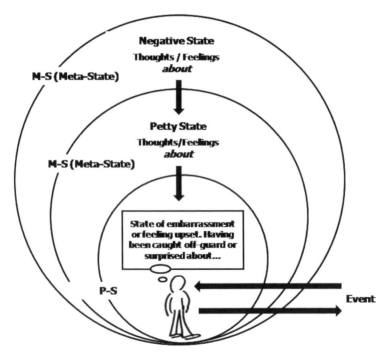

Consider that experience for a moment, what would that person think and feel?

At the core of the experience the person would be feeling surprise and shock. And how does the person *respond* to those feelings? With a self-conscious sense of embarrassment along with some upset feelings (perhaps he or she felt uncomfortable, out of sorts, weird, etc.). To that the person then entertains some petty thoughts and feelings by which he or she made a big deal about things, thus complicating matters. Later, as the person processed through all of this, more thoughts and feelings arose which evaluates and judges the person's response in a negative ("bad") way. And with that, the person has successfully generated a tremendous *meta-muddle* of thoughts-and-emotions.

The Mechanism that Creates Meta-States

What creates meta-states? What mechanism, function, or process allows us to layer one state upon another? What is this conceptual ability of being able to go meta? How are we able to go meta, conceptually move to a meta-level, and abstract (i.e., create an abstraction) about a previous abstraction (Korzybski, 1933/1994)?

> The answer lies in our special kind of consciousness—*self-reflexive consciousness*. In exercising our self-reflexive consciousness we use the very capacity which enables us to create and experience meta-states.

And what is self-reflexivity? To say that your consciousness is self-reflexive means that you can *reflect back onto* the very processes and products of your consciousness. That is, after you have said something, thought something, or felt something, we can then reflect back upon these responses, and think, feel, say something about your first responses. You are now responding to your earlier responses.

This dynamic creates numerous meta-responses, layers of them. Reflexivity leads to meta-thinking, meta-communicating, meta-feelings, meta-modeling, and meta-analyzing.

And with these meta-cognitions, meta-feelings, meta-responses, you begin to create multi-layers of states, states-upon-states. Not only that, but you can do so over and over again to create ever increasingly layers of complexity. And because this process is infinite inside you, it has no end; you can always think something else about all of your previous thoughts.

> *"We call it 'self-awareness'*
> *or the ability to think about*
> *your very thought process.*
> This is the reason why
> man has dominion over all things in the world
> and why he can make significant advances
> from generation to generation.
> This is why we can evaluate
> and learn from others' experiences . . .
> This is also why we can make
> and break our habits."
> Stephen Covey
> *Seven Habits of Highly Effective People*
> (p. 66)

Reflexivity as a process of your consciousness inevitably results in meta-states. This inescapable process also results in the building of highly complex states of consciousness. And best of all, this unique human ability to think about yourself and your expressions (e.g., your thinking, feeling, choosing, and behaving) enables you to *transcend* your immediate time, space, being, values, and experiences. You can and do continuously transcend your current experiences and include them inside of other awarenesses. In this way you keep embedding one level of reality inside of higher frames that operate all sorts of altered states, some which are problems and others which are resources.

When you resourcefully meta-state, you create the richest and highest of states—states of genius, flow, transcendence, self-actualization. When you unresourcefully meta-state, you create neuroses, psychoses, "dragons," limitations, diseases, and all sorts of human "evil." The reason this becomes destructive is simple: you are turning your energies against yourself and thereby putting yourself in self-attack.

Self-reflexive consciousness gives you this strange ability to *go meta* which lies at the source of the mystical and spiritual feelings of transcendence which inevitably follow. Reflexivity is what endows you with a transcendental consciousness, an awareness of conceptual realities that transcend the immediate sensory world so that you feel and sense and believe in other and higher worlds.

It is this inner *transcending capacity* that's the basis for all the experiences we label as existential, ontological, and spiritual. To the extent that Meta-States provides a way to model the structure of your meaning-making, it takes us beyond mere information processing, to the developing of *beliefs* about all kinds of things: self, purpose, destiny, meaning, existence, etc. It also takes you to the domain where you create *beliefs about your beliefs* — to belief systems — and with that it takes you up into the realms of potentialities and possibilities of human potential.

Consider this wondrous human ability you have to *go meta,* and to abstract repeatedly to ever new levels above and beyond your current state of consciousness. This *meta-move* as your ability to transcend your current thinking-and-feeling provides you the foundation for creating a great many levels of states upon states. It creates your Matrix of meaning frames about life and reality. And with that, you begin to do what we humans do best, you layer concept upon concept creating ever larger and more semantically significant layers. In this way you create all kinds of meta-states: *simple* and *complex* meta-states, *conscious* and *unconscious* meta-states, *congruent* and *incongruent* meta-states, *floater* meta-states, gestalt states, etc.

Korzybski's Prelude to Meta-States
When Alfred Korzybski, the founder of General Semantics, developed neuro-linguistic trainings in the 1930s and 1940s, he described the functioning of self-reflexive consciousness as "consciousness of abstracting." He said this was the key to both personal sanity and human science. To explain this, he articulated a model of the levels of abstraction which he called the *Structural Differential.* In this model, he tracked the construction of information from the outside world to the highest constructs. This allowed him to specify different levels:

Level 1: Energy Manifestations
Outside the human nervous system is the world of energy manifestations of the electromagnetic field. This world never enters consciousness. What does enter is information or data about that world. It enters in *as you map the world* "out there" using neurological *transforms* and *abstracts.* Korzybski used the term *abstracting* to

describe how you select some pieces of the information to attend and to use as your neurological mapping.

Level 2: Human Sense Receptors

From the energy forces "out there" in the world, you pick up clues and data about them via your sense receptors. From these sense receptors you abstract at the next level. That is, you summarize and transform that information as you create an internal facsimile or map of what you sense out there. By their nature and structure, the sense receptors (your eyes, ears, skin, tongue, etc.) can only abstract a small portion of what exists. Your nervous systems, for example, lack the equipment to see very much of the electromagnetic light spectrum, or experience other stimuli (e.g., pharemones). Consequently, you leave characteristics out as you delete them from your mapping.

Level 3: Event Level

Your nervous system with its structure of axons, neurons, dendrites, nerve impulses, neuro-transmitters, and specific sense receptors work to abstract certain patterns of nervous impulses and energy. The event level is also a level prior to your conscious awareness and the words you use to talk about it. At this level of abstraction, while you are able to *sense* the world, you are not conscious of it. It is encoded at subconscious levels of awareness. This is a pre-language level of awareness.

Level 4: Conscious Level

As the impulses and neurotransmitter stimulate differing parts of the brain (thalamus, cortex, etc.), these parts of the brain abstract to create various internal representations of the outside world. It is at this level that you first experience conscious awareness of the world of sensory stimuli. You now become conscious of the stimuli.

Level 5: The first linguistic level

As sensory-based stimulations (e.g., sights, sounds, sensations, smells) occur, giving you your representational movie of the world out there, you abstract another level. You do this by constructing words and linguistic descriptions about the movie that you play in your mind—your internal representations. As you then label your representations with descriptive or sensory language you move to your first linguistic level.

Level 6: Evaluative linguistic level
The next shift and the next level occurs as you use more conceptual and symbolic language. Here you evaluate using higher level abstractions and concepts. With evaluative language you use more conceptual words about your first words, as you categorize, classify, invent theories, etc.

Level 7: Etc.
And on it goes. We continue this abstracting process infinitely. Korzybski used the extensional device of "*Etc.*" to describe this as an unending process. Whatever you say about anything, you can always then say more words about those words. This capacity for abstracting, for going meta, and for reflecting back onto your previous abstractions never ends. It is an infinite process.

Figure 9:4

The more you abstract, the more you move into the land of

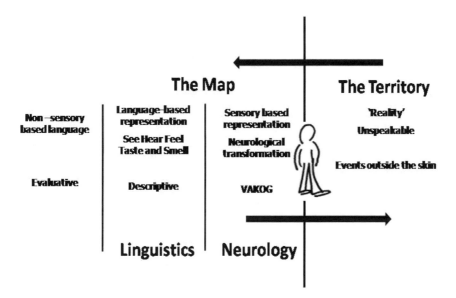

abstractions, the mental world of ideas, and ideas about ideas. This leads to higher and higher understandings, schemas, models, theories, hypothesis, etc. about the world, and takes you further and further away from experiential reality at the sensory level. This progress from empirical to abstraction is an essential part of the scientific process.

And in this way you create your "mind." That is, you construct the meta-levels of your mind from your conceptual understandings while you lose awareness of your senses. This is the reverse process that Fritz Perls referred to when he urged awareness focus in Gestalt Therapy, "Lose your mind and come to your senses."

As you abstract in this "going meta" process, you begin living through definitions, ideas, concepts, abstractions, beliefs, hallucinations, etc. If you do this as your primary way of relating to the world, then you develop what Korzbyski described as "an intensional orientation." This means you relate to the world by *the word definitions in your head* (intensional). He contrasted this to an "extensional orientation" which refers to orienting yourself to the empirical world of sights, sounds, sensations and smells (the VAK world of sensory experience—visual, auditory, kinesthetic).[1]

If you ask me where you can find meta-states in Korzybski's General Semantics, or in *Science and Sanity,* the answer is easy. You will find it in his descriptions of the following which were ways Korzybski attempted to map out Meta-States:
- Second-order abstractions
- Third-order abstractions and so on
- The Structural Differential
- The Theory of Multi-Ordinality

Meta-States — A Higher Level Domain
The field of NLP has several domains of knowledge and skill. These include Modeling (strategies), the Meta-Model of language, Meta-Programs, Meta-Modalities (the so-called area of "Sub-modalities"), Time-Lines, Reframing, and Hypnotic Language patterns from the Milton Model. In each of these domains of study there's a basic model that describes an area or discipline. That is, in each, there's a theoretical explanation about the model, how it works, what it's about, a set of guidelines that govern its operation, the elements, components, or variables that make up the unique pieces within that domain, and a set of patterns that provide practical applications for using the model.

When Bandler and Grinder first offered the model of the representational systems of sensory modalities, they presented something new to psychology in terms of tracking human subjectivity in terms of specific representational steps. By utilizing something so simple (and obvious) as "the sensory senses" for the component parts of "thought," *they turned these modalities into the languages of thought*. This transformed and endowed the sense modalities of visual, auditory, kinesthetic, olfactory, and gustatory so that they became the cornerstone of the NLP model. Gregory Bateson noted his surprise about this creative innovation in his Introduction to the first NLP book, *The Structure of Magic (Volume I)*.

They then supplemented the representation systems with *a meta-modality,* namely the linguistic representational system (often called auditory digital or A_d). If you map the territory of the world by generating internal sights, sounds, and sensations with your *neurological* representations, you map the sensory map *linguistically* as you use language and words about those first level representations.

Sometime later, Richard Bandler and Todd Epstein introduced the domain that Bandler eventually dubbed "sub-modalities." Yet before they invented that term, they called it *pragmagraphics*—a much more accurate term. It means the *graphics* or images that have *pragmatic* effects in your inner movies and in your neurology. But Bandler said that term was too cumbersome, so he came up with the term, "sub-modalities," as if that isn't a cumbersome term! Of course, the problem with that term is that it falsely implies that there is a sub-level to the sensory-based modalities. In actuality, these only refer to the qualities, properties, distinctions, or components and so are *the cinematic features* of our mental movies and representations.[2]

In spite of this misunderstanding and unfortunate terminology, "sub-modalities" opened up an entirely new domain in NLP which led to numerous refinement of patterns, insights, and technologies. These quickly emerged as the model provided new and different ways to think about the features and qualities of the representational systems.

As an aside, to demonstrate that "sub-modalities" actually operate at a meta-level, you only need observe that some "sub-modalities" are also meta-programs. For example, zooming in is specific details and zooming out is global or general. How could that be? The higher logical level that makes something a meta-program is consistent with the Meta-State principle that *higher frames govern lower levels*. What this means for those trained in NLP is that the "difference that makes a difference" actually occurs at a meta-level. The actual power of the so-called sub-modality shifts and interventions arise from the meta-level frame. The categories and conceptual classes that we have called "sub-modalities" (like distance, location, clarity, intensity, etc.) are actually *meta*-qualities and distinctions.

Figure 9:5

Meta-States
(Presuppositions, meta-frames, meta-paradigms, narratives)
↓
Sub-Modalities
Specific qualities, distinctions, features in the Representational Systems

Evaluative Based Language
↓
Sensory Based Language
↓
MODALITIES
Sensory Based Representations

Similarly, Meta-States enables us to move up to larger distinctions and to gain a broader perspective about things. At those meta-levels of cognition are the presuppositions, frames (meta-frames), paradigms (and meta-paradigms), and narratives (White and Epston, 1989), which actually govern and drive modalities and their distinctive features.

Simple and Complex Meta-States
Directly experiencing thinking and emoting about things "out there" in primary states evokes direct and immediate emotions in you that allow you to easily anchor these states. The sensory based modalities govern your primary states.

Things change when you go meta because meta-states operate as very different phenomena. Given the kind of complex and layered consciousness involved in meta-states, the thinking and emoting becomes more systemic and embedded. This makes for more complexity. It also makes for higher frames-of-references and, therefore, more unconsciousness. You simply assume them as your presuppositional reality.

As you think-and-emote at meta-levels, your state of mind becomes more complex. As a meta-state, it usually becomes less kinesthetic. I say *usually* because it can just as well become much more emotional and kinesthetic which I'll get to later.

The usual effect is that the "feelings" you experience at meta-levels (i.e., our meta-feelings) shift in nature and quality. They take on a more conceptual feel. The result is that you then experience these conceptual states of consciousness in a way that makes them feel more "heady" and intellectual. As a general rule, your meta-feelings are more cognitively informed than kinesthetically. Here *while you say* that you "feel" something, you are actually making an evaluation about some conceptual abstraction.

"I feel dumb."	"I feel judged."
"I feel weird."	"I feel out of sorts."
"I feel great."	"I feel I'm on top of things."

When you consider these expressions, and the states to which they refer, these do not express *emotions,* but *judgments.* They express higher level evaluations. And as the evaluative part of your mind dominates, the kinesthetic weakens until there's hardly any discrete set of body sensations which correspond to them. You can test this out on some of the previous feeling statements by asking:

- Where in your body do you feel this?
- What is the feeling of it—cold or hot, pressure or rhythm, tense or relaxed, etc.?

When you ask these feeling questions about meta-feelings, which are more judgments than feelings, people will look at you as if you've lost your mind. They will shake their head in disbelief, begin stuttering as they try to find some words, or be stunned into silence. Why? Because the feeling questions reveal that the experience is not experienced somatically as a feeling located in the body at all. These feeling statements are *pseudo-feelings* which typically makes it more difficult to anchor these meta-states kinesthetically.

Consider the state of "fearing your fear." What would you call that state? When President R.D. Roosevelt said, "The only thing we have to fear is fear itself," he referred to a profoundly dis-empowering meta-state of *timidity mixed with paranoia*. Here the object of fear does not refer to anything beyond the skin—a wolf, a dangerous place, an angry spouse, getting hurt in a sport, etc. The structure of fear-of-fear sets you up to be afraid of *your state of fear*. You become fearful of your inner experience with all of the thoughts, emotions, sensations, neurological processes of fear. Here you experience all of the energy of the meta-fear which is directed against your state of fear itself, turning your energy *against* yourself. The energy has nowhere to go except *against* your mind and body.

Figure 9:6

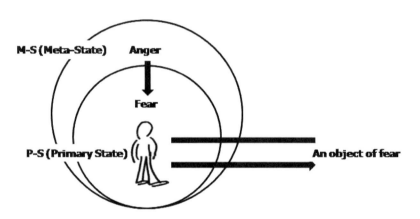

Or consider the state of *feeling joyful about anger*. Over the years of psychological practice, I encountered numerous clients in that meta-state. For example, my client was a woman who had lived for years feeling conned out of the right to own, feel, and acknowledging her anger.

> "It's not lady-like." "You shouldn't be angry." "Anger never solves anything."

Then something shifted and she decided to accept anger as a God-given human emotion. She gave herself permission to experience anger. And with that new permission, she experienced *a sense of joy and delight* in the freedom to finally express and release her anger. Frequently such individuals experience this joy-of-anger state as a personal liberation, a transformation to not cower to everybody's anger, displeasure, or disapproval.

Of course, it could go the other way. A person could enjoy and thrill in anger due to the sense of power, intimidation, and dominations it gives. That's what I found during the time that I worked with the men being released from Federal Prison who were required to attend a "life skills" class. *Everything depends upon the attributed meanings the person creates.* What joy do you derive from the anger? The joy of anger results from the conceptual meanings, or the neuro-semantics, that you construct about it.

This moves us from a simple meta-state to more complex ones. A *simple* meta-state refers to a structure of one basic state about another basic state: sad about anger, angry about sadness, fearful about sadness. The possibilities go on and on.

Complex Meta-States

As you develop ever higher levels and layers of states-about-states-about-states, you abstract about your abstractions, and then draw even more conclusions. Notice what happens when you begin using secondary thoughts-and-emotions and apply them to primary thoughts-emotions or other secondary states.

Consider the meta-state of guilty anger, that is, feeling guilty about feeling angry? What would you call one? When you experience thoughts-emotions of guilt about the state of anger, guilt of anger is the meta-state.

Now in guilt you experience a sense of "wrongness." You engage in thinking-feeling-and-acting "wrong" (which is a concept) regarding to some set of actions. At the primary level you have violated some standard. You have "missed the mark" of some targeted value or goal. You have demonstrated fallibility by making a mistake or committing an error of some sort.

How do you respond after you experience a state of wrong-doing? You inevitably will move up to a higher awareness about your concept (your ethical self) to create another generalization. You create mental constructions about *yourself as a person* who has done wrong.

Suppose the wrong involved simply "feeling angry." Yet if you do not ask, "How is that wrong?" you will merely assume it because you have a rule about when to anger, how, in what way, toward whom, etc. So now you *guilt* yourself for thinking and feeling angry about something. In doing this you turn your psychic energy *against* yourself.[3]

Figure 9:7

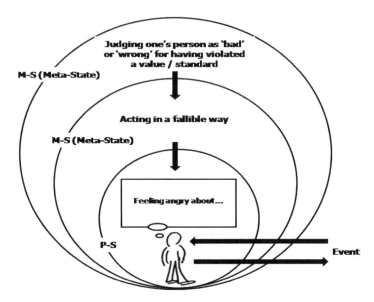

Summary

- Beyond your primary states of consciousness, you create and experience meta-states as higher states of mind and emotion reflexively referring to your previous states.

- As a meta-class of life, you cannot help but make conceptual moves to a higher frame of reference and react to your own reactions. The mechanism that makes this possible is self-reflexive consciousness.

- Transcending primary states moves you up into conceptual and semantic states full of "beliefs," "values," "understandings," etc. And these define and describe the essence of "being human."

- In your higher executive states you are reacting to yourself and thereby setting higher frames of reference that become your reality strategies for moving through life. That's why you never leave home without your meta-states. You take them everywhere you go.

- The higher level states operate either *for* or *against* you. They can function as glorious states of your higher mind, supporting your genius and evoking the best in you, or they can function as fire breathing dragon states, sabotaging and toxifying life. Awareness is what enables you to choose.

End Notes:

1. For more about these linguistic distinctions, see *Communication Magic* where I extended the Meta-Model with seven distinctions of Alfred Korzybski that are at the heart of General Semantics.

2. For the story about sub-modalities, see *Sub-Modalities Going Meta* (2005), the original title was, *The Structure of Excellence: Unmasking the Meta-Levels of "Sub-modalities"* (1999).

3. Here I have phrased the emotional words as verbs instead of nouns. This more accurately communicates that the phenomenon here are processes, not things.

Chapter 10

THE NATURE OF
META-STATES

Part A

Moving Up into a Different Kind of Reality

"Language is the house of being.
Man dwells in this house."
Heidegger

Journeying into the Meta-States model expands your understanding that *meta-states involve higher levels of abstracting and experiencing* (thinking-and-feeling) than what we typically experience in primary states. This makes your higher levels of states more complex, complicated, and layered. It also creates other systemic dynamics that is challenging as you work with these higher states, design and refine them, anchor and solidify them, install and uninstall them, etc.

Given these differences between primary and meta-states, to become competently skillful in working with your meta-states, and those of others, requires that we make explicit the nature of meta-states and delineate the key critical differences. The goal of this chapter and the next is to explore in more depth the nature of meta-states and how to work with them. In doing this, we will answer three questions:

- What is the nature of meta-states?
- How do they differ from primary states?
- What does this mean for us in managing these higher level states?

1) Structural Complexity

Meta-states involve a structural complexity that arises from the layeredness of thought upon thought, feeling upon feeling, concept upon concept, etc. From this layeredness we experience our meta-states as textured with other variables. Some of these are from specific thoughts and feelings that we add, some arise as emergent properties of the system. Typically this makes it more difficult to quickly establish a meta-state. I say *typically* because this

The Nature of Meta-States
1) Structural Complexity
2) Kinesthetic texturing
3) Anchoring artistry
4) Systemic interfaces
5) Integral Coalescing
6) Meta-level framing
7) Reflexivity
8) Linguistic
9) Unconscious

does not mean that, at times, we can and do establish a meta-state suddenly and immediately. Sometimes that happens. Yet that is the exception, not the rule.

Herein lies a basic difference in the very nature of meta-states from primary states.

> *Meta-states represent a higher level phenomena which involve structural layers created by the transcending-and-including process and so typically needs higher level symbols and linguistics for coherence.*

2) Kinesthetic Texturing

When I first began exploring meta-states, it actually surprised me to discover that these higher states typically lack the kind of strong and driving kinesthetic sensations that we experience in primary states. In primary states you experience primary emotions (e.g., anger and fear, joy and sadness, tense and relaxed, attraction and aversion). Usually you can quickly access the feeling experience of these states and *how* they feel in your body and *where* in the body you experience them.

Primary states have definite and clear kinesthetic sensations that make them easy to anchor with a touch.

These distinctions between primary and meta-states distinguishes emotions from feelings. Emotions involve somatic sensations—feelings or kinesthetics plus a cognitive evaluation. The kinesthetic qualities involve various sensations or feelings—the sense of touch, temperature, pressure, location, breathing, etc. This set of distinctions about our kinesthetics describes our primary states in behavioral terms. By operationalizing our terms in this way we are now able to replicate the state in ourselves and others. We do this while avoiding the abstractions of "emotional" terms (e.g., excited, centered, joyful, frustrated, etc.), which, in reality, are meta-states. In this way, we distinguish *kinesthetics* (K) as body sensations from *emotions* (K^{meta}) as higher level evaluations about sensations.[1]

As an aside, even the primary "emotions" already operate as a meta-level phenomena (K^{meta}). Technically we could tease out yet another *lost level* inside the primary state level. Since we usually do not need this depth of analysis, the designation of primary state versus meta-state here provides a sufficient distinction for our purposes. *The primary emotions,* since they already involve cognitive evaluations, *result from that previous meta-level having coalesced into a primary state.* As meta-levels coalesce into lower levels, they eventually come to operate *as if* they are primary states.

In kinesthetic experience, meta-states differ from primary states. While meta-states may have kinesthetic qualities, more typically they are not driven or primarily characterized by such. Their construction involves more layered and complex consciousness which makes them more "conceptual" and "mental." Something else comes from this, namely an inability, or at least a greatly reduced ability, to easily specify what the meta-state feels like. Have you noticed this? Try your hand at it.

- What specific kinesthetic sensations in your body does the state of self-esteem involve?
- Where specifically in your body do you feel resilience?
- Describe the unique breathing that is involved in proactivity.
- Where do you feel "being mischievous?"
- How about feeling protective, stubborn, argumentative, etc.?
- Does forgiveness have any special qualities of warmth or

coolness in any of your muscles?

When you try to identify *where* in your body you feel such states and *what* specific kinesthetic, somatic feelings correspond to these meta-states, you discover that the kinesthetic sensations are not definitely clear and immediate as primary states and emotions. Typically they are not.

3) Anchoring Artistry

Because many meta-states are not kinesthetically driven, we cannot anchor them with the same ease that we anchor primary states. That's because with a primary state, we are essentially setting up a simple association between stimulus and response. Once a person responds with certain thoughts-and-emotions to a trigger, we link another sensory stimulus to it, like a kinesthetic touch on the elbow, so that it becomes an anchor of that response.

For a meta-state anchor, however, we set up a link between one internal response and another internal response. We establish a higher and more effective reaction to our first reaction. And if that second response is more cerebral, more conceptual, if it involves more a mental evaluation or judgment, then the second response will typically have less kinesthetic impact. That then means there will be less energy in it so anchoring the meta-state to the first state will involve more finesse.

Does this mean that we cannot anchor them? No. Not at all. *We certainly can anchor meta-states.* We can even anchor them in any of the representational systems—with sights, sounds, sensations, words, symbols, metaphors, etc.

If you have worked with meta-states, you may have found that sometimes you have difficulty even getting the meta-state back when you "fire off" the anchor. In spite of accessing, building, and developing a meta-state, you may suffer the disappointment of not being able to re-trigger it with the anchor. How then do you install and anchor a meta-state? There are several ways.

First and foremost, it is critical to solidify the meta-state through questioning, rehearsal, and feedback summaries. This requires that you will keep reflecting back the words, ideas, and the meanings that help the person to formulate the experience and to find the very best words and symbols for him or her—that person's "right words." As you do this, set multiple anchors in as many representational systems as possible. This will create redundancy. You'll also want to use the meta-representational systems of language and symbolic imagery as you integrate and solidify the conceptual understandings and meanings of the meta-state.

Consider the meta-state of self-esteem, or to express it more accurately, the state of self-*esteeming*. To discover that this state involves meta-feelings, ask, "*Where* in your body do you feel self-esteem?"

Self-esteem consists of a set of thoughts, evaluations, judgments about another high level abstraction—your mental mapping about your *self* that is, *your concept of yourself as a human being or a person of worth and value*. This explains why the meta-level phenomena of self-esteem does not so much involve a feeling as it does a complex set of thoughts, evaluations, understandings, etc.

To anchor this higher level state you could use the Circle of Excellence pattern. First elicit an experience of unconditionally valuing yourself. Then via lots of questions and meta-questions, facilitate esteeming oneself as unconditionally worthy. Finally elicit meta-level belief structures that encourage you or another to step in and fully experience these inside an imaginary sphere.

As the person integrates all of the higher levels of frames, coach his or her body to feel and express them. The person could integrate and solidify this meta-state using the color of the sphere and the physiologies involved. Then any or all of these variables (the color, the sphere, the posture, etc.) could anchor it. All of this will depend on your ability to call forth in the person *higher level concepts* that elicit robust emotions of meaning and meaningfulness and then link them to various visual, auditory, kinesthetic, and linguistic anchors.[2]

4) System Interfaces
If you have worked extensively with the NLP model, I suspect that you have already noticed this difficulty of setting "touch" anchors for meta-states. Over the years, I have met a great many NLP practitioners and

trainers who were frustrated by this. No one ever told them that meta-level phenomena and meta-feelings involve different anchoring processes from what works with primary states.

If you set out to anchor self-esteem, resilience, forgiveness, or any other meta-structured state with a kinesthetic touch on the arm, and then "fire off" that anchor, typically you will not get back the same state, intensity of state, kinesthetic strength to the state, etc. In fact, sometimes attempting to anchor meta-states in this way will backfire so that you will actually disperse the neurological energy of the state. It would have a similar effect to collapsing anchors. Rather than building up a neurological energy pattern, the "anchoring" will dissipate it.

Have you noticed this? Do you know what explains this phenomena? *This phenomena arise from the interface of state upon state.* It arises because you are working with logical levels and between logical levels. That is why there are going to be various interfaces between the states and that there may be higher states or frames also influencing things.

For example, what happens if you anchor confidence and apply it to the state of anger? The result of anchoring as you apply confidence to anger *depends on the meanings that "confidence" has to you or another person at the meta-level.* That's why we can get a wide range of semantic constructions:
• Confident that I'm an angry person and can't get over it.
• Confident that I can effectively handle my anger.
• Confident that I have to express my anger when I feel it.
• Confident that anger runs my life.
• Confident that I am in charge of my anger, creating it and expressing it.

By setting forth the situation in this way, I am highlighting the role that higher frames, meaning frames, and frames-by-implication play in meta-stating. Merely accessing and applying *confidence* to another state does not guarantee anything. It's too simplistic to suppose that such will solve the problem of out-of-control anger.

> *It is the way the person interprets the confidence state as the higher frame that determines everything. It controls the meaning which, in turn, controls the texture of the primary*

state.

The person's interpretations arise uniquely from his or her belief frames at a higher level. The interface between the levels could also have the effect of reducing the neurological build-up of tension as it does in the collapsing of anchors. So bringing confidence to anger may result in the gestalt meaning:

- I'm confident that I don't need my anger, that anger is bad and wrong and that if I deny it, I will effectively control it.

Of course the problem with a frame like that, operating as a higher or meta-state, is that it will reduce a person's ability for experiencing healthy anger and using it effectively for learning and action. That frame turns the person's anger energies against himself as he censors it as "bad," thereby turning it into a moral issue.

In a later chapter (Chapter 19) we will explore the system interfaces and identify the numerous interactions and system properties that arise from states-upon-states structures.

5) Integral Coalescing

Working with the nature of these layered meta-states means working with a dynamic complexity. Given that meta-states contain an interactive structure involving several layers of states, and sometimes of states-embedded-in-states-embedded-in-states, the challenge always is to facilitate a coherent integration. Without coherence, you could work with every critical variable and still not elicit the inner consistency required for all of the variables to cohere as a single unit. And that's critical if you want the meta-state to last over time. So what are the processes and factors that play a role in creating stability at meta-levels?

In working with mental and emotional states, there's no problem in *applying* another thought, another feeling, or another physiology to a state. We do that all the time. We do that day in and day out. That part is easy. Just ask a question about something else and relate it to the first.

- Would feeling more appreciation about life, yourself, and others be valuable to you? This meta-question invites the creation of a meta-state of *valuing appreciation.*

•   Can you see yourself as the kind of person who integrates a charming negotiation style as you provide information for your customers? This meta-question invites the creation of a meta-state of being a *charming negotiator*.

Relating, or linking, one state to another isn't the challenge. The challenge is *how* to do so in a way so that the two becomes one integrating to become part and parcel of each other, even unseparatable. The keys to this are repetition and intensity to coalesce the states to create a new whole, a new gestalt. When you can do that, you can anchor and stabilize the meta-levels of the states and create an integral coalescing.

Most people devoted to their own self-development and self-actualization have created the meta-state of *joyful learning*. Over time they take joy and learning and combine them to establish the state of mind wherein they enjoy learning. They love it. They find it highly valuable. And they get multiple pleasures out of it—growth, insight, improved efficiency, wisdom, productivity, etc. Eventually the *joy* of learning coalesces into the experience of *learning* so that the person can no longer even imagine learning apart from joy. All that's left is *joyful learning* as a single unit—the two coalsced into a new synergy.

What I'm describing here is *the coalescing process* and this is the power of meta-states which become gestalt states. In this way we can design, set, and anchor meta-states so that the meta-levels of our mind become so stabilized as an integral experience that we can carry it with us for decades, even for the rest of our life.

This coalescing characteristic of meta-states plays a critical role as we work with higher levels and set multiple frames. It means that once installed as our frames-of-references, and anchored as our felt reality, meta-states become extremely stable phenomena. This can make them more sustainable, more durable, and more resistant to change.

Both Korzybski and Bateson noted this phenomenon. For Korzybski, it emerged from the differences between lower and higher brain functioning. Our thalamic abstracting leaves us with dynamic, ever-moving and changing representations that we experience as ever shifting emotions whereas the higher cortical functioning of the cortex generates stable concepts. From this emerges the more stable higher levels of states.

By abstracting and going meta to higher levels, we create our conceptual and presuppositional reality which make up our unconscious frames-of-references. This creates the reality structures we believe in and value, those we simply take for granted as "real." This framing stabilizes them and commissions them to operate as our canopy of consciousness. They become the mental and emotional atmosphere within which we live and breath and have our being. As we create these higher frames by thinking and abstracting this develops our executive states that we more commonly refer to by scores and scores of meta-terms such as "understandings," "beliefs," "decisions," "values," etc.

6) Meta-Level Framing

With the process of repetition, we store our learning history and references for understanding as higher-level frames. Using the height metaphor (going up) rather than the depth metaphor (going down), orients us to think about the meta-move as going up as we engage in what Transformation Grammar call a *Trans-Derivational Search* (TDS) for meaning. In that model, the *deep* structure operates as our *higher* frames of reference, frames of meaning, and frames of mind. It initiates the frame game (the inner game) that we then play out in our emotions, behaviors, talk, and skills (the outer game).

As repetition continues to streamline these frames, they become increasingly outside of our awareness. These frames-of-reference then operate as attractors in our neuro-linguistic system of meaning making. Then as we lose awareness of our frames, this reinforces them as "reality" leading us to conclude, "That's just the way it is." As this reality strategy solidifies over time, we simply do not think about calling these assumptions into question.

After this, as we move out into the world, we take our conceptual realities (these meta-level frames-of-references or meta-states) everywhere we go. Now they operate as our perceptual or attentional filters (meta-programs). In this way, meta-states become solidified meta-programs.[3]

This explains why after a meta-state coalesces into a gestalt state, there are fewer things that can mess them up or pull them apart. At the heart of the process is the meta-state of *believing in our beliefs*.[4]

At first, believing in our beliefs sounds like a great strategy. But there's a problem with it—it creates fanaticism. True enough, we can solidify our meta-states by believing in them. Yet when we *believe* in our belief frames, we set a frame of validation about the belief that thereby locks the belief in. And while it makes the belief cohere, it also transforms the belief so it closes to feedback thereby making it rigid and even defensive. This is how we close beliefs off from ongoing feedback.

The belief then not only operates as our model of the world, *it also boxes us into that world so we cannot question it*. After all, "Why question reality?" And typically if we become conscious of this, we have the sense that it is silly, ridiculous, and even stupid to question it. So in the end we become dogmatic and stubborn. Now we "know." We say that we don't just "believe," we say that *we know*. Of course, then when the territory changes, we are left increasingly out-of-touch with reality and less flexible enough to adopt or update our belief. We feel that we cannot alter, shift, or change. We begin to fear change, dislike change, and wish things would not change.[5]

The stability of established meta-states explains why we can use the most powerful models and technologies from NLP, or other disciplines, to try to create an empowering meta-state and still not succeed. If a person has a meta-level frame-of-reference *that doesn't allow* a state, idea, belief, etc., that eliminates it, discounts it, or nullifies it—the change pattern will not work. The higher levels governing the lower levels will disable and nullify it.

Perhaps you elicit an empowering meta-state with a client in your office, but when the person walks out, or goes into a different context, the higher state evaporates or is unaccessible. The person may have accepted the frame during the experience when he was "trying it on." But then, apart from that environment, back in "the real world," higher meta-frames kick in to veto or eliminate the new resource. This explains one of the ways that some people have "tried NLP and found it wanting." They were attempting to manage a subjective experience containing meta-levels while unwittingly treating it as if it was a primary state.

7) Reflexivity

Given all of this, you can see that while we can simply anchor a primary states kinesthetically by a touch, gesture, or movement, and apply it as a resource to another state, things become more involved when we work at meta-levels. Inasmuch as several embedded states come together to comprise a meta-state, sometimes we have to un-connect those states-upon-states before we can build up a new meta-strategy with new life-enhancing hypnotic inductions. We have to break up the anchored chains of state-*after*-state and state-*upon*-state. In both cases, we have a sequence of representations and states, or a strategy.

Meta-states function in a similar way to a strategy sequence. Similar, but not the same. That's because whereas a strategy sequence following the NLP-enriched TOTE model, moves out linearly, sequentially, and horizontally, *the sequence of meta-cognition in meta-states moves up and down logical levels vertically.*

This explains why some interventions in NLP strategy work (eliciting, unpacking, interrupting, designing, redesigning, installing, and utilizing strategies) rather than simply having a person "think of a time when . . . " anchor it, and zap them with a swish or reframe.

The principle is:

> *Different NLP patterns and interventions work in diverse ways with regard to primary and meta-states.*

Some patterns work only on primary states. Others work best on meta-states. Yet others work best on complex meta-states.

To distinguish strategies, states, and meta-states think of strategies as a way to work with consciousness. That is, with strategies we track the sequential, step-by-step linear process of where consciousness goes to generate various outputs (behaviors) in terms of emotions, actions, gestures, skills, perceptions, etc.

With states, by contrast, we work much more with neurology than consciousness even though within every state we will find an explicit set of internal representations and cognitions. Because states result from the streamlining of strategies, we only need one piece of the configuration of the strategy to set off the entire mind-body experience. We therefore manage states and experience states much more dynamically and holistically than we do strategies.

The dominant and determining factor in meta-states is your self-reflexive consciousness. As you think about your thinking, feel about your feeling, evaluate your evaluations, etc. you simultaneously transcend your current level of thinking-feeling. This vertical jump creates the next higher level and builds within the very process conceptual frames. The resulting *system* is your neuro-linguistic and neuro-semantic system of meaning. Transcending your levels of mind and feeling describes the direction and flow of consciousness as it moves up and then back down.

Consciousness now does loops, spirals around, and moves in non-linear ways so it goes in circles. In this way you use various feed back processes and feed forward processes as you continue to create your sense of reality. From this emerges numerous systemic properties—gestalt states, coalescing, attractor frames.

This explains why you need two specific skills, first to be able to elicit meta-levels and second to be able to track the results of the meta-processes. You do the first with meta-questions and you do the second with the Matrix Model. Thinking systemically with meta-states means you think with both the horizontal and the vertical communication loops: feedback into yourself as information and feed forward through ourselves and out into the world as energy.

Summary
- Meta-states not only differ from primary states, they differ from one another. Recognizing this enables you to work more intelligently and purposefully with these layered states of consciousness.

- The nature of meta-states differ in nature from primary states in numerous ways. This is important when you want to understand, model, or transform these higher conceptual and semantic states.

• While meta-states are more complex in numerous ways, meta-states are also made out of the same "stuff" that makes up primary states: thoughts, emotions, drives, desires, hopes, expectations, information processing, languaging, etc.

End Notes:

1. This distinction between feelings as our kinesthetics and emotions (K^{meta}) goes back to the beginning of the NLP model.

2. I use the *Circle of Excellence* pattern as one possibility of using an NLP pattern for self-esteeming. For that pattern see *The Sourcebook of Magic* (1999). For the newer and more direct meta-stating processes for self-esteeming, see the APG (Accessing Personal Genius) manual and the book, *Secrets of Personal Mastery* (1999).

3. In the book *Figuring Out People* (2006) chapter 4 is devoted to detailing the processes for how meta-states become meta-programs.

4. As an aside, this explains why change or therapy can take so long. It explains why people have a tendency to slide back to old habits and why a valued change might not last. Why? Because we've changed frames at too low a level and have not found the higher leverage point of change in the person's reality strategy.

5. This describes *the neurotic process* by which we become less and less sane. We become less flexible and able to adjust to reality because we are less and less open to continual learning. Consequently, we become more and more defensive and insecure. Then, to protect ourselves (or more accurately our ideas and beliefs) we adopt various defensive mechanisms. And all because we started to *believe* in our beliefs which created a false sense of security.

Chapter 11

THE NATURE OF
META-STATES

Part B

The Language and our Higher Unconscious States

Seven distinguishing factors of meta-states were identified in the last chapter that began our exploration into *the nature* meta-states. Here our exploration turns to two additional facets of the nature of meta-states. First, the role of language in meta-states—a meta-state is a phenomenon which is linguistically informed and driven. Second, their nature as unconscious frames that make up our hidden matrix or canopy of consciousness. Meta-states describe your "unconscious mind."

Linguistically Informed and Driven
Unlike primary states that are representationally driven—driven by the sights, sounds, and sensations of your inner moves, meta-states are primarily informed and driven by linguistics. With primary states you experience your consciousness as directly related to and about something "out there." This initiates immediate somatized sensations in your body. And such primary states may be entirely wordless.

Not so meta-states. By contrast, as linguistically driven phenomena, *meta-states need more complex symbols, representations, and meanings.* This suggest numerous things regarding how to work effectively with these higher executive states.

The complexity of the layered nature of meta-states explains why we are not able to easily anchor them with kinesthetic, visual, and auditory anchors. With meta-states we will need to use the meta-representational system of language and linguistic symbols. Obviously, meta-states involve more variables than just somatic or kinesthetic components. Sensory-based elements alone cannot manage all of the layered learnings and frames in a meta-state.

The Nature of Meta-States

1) Structural Complexity
2) Kinesthetic texturing
3) Anchoring artistry
4) Systemic interfaces
5) Integral Coalescing
6) Meta-level framing
7) Reflexivity
8) Linguistic
9) Unconscious

To access and build up the embedded layers of a meta-state requires greater skills at symbolic anchoring. Typically, anchoring a meta-state will not occur by simple linkage, but by linking each of the conceptual layers of thoughts-and-feelings with the necessary words and symbols to encode the embedded framing. This requires symbols sufficient to link the syntax of the embedded layers of these states that are more symbolic or conceptual.

To do this you will use images, sounds, or touches at meta-levels to symbolically stand for the required concept. The sight, sound, or sensation will not stand for itself, will not be literal, but symbolic. You will connect an anchor to these embedded layers as *a symbol of* the belief, understanding, value, etc. Because meta-states take us into the abstraction level of language, words, and other symbolic systems (i.e., mathematics, music, poetry, story, etc.), words will predominant in this domain as the meta-representational system.

Language, as a mental-neurological phenomenon, allows you to stabilize meta-states and sustain them over time to maintain them as enduring phenomena. That's why you need to find the right words or symbolic system to effectively anchor a meta-state. The right words and language patterns will induce you into the desired semantic state. In this, the right words essentially provide a hypnotic induction of the meta-state. This level helps you more fully appreciate the role of your neuro-linguistics because through them you can link and coalesce the levels that make up a meta-state.

Some NLP trainers have what amounts to a discounting of, and even an outright contempt for, the meta-representational system of language. Their belief is that the languaging dimension is inferior to the level of the senses and to the silent level (Korzybski's Event Level). This seems to be the attitude today of both Richard Bandler and John Grinder which, I think, they got from Fritz Perls.[1]

> ". . . the essential thing in Gestalt therapy, is, the non-verbal is always more important than the verbal. Words lie and persuade; but the posture, the voice, and the non-verbal behavior is true." (*The Gestalt Approach and Eye Witness to Therapy,* 1973, p. 157)

Yet there's no need to elevate your senses over your mind. What you need is to keep open the feedback loop between mind and experience so that you maintain flexibility as you map and re-map your model of reality. Consciously choosing to lose your higher level "mind" from time to time enables you to re-access and re-gain the resources in the sensory systems. Yet even as you do that, the problem is not language.

Developing the ability to turn off the language system and access a pure and *primal uptime* state where you get "the words out of your mind and eyes" is a highly valuable skill. I sometimes use various "Stopping the World" exercises in trainings precisely because it offers a rich resource for deconstructing old meaning structures that create limitations. Yet the uptime state of "pure sensory awareness" is not your only resource. Nor are all resource states wordless. Quite the contrary, many of the most resourceful states of all involve language driven meta-states—self-esteem, proactivity, resilience, forgiveness, etc.

Sometimes it is good to lose your higher level "mind" and return to your senses and re-map with new words to create new enhancing meta-states. This is part of the *unlearning* process.[2] As language informs and structures meta-states, you will need empowering and transformative linguistics. Without the higher level abstractions of language, you will not sustain, maintain, or stabilize these executive states.

If you are wondering about the reason for this, the answer is simple. At the meta-levels our higher states involve beliefs, understandings, values, interpretations, evaluations, judgments, etc. These conceptual experiences, as meta-states, involve abstract understandings which require language. And while we can sometimes do this with single words, it usually requires sentences involving more complex linguistic structures. This takes us up to the level of beliefs, understandings, paradigms, etc. —understandings that we develop about principles, laws, processes, causation, etc. And, of course, this is the domain of the Meta-Model about how language works as you construct your model of the world.

As semantically constructed states, that which holds your meta-states together and anchors them, are your linguistic symbols. Your words operate as inductions, conceptually gluing your ideas together into a coherent story. Words hold your thoughts, ideas, meanings, abstractions, etc. together.

Self-Esteem

Consider the "linguistic glue" that you use to meta-state self-esteem. How do you apply a state of mental/conceptual esteem (value, high appraisal of worth and dignity) to yourself, that is, to your concept of "self?" Do you not have to use words and abstract understandings to encode your believing and valuing about your "esteem" as a human being? Do you not need several layers of complex language to encode your criteria and meaning of self-esteeming?

To engage in self-esteeming, you inform and direct your consciousness by such self-esteeming languaging patterns as the following:

> "My worth as a person is unconditional; it is not conditioned on anything—not looks, intelligence, money, degrees, etc."
> "Conceptually, my worth as a human being is a given."
> "I am a somebody simply because I am a human being."
> "I refuse to be or consider myself as 'a human doing' and measure my human 'worth' by my achievements. I claim my innate value as a human being."

> "I refuse to rate myself as a human being."
> "I bear a divine image (made in the likeness and image of God),
> therefore I have immense value irrespective of my
> accomplishments, looks, money, status, degrees, etc."

To encode these conceptual understandings, language is required. We can't even think about them without words. Try as you may, how could you encode such abstract understandings merely using pictures, tones, volumes, or bodily sensations? While you may eventually encode your conceptions in a single image, first, you have to conceptualize the ideas and that demands language. Afterwards, you might summarize the concepts with an image, or sound, or touch. As a complex piece of consciousness, the idea of "self" and of "rating" one's self as valuable, worthwhile, and having dignity involves several levels of abstract concepts. These concepts are beliefs about numerous meanings—the attribution of value, the self as a special and valued person, the criteria of esteeming, etc. Is there any question that a meta-level state of this nature needs the representational system of language to encode them?

Linguistically Decoded by Meta-Modeling

If you *glue* meta-states together by the words and linguistic structures, then how do you *unglue* the words of a negative and toxic meta-state which you find dis-empowering and limiting? What is the process for pulling language apart when it is toxic?

The answer is the *Meta-Model.* That's why meta-modeling utilizes a set of explicit questions for exploring and challenging the ill-formed structure in semantic structures. Asking indexing questions has the effect of *undoing* the construction of meaning. If you have a meta-level toxic belief or a non-enhancing value, *meta-modeling unglues the words that hold the construction together.*[3]

Using the Meta-Model questions effectively enables you to take the fluff and vagueness out of your abstract ideas. The questions defluff and de-abstract. You pull apart the component pieces and undo the construction of the concept. If you de-nominalize a process term (a verb) that's been nominalized, you essentially break an old meta-state apart. Your questions send you or another back to the sensory-based experience from which the toxic map was made and that gives you a chance to remap. It allows you, or another, to create new and better meta-states that utilize a more empowering abstraction (transformative language) from the same sensory based data.

Re-anchoring alone will not do it. Nor will swishing, or even desired outcome development. What works best here is meta-modeling. *In indexing specifics you take the fluff and non-sense in the linguistic construction that has solidified and sustained the negative state and meta-model it.*

Using Meta-Model questions is the method of choice for ungluing negative and limiting meta-states. This is what the Meta-Model does. It breaks up the linguistic structures of complex equivalences, cause-effect linkages, presuppositions, mind-reading, etc. Which contain the old negative inductions.[3]

Pull the meta-level meanings apart and the conceptualization cannot be sustained. It will disintegrate. This deconstruction of the morbid ideas then frees you from the old word and language cages that have imprisoned you. As the unenhancing meanings cease to cohere, the hypnotic state dissolves.

Ungluing the Meta-State Linguistics of "Failure"

Consider failure as a meta-state. Where do you feel "failure" in your body? Pretty nebulous, right? How would you anchor that meta-level state?

"Failure," generally, does not involve a set of somatic sensations. It primarily involves evaluative judgments about some other state—typically the state of not reaching a desired outcome. "Failure," as a state, arises as a human experiential phenomenon as we speak it into existence. As you language it, you represent it. And as you represent it, it becomes an induction, a belief, a meta-level frame of mind and your neuro-linguistic reality. Yet failure does not exist "out there." *It only exists in the world of communication in a mind.* By language, you encode it and then believe in it. Then you apply it as you personalize it as your self-map: "I am a failure." Here linguistically we combine a nominalization ("failure") and an identification ("I am") to create meta-level poison that feeds this dragon state.

Now suppose, you meta-model that non-sense with the intention to slay that toxic meta-level dragon. Perhaps the conversation would go as follows:

Speaker: "How do you know that failure exists in the first place?"
    Client: "I feel like a failure?"

Speaker: "Where do you feel this?"
    Client: "Well, I say to myself, 'Nothing I ever do turns out right! Everything I do flops. I'm just a failure.'"

S: "What specifically did you fail to accomplish?"
    C: "Everything!"

S: "Like what specifically? Give me an example."
    C: "I didn't finished college. I dropped out."

S: "So at some point in time, you dropped out of a class or did not sign up for the next semester, right?"
    C: "Yeah, I did not sign up for another semester."

S: "So what did you do?"
    C: "Well, I began working with this company; I thought I would make a fortune and did not need a college education."

S: So you chose to redefine your goal as you developed another vision?"
    C: "Well, yes, I suppose you could say that."

S: "Does anything stop you from signing up for a class at college?"
    C: "I'm too old."

S: "The collage has an age limit? Forty-year olds are forbidden to attend?"
    C: "Well, no. I suppose I could."

S: "If you signed up and kept at it, one class at a time, could you really maintain this belief in your failure-hood?" Etc.

The magic in asking the meta-modeling questions occurs in *indexing the specifics.* These questions challenge, shift, and expand a model of the world. Inquiring about how a map works, how a person has constructed a given idea about another idea invites you to *de-construct the post-hypnotic induction*. It is like pouring the acid of clarity on the old hypnotic language patterns that keep the old post-hypnotic suggestions activated. Meta-model questions de-hypnotizes. As long as the person keeps repeating the hypnotic induction encoded in the words, "I'm a failure; nothing ever goes right" and keeps using this as a frame of reference, it keeps the toxic and morbid meta-state functionally alive. And as language encodes it, re-languaging can re-code or reframe it.

When Meta-States Become Unconscious

Building and utilizing meta-states as higher executive frames invites many complications and complexities to your experiences. Beyond simple meta-state, are complex meta-states. There are also *congruent* and *incongruent* meta-states — states that involve inherent contradictions and conflicts or those that express alignment and congruency. Another systemic property that emerges out of these configurations is what we call the "unconscious" or "the subconscious mind."

As repetition and habituation drives higher frames up the levels, they move outside your awareness. Metaphorically, *they become a canopy of consciousness* — the mental and emotional atmosphere within which you live. When this happens, you take them for granted. You just assume them as your conceptual atmosphere, the Matrix you live in.

How do you then experience your state of consciousness with all of the mind-body, neuro-linguistic energies of perceiving, feeling, valuing, interpreting, appraising, posturing, breathing, etc. when your higher frames are outside-of-awareness or unconscious? You simply experience the concepts as your felt reality, as the texture and quality of your everyday life.

Now if you want an elegant linguistic marker to flush out these unconscious frames, *simply ask about the kind and quality of a state*. The answer will give you clues about the higher unconscious frames that texture and qualify the state.
•   What is the quality of X (your anger, your fear, your relaxation, your love, etc.)?

- What kind of anger do you typically experience when X occurs?
- How would you describe the quality of your X?

The adjectives and adverbs that emerge will tell you about the higher meta-states. Knowing about meta-states enables you to hear the first statement and know, by implication, that the person is saying the second:

- *Statement:* "You wouldn't like me angry. My anger is rageful."
- *Translation:* "I have embedded my anger inside of a frame of dislike and hatred. I taboo my anger, forbid it, push it down, repress it and I only see signs of it when it explodes in rage."

Again:

- *Statement:* "I have guilty anger. It's not good to be angry. It never solves anything. I grew up with two hostile parents and swore that I would never be that way."
- *Translation:* "I shame and guilt myself about anger. I have a belief frame that says it is worthless, it does not contribute to solving anything, and so I avoid it. I have a memory frame of two angry parents who did not know how to communicate anger effectively, with love and respect. I have a decision frame that says an absolute 'No!' to allowing anger any place in my life."

Above and beyond almost every state, belief, idea, understanding, self-definition, etc. you can count on the presence of higher states that reference it and set frames about it. These are the operational *frames by implication* that are typically outside your conscious awareness. (We call these FBI frames in Meta-Coaching.) Here you store those parts of your "mind" which lie outside of awareness (your unconscious or subconscious).[4] If this part of "mind" operates as *pre-conscious* form, you can gain awareness of it with a little effort. If it arises from *repression,* then you have blocked it off from awareness by tabooing it as your higher frame about it. You've done this as a way to defend yourself against it and against knowing it.

For example, imagine that Jim decides to surprise his wife Shirley by coming home early one afternoon. He comes home to cheerfully greet Shirley. Here we have a simple set of events. And yet these individuals can experience them in very complex ways. That's because mere representation does not fully explain them. We have to also ask, "What meanings do the individuals give to these events?" "What states do they access?"

Suppose Shirley feels pressured and upset to Jim's surprising early arrival. Suppose that the immediate and automatic thoughts that go flashing through her awareness are fearful apprehensions.

> "Why is he home early? Is he checking up on me again? Why does he always have to check up on me?"

Suppose that she consequently then feels manipulated and responds in a less than friendly way. To the innocent event, she then feels strangely uncomfortable, somehow out of control and a sense of pressure, even stress. None of these are primary states. These therefore reveal meta-level frames and meta-states. At a less conscious level, she might feel fearful, "He will be critical about the house still being a mess." What then? Perhaps she would then get into a defensive mode.

Figure 11:1

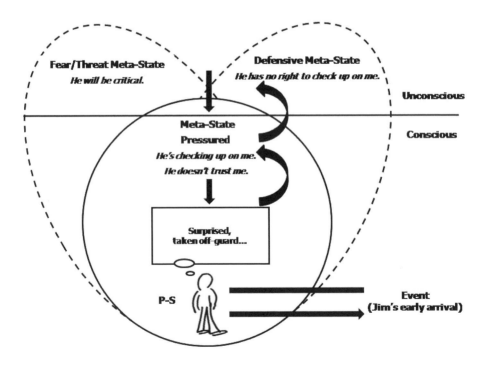

Above and beyond her unresourceful state there are higher frames. Yet because these occur outside her awareness, she has no access to them. She simply thinks and feels upset.

> "I hate feeling pressured, checked on, controlled; it makes me feel like a little girl. He has no right to pressure me this way!"

Now suppose that the state of anger is somehow a feeling of being violated, which she attributes to Jim. It is a state that she taboos thereby preventing herself from experiencing. She does not give herself permission to experience.

> "A good wife/woman shouldn't feel anger. Anger is not lady-like. Anger is dangerous."

As such, this meta-state of anger-about-feeling-pressured generates emotions and behaviors that come out as defensive anger in disguised form. It comes out as coldness, upsetness, negative perceptions of manipulation, silent treatment, etc. (passive-aggressive responses).

Unconscious meta-states are a complex of states about states to which we have little or perhaps no access. This makes them even more powerful over our perceptions, memories, learnings, communications, and behaviors. They *have* us. Yet we can explore them by using meta-questions:[5]

> How do I think-and-feel about that state?
> And how do I think-and-feel about that?

Meta-States as a Matrix or Canopy
Primary states come and go. They never stay around very long. You feel up, then down. You get curious, then bored, then nervous, then playful, then hungry, etc. All day long you go in and out of multiple states.

By way of contrast, the stability of meta-states enable you to perpetuate them and to carry them with you everywhere you go and to do so for years. You can even adopt them as an attitude or frame of mind, and carry it with you for decades, even for a lifetime. It's as if the attitude or state floats above you all the time giving you ready access to it. When this happens, you can at a moment's notice really "fly into a . . ." rage or calm, or resilience or self-esteem. It's as if the state is a frame that all of your life is embedded within, and that's not far from the actual case.

Your wild and wonderful reflexive self-consciousness allows you to recursively have thoughts-feelings about thoughts-feelings through many levels. This allows you to build lasting meta-states as internal mental contexts that you take with you everywhere and use to process the events of your lives. These meta-states make up your Matrix of meaning frames.

Executive Quality Control

There is one powerful meta-state, as an internal context or canopy of consciousness, that enables you to quality control your experiences. How do you create this state? Simple. Rehearse the following questions until this qualify focus becomes habitual as the way you think.
•   Does this experience empower me as a person?
•   Does this enhance my life, relationships, healthy, etc.?
•   Does it serve me well?
•   Does that way of acting get me the things I really want in the long run?
•   How useful is this state?
•   Is that where I want to go?

When you repeatedly use these questions to check if a given behavior, emotion, thought, belief, circumstance, etc. fits with your highest values, you create a meta-state that sets an executive decision at a higher level to make sure that you are living in a life-enhancing way.

This meta-evaluation provides you a meta-state for automatically quality controlling things for balance, health, and well-being. Having coached hundreds of people in constructing this meta-state, I have seen how it delivers people from a bad habit of negatively evaluating everything one does. Those who have a tendency to harshly judge themselves and yet who can show love, gentleness, and kindness to others, have a meta-state of self-criticalness. As a dragon state of pain and distress, self-judgment unconsciously floats above every experience.

To stop this, set the quality check as a higher frame of mind, to evaluate your evaluations. This gives you a way out of the endless looping around bad feelings.

>"Oh, there I go looping around judgments . . . I don't need that." "Does this way of thinking and feeling serve me very well? Hell no, it does not!"

Many have reported that this higher level awareness gives birth to a significant miracle in their lives. Now they can step out of the old frame of self-contempting, blaming, discounting, and judging.

Strategically Thinking and Speaking

In the 1980s I unwittingly created a powerful meta-state matrix of thinking and speaking strategically. I didn't understand what I was doing, nor even intended to do it, and yet I did it. It happened through the process of training assertive communication skills. Over and over I repeatedly set a frame in my mind that came to govern my communicating and relating. I even put it in the book title, *Speak Up, Speak Clear, Speak Kind* (1987). For me, thinking and speaking strategically developed a resourceful focus, orientation, and attitude because it set up a perpetual curiosity in me.

- Where do I stand with this person?
- Where does this person stand with me?
- What is the present state between us?
- What state do I want and desire us to move toward?

As I repeated this theme of strategic thinking and feeling, it habituated the state and eventually became my frame-of-reference. If you like the idea, try it out for yourself. It will empower you to navigate through relationships, business, negotiations, etc. more purposefully.

- Where do I stand with myself?
- Where do I stand with regard to my goal for this task?
- With this reality that I wish to handle more effectively?
- Where does this person stand with me?
- What relation does this force, influence, etc. have with me?

Strategic thinking induces a meta-state of awareness of a larger relational perspective. What meta-states would you like to build and install as your automatic executive states as you move through the world? The possibilities are limitless. You can take any of your highest core values and beliefs and set them as an executive frame or state.

Conceptual and Over-Generalized

Because meta-states involve thoughts-feelings and responses about other thoughts-feelings and responses, *every new meta-stating moves you up into a higher logical level.* The experiences that we typically describe using a hyphenated *self-* involve meta-state constructions. Hence, self-confidence refers to confident thought-feelings about one's self—one's concept of self.

As you develop solidified states about states-about-states, they become transcendent mind-sets as your frames-of-reference. They then operate as your canopy of consciousness. They become the conceptual and semantic atmosphere within which you live. When this happens, you take your meta-level attitudes with you everywhere you go. You may "never leave home without" self-pity, self-criticism, an un-defeatable spirit, pessimism, optimism, etc. Because of these dynamics, negative meta-states disempower and sabotage you and positive meta-states typically empower and transform your life. As meta-level experiences, meta-states drive and govern all the lower states and experiences.

This atemporarity of meta-states explains how they transcend specific space-time events and make it possible for you to create meta-states matrices out of specific frames. As you can create a meta-state, you can then generalize and detach it. This enables you to refer it to anything or everything. Then it becomes a state *meta* to every thought, feeling, experience, behavior, etc. It becomes a larger matrix of concepts. It is as if you have taken a cognitive understanding, belief, or emotion and made it a generalized frame. You can then use it as an executive state.

Summary

- It's the nature of meta-states to be intimately related to the meta-representational system of language and linguistic symbols. Recognizing this enables you to more elegantly access, create, and anchor meta-states.
- Meta-States are both conscious and unconscious. However, they are more likely to be unconscious than conscious. This explains why they can operate in such a powerful way in our lives. Unconscious meta-states involve the presuppositional frames and mental contexts that govern and organize your experiences without you even knowing.

End Notes:

1. See the Neuro-Semantic website, www.neurosemantics.com for the article, "Ten Years and Still No Beef."

2. *Un*learning is as important as learning, and sometimes even more so. The best process for unlearning in Neuro-Semantics is the Crucible. See *Unleashed* (2007) for a chapter about the Crucible and the training manual, *The Ultimate Self-Actualization Workshop*.

3. The Meta-Model is an extremely powerful model in spite of its simplicity. See *The Structure of Magic*, 1975, *Communication Magic,* 2001). The terms complex equivalent, cause-effect, mind-reading, nominalizations, etc. are Meta-Model distinctions that cue us for the need for specificity and indexing.

4. "Unconscious" is an exceedingly broad and vague term. There are numerous aspects of our consciousness that are unconsciousness. See the article, "Which Unconscious Mind do You Train?" www.neurosemantics.com.

5. Meta-questions are obviously a key and central facet of the Meta-States model, for a list, see *Coaching Change, Volume I of Meta-Coaching Series*.

Figure 11:2

Primary states differ significantly from meta-states. The following identifies the most significant contrasts and specifies numerous meta-level distinctions.

PRIMARY STATES	META-STATES
First-Level	Second/Third Levels, Etc.
Simple/Direct	Complex/Indirect
Immediate, automatic	**Layer** levels of consciousness
	Mediated by symbols
Synesthesia (V—K)	Meta-level synesthesias— created by the
	Collapsing of Levels
Modality (VAK) and	*Affected* by Sub-modalities, but not driven
Submodality-Driven	**Linguistically-Driven**,
	Linguistically-located
Kinesthetically Exper. +/-	No Immediate or localized
Easily Anchored	Chains of Anchors—glued together by words
	Chains connected by multiple anchors
Primary Kinesthetics	**Meta-kinesthetics** or "emotions"/
	Evaluative Emotions
(primary feelings)	— judgments coded in the soma (body)
Intense to very intense	Less intense: more thoughtful, "*mindful*"
Strong, primitive, deep	Weaker, less primitive, more modified by
	cognition
Quicker, Shorter	Lasts Longer, more enduring, stable
Animal	Human: dependent upon symbol-using capacities
More Focused	Multiple-focuses simultaneously
One time learning	One time learning very infrequent
	Repetition generally **needed** to drive in & install
No layers of cons.	Several or many layers of consciousness
First Position	2nd., 3rd. or other multiple positions
	consciousness expanded and transcendental
Associated!	Dissociated from primary emotions
Thought about the world	Thoughtfulness/ mindfulness, thought about thought
Object: external -in world	Object: internal — in mind-emotions
Empirical Qualities	Emergent qualities/properties:
	Having no lower-order counterparts
Somewhat projective	Highly projective
	Once collapsed — begins to operate as a primary
	State with a seemless logical-level synthesis

Chapter 12

TEXTURING STATES

Qualifying States for Higher Quality

- Is it possible to *texture* a mental and emotional state?
- If it were, suppose you could add various tastes, feels, and qualities to your current frame of mind. Would you like that?
- Suppose you could make the way you move through the world richer and fuller so that it radiated with a delightful and fascinating aroma?
- Suppose that you're not stuck or limited with just the plain vanilla states, but that you can qualify your states with all kinds of higher resources, frames, and states?

These questions about the quality and nature of our everyday mind-body states implies something very powerful and important. *You can design the very quality of your life by texturing the quality of your states.* When you do this, you move to one of the most exciting and captivating features of the Meta-States model.

Plain Vanilla States
Consider the nature and quality of some of the following states. I have

created the following list of terms to summarize everyday states. As you explore them do so in terms of how you experience the quality of your common states. So, considering the states you typically experience, evaluate them in terms of the following:
- Intensity and strength
- Accessibility and development
- Features and feel
- Ecology and balance
- Synergy to jump to a higher gestalt

States are just states until you meta-state them with various qualities, resources, limitations, permissions, prohibitions, etc. Then they become rich complex states, in fact, they become attitudes that influence your personality. As you texture your states with other states, the new combinations begin to add a systems complexity to your experiencing so that as your higher states set the governing frames it transforms your way of perceiving and being in the world.

If you start from a list of some basic states and think about using them not merely as a state, as *a framing state,* that is, as a meta-state frame for other states, then what happens when you apply these to each other?

Confidence	Anger	Joy
Clarity	Fear	Playfulness
Commitment	Anxiety	Respect
Courage	Sadness	Interest
Congruence	Discouragement	Enthusiasm
Curiosity	Tension	Relaxation

If you use these to *texture* your states with these states, what are some of the interactional possibilities? To answer, let's play with the emergent experiences. As you read each possibility, slow down to take a moment to imagine the texturing of the state.

Confidence:
- Hesitating confidence
- Courageous confidence
- Foolish confidence
- Playful confidence
- Bold confidence
- Anxious confidence

Clarity:

- Slow clarity
- Dull clarity
- Bright and brilliant clarity
- Developing clarity
- Curious clarity

Commitment:
- Fearful of commitment
- Total commitment
- Stressful commitment
- Playful commitment
- Miserable commitment
- Insecure commitment

Curiosity:
- Aggressive curiosity
- Rigid curiosity
- Humorous and silly curiosity
- Serious curiosity

Anger:
- Hostile anger
- Dreadful fear of anger
- Shameful guilt for being angry
- Joyful anger
- Respectful anger
- Loving anger

Fear:
- Shameful fear
- Bold fear
- Curious fear
- Playful fear

The Meta-State Flush Out

That you experience your mind-body states in terms of so many other qualities and properties as indicated in these lists reveal, and flush out, hidden meta-state structure in your experiences. Typically, however, you don't experience them as *meta*. Instead, it all seems part and parcel of one state—one experience. You experience the higher level thoughts and feelings as having completely coalesced into the state so that the experience is simply the embodied texture of your state.

It is this coalescing of the higher state into the primary that integrates the levels and so incorporates the qualities of the meta-state into a singular experience. In this way, meta-states get "into your eyes."

They coalesce and percolate into your muscles. And as this happens, you cease to notice them as separate states. They become *a part of* the state and no longer *apart*. The higher levels enter into the experience as the frames that qualify and govern the experience. Then textured into your state, your meta-states are hidden and invisible to you even though you never leave home without them.

This coalescing process literally *incorporates* higher level concepts and abstractions into the primary state. That is, what was just a mental awareness becomes *embodied* within your neuro-pathways and becomes part and parcel of your physiology. The end result are higher levels of consciousness textured into your emotional states.

In this the "state" is a holistic dynamic that includes state of mind, state of body, and state of emotion. And although the state is holistic, we can tease out the higher levels to identify its component elements. You can do this easily if you know what you're doing. You can use the qualities of your states as a way to flush out meta-states (whether your own or those of someone else). How? Simply inquire about the quality of a state.

- When you get angry, what's the quality of your anger?
- Would I like you angry?
- Are you respectful and thoughtful when you're angry?
- Or do you lose your head and go ballistic when you get mad?
- Can you maintain civility and patience when you're feeling upset and angry?
- Or do you become impatient and insulting?

The answers and responses that emerge from these *quality questions* about a state flushes out the higher frames that currently texture the state. Typically, you will find many of them. You can also ask about other meta-level phenomena.

- What do you believe about anger?
- What memories in your personal history informs you about this?
- What values or dis-values do you have about experiencing anger?
- What moral judgments do you make about this?
- How does this affect who you are?
- How does anger play into or fail to play into your destiny,

mission, and vision?
- What do you expect about anger?
- What do you expect regarding people when they get angry?

As meta-questions, these questions about an inner experience enables you to move up and flush out the matrix of frames of meaning governing your life.[1]

Understanding the Meta-Levels in States

Far from exhausting the subject, these questions just get you started in this domain of the meta-levels of our neuro-semantics. To fully understand the layered textures of meta-states, step back and think about your everyday states. At first reckoning, they seem ordinary and plain—vanilla states. But they are not.

They are textured. They have properties and features and characteristics that go far beyond plain vanilla. Over the years, via everyday experiences, you have been qualifying your states. You have been setting your states inside of many other frames-of-reference. And every time you do, you thereby create another meta-level state.

Using anger as a prototype, you come to experience thoughts-and-feelings and neurological somatic sensations about your state of anger. You like it or dislike it. You fear it or love it. You dread it or long for it. You believe it can serve you; you believe it only turns things ugly. All of these thoughts and feelings of anger are themselves meta-states. *They are dynamic, ever-moving and changing mental and emotional states about other states.*

Structurally, the special relationship that a meta-state stands to another state involves *classification.* They relate to another state as a higher state of awareness and *they classify the lower state.* The junior state functions as a member of the class that the meta-state creates. The higher or meta-state functions as a category for understanding and feeling about the lower state.
- No wonder then that "fear of our anger" (i.e., fearful anger) differs in texture so much from "respect of our anger" (e.g., respectful anger).
- That's why "shame about getting angry because it only turns things nasty" differs so much in its texture to "appreciation of

my powers to get angry because it informs me that some perceived value or understanding feels violated and allows me to respectfully explore the situation surrounding any anger."

As a higher logical level, the mental and emotional *frames* that you bring to your primary experiences represent the governing influence in your life. The higher frame, as a message about the lower experiences modulates, organizes, and governs the lower. This explains why it functions as a self-organizing attractor in the human mind-body system, thereby making your meta-states so important. They are important because in your meta-states are all of your values, beliefs, expectations, understandings, identifications, etc. Within them are all of the meta-phenomena that make up the landscape of your conscious and unconscious mind.

The Systemic Nature of Meta-States

While I have described teasing apart the structure of our higher frames-of-references (or meta-states) from the primary experiences, we can only do this for sake of analysis. In actual practice primary and meta levels of experiences merge together so we experience them as one.

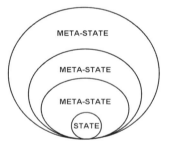

Research scientist Arthur Koestler introduced the term "holons" to describe reality as composed of *"whole/parts."* These whole/parts *holons* refer to any entity that is itself *a whole* and yet simultaneously *a part* of some other whole.

Consider your states and their textures as holons. Experientially you experience your states as a whole. Confidence, courage, commitment, playfulness, joy, flow, etc. each state seems fully contained and meaningful in itself. And yet each of these states also exist as a part of some larger whole. The next larger whole is your neurology. After all, you would have no state without a body, a functioning nervous system, a thinking brain, "life," oxygen, an atmosphere, etc.

Your mind-body state also occurs as a holon within multiple higher mental and emotional frames of beliefs, values, expectations, and scores of other meta-levels. The state of confidence is *a whole* and yet at the same time it is *a part* of other higher level frames: your sense of self, your beliefs about the skill that you feel confident about, your health, etc.

Ken Wilber speaks about holons in terms of two factors: *1) agency and communion,* and *2) transcendence and dissolution.* First, *each holon has its own identity or autonomy.* It has its own "agency" or identity as a whole. Yet because it is a holon within a larger whole, it also communicates with the larger system. That is, it has communion with other wholes. As an example of meta-states, we have a holon of confidence within the holon of esteem for self, which is within the holon of possibilities for growth and success, etc.

Second, this holon structure allows us to *transcend* any state or meta-state and to go beyond what we have been to become more of what we can be. We can add novel components to our layers of states. Or we can dissolve a whole category of being. In other words, we can build up a holon or pull it down.

Yet when a state as a holon moves up and experiences a transcendence of itself (self-transcendence) something new emerges. This occurs when you develop a compelling outcome so that you are empowered to boldly face a fear. In this case, the gestalt state of *courage* emerges. And while the lower state of fear is transcended so that it included in the higher state, this continuous process produces discontinuities. It is a discontinuous change rather than a continuous one building on what went before. Yet in this the leapupward does not work in reverse.

The principle in systems theory is that the new gestalt is "more than the sum of the parts." A new configuration emerges. That's why merely adding all of the parts together cannot explain it. *This is emergence* —a leap upward to a higher form of organization and structure. Wilber (1996) writes:

> "So there are both discontinuties in evolution — mind cannot be reduced to life, and life cannot be reduced to matter; and there

are continuities . . ." (p. 24)

Wilber also asserts that "holons
emerge holarchically" (p. 27).
Koestler invented this term,
holarchy (holarchically), to
r e p l a c e   " h i e r a r c h y . "
Holarchical describes what we
mean by a natural hierarchy,
not the ones that we create
which involve domination.
Natural hierarchies describe *an
order of increasing wholeness:*
particles to atoms to cells to
organisms, or letters to words to sentences to paragraphs. The whole
of one level becomes a part of the whole of the next.

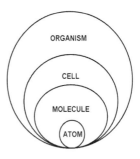

Each higher level embraces and engulfs the lower. That's why when
we take a primary everyday state like anger or confidence and set it
within various frames or states, we create new emergent properties that
nurture the first mind-and-body system.

- Imagine embracing your anger with acceptance, appreciation,
  and wonder. Imagine engulfing it in love, respect, and honor.
  Imagine applying mindfulness, values, and patience to it.
  Imagine bringing ecology concerns, moral uprightness, and
  honor to it. What would your holarchy of anger be like then?

- Imagine embracing your power to take action in the world with
  acceptance and appreciation. Imagine engulfing it with
  ownership, excitement, and joy. Imagine applying hope,
  desired outcomes, willingness to take intelligent risks, love, and
  concern for others, to it. Now let all of this coalesce in a state
  of contemplative relaxation.

The texturing of meta-states occurs in a holarchy of levels of states.
With meta-states, you can now take charge of this natural process
which means that you can design the kind of quality states that will turn
you on to life in new and exciting ways.

Transcending and Including to Create *States Plus*
To transcend any everyday plain vanilla state, begin at the primary level of consciousness as you notice your thoughts and feelings about something "out there" in the world. This is your primary state. Your awareness focuses on something external to yourself.

As you now transcend this experience, include it in a higher level of thought, emotion, and awareness to enrich it. Doing this will create a new level of your own mental-emotional organization. You will be commissioning your higher consciousness to contain the lower.

> In respectful, considerate, and patient anger—you still have anger. You still have the sense of threat or danger to your person or way of life, yet your *anger* is now textured in higher levels of mind and emotion. This is what causes something new to emerge. You have the anger state *plus* something that transcends "mere" anger (that is, animal-like, brute anger). Now you have a higher kind of *human* anger, even spiritual anger.

You have a hierarchy of levels of states as a *holoarchy* because as Aristotle first pointed out:

> "All of the lower is in the higher, but not all of the higher is in the lower."

Molecules contain atoms, but atoms do not contain molecules. As you move up levels, the higher level *includes* the lower while simultaneously the higher *transcends* it. As we transcend the lower, we *add* new features, qualities, properties, and characteristics to our states. In Meta-States this provides the ability to engineer new emergent properties for your states. It gives you the key to the structure of subjectivity as experiences become more complex and layered.

> When your learning is *taken up into* playfulness and appreciation, when you *engulf* it with passion and the intention to improve the quality of life—something new emerges. You have a passionate learning state that's tremendously accelerated so that it creates a real turn-on attitude. One's mind-set now takes on more of the qualities of "genius." Each higher level has added new components that enrich the emergent gestalt. Now something bigger and more expansive arises. Now we have the learning state *plus*.

Summary

•   The powerful process for texturing your states can give you the ability to create high quality states textured with your best resources. When I first discovered the Meta-States model, I didn't understand how higher levels operate as holons. I didn't understand how they *transcend* in order to *embrace and include* the lower levels.

•   This now explains how higher states permeate the lower levels giving them rich textures, tastes, aromas, etc. And this has led to the development of a whole series of patterns to empower you to translate what you know in mind into your body (embody).

•   This mind-to-muscle process facilitates a mind-body integration allowing the higher levels to texture the lowers levels. It allows you to work with layers of thought and feelings as a holon structure—whole/part states within a holarchical system.

End Notes:

1. From the Meta-States Model we have been developing a list of *Meta-Questions*. A list of 32 is in the book, *Coaching Change* in the Meta-Coaching series.

Chapter 13

THE META-STATING

PROCESS

The Process of Eliciting, Accessing, Creating, and Embodying Meta-States

*S*o *how do you do it?* That's the question. Now that you know about meta-states—their nature, operation, and power, how do you do it? How do you meta-state?

As a layered state of mind-and-emotion, the power of a *meta-state* is that it endows you with a higher state of mind for seeing and interacting with the world. Every meta-state facilitates a higher state of consciousness. This higher state may help you or it may hurt you. Yet either way, it constructs for you *an attitude* that you can then carry with you as a frame-of-reference. Whether it serves you well or limits you, whether it empowers and enhances your skills, or locks you up in self-sabotaging thoughts and feelings, a meta-state represents a highly evolved and complex development of human awareness.

With this as a background, how can you deliberately structure your "mind" to create high quality attitudes?
*   How do we *elicit* an existing meta-state?
*   How do we *create* new meta-states?
*   How do we structure layers of thinking-and-feeling for a fully

integrated *attitude?*
- How do you meta-state yourself and others *conversationally?*
- How do you develop skill and expertise in reflecting back onto your states and build empowering higher executive states to unleash your highest potentials?

You undoubtedly already know that sometimes the meta-stating process takes only a few seconds. Sometimes it only takes as long as it takes to inquire about another feeling:

- How do you feel about your self-pity?
- What is your sense of elation like when you land your dream job?
- What would it be like for you to find all your skills for learning and modeling increasing at an accelerated rate?
- How much would you enjoy running your own brain?

The Meta-Stating Process
1)Awareness
2) Access
3) Amplify
4) Apply
5) Appropriate
6) Analyze
7) Accelerate

At other times the meta-stating process can involve hours, if not days to construct, refine, tweak, sequence, and "install" so it becomes fully embodied. This is especially the case with building complex meta-states like resilience, un-insultability, seeing and seizing opportunities, committed visionary leadership, coaching expertise, and the like.

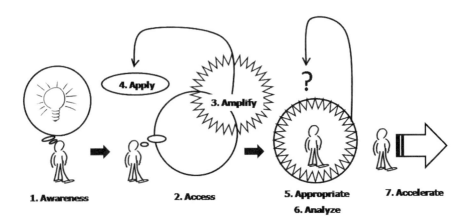

1. Awareness   2. Access   5. Appropriate   7. Accelerate
                                     6. Analyze

The complexity of a many-layered piece of consciousness that you have sequenced so that out of it emerges a new gestalt like self-efficacy, courage, seeing opportunities, etc. may at first seem very complex. And it may be. Yet within that complexity there is something so simple, namely, *the simplicity of layering one thought or emotion upon another thought or emotion.* This is the ultimate simplicity regarding the composition of our experiences.

> *Ultimately, all of your states, meta-states, and gestalt states are comprised of the same stuff—constructed representations that you layer upon each other.*

As you meta-state and build up meta-state constructions, you ultimately only have to work with putting together different thoughts and emotions so that in the process they give rise to new configurations or gestalts. This chapter will describe these meta-stating processes and do so by beginning with the processes that we use at the primary level.

1) Awareness
Becoming aware of where you are, where you want to be, and making a decision about your desired higher level state is the first step of consciously meta-stating. What frames and resources do you want to apply to your primary state?

1. Awareness

In this step, you pick your magic. "Magic?" Yes, when you meta-state you engage in neurological processes that involve your internal psycho-logics that will perform what Bateson called "magic" at the meta-levels. Due to the plasticity of symbols and how that you can use your thoughts-and-emotions as frames, it operates as if by magic. Since believing, expecting, valuing, attributing, etc. can sometimes call something into being, meta-states can seem magical at times.

In the *awareness* you step aside from yourself for just a moment and embrace a present state awareness for picking your magic.
- What higher level mental-emotional state would you like to develop? Resilience? Un-insultability? Self-esteem?
- What frames of references would you like to set and establish in your life? "Today determines my future, not the past." "I

am more than my thoughts and feelings."
- What attitude would you like to build to use as your perceptual filter from this day forward? "Problems make life fascinating." "I always have choice and can always do something."

Actually you are meta-stating *awareness* and *perspective* as you ask and answer these questions. Did you notice that? Often when you are

1.   Present State Awareness
Access State and Context (grounding and ecology check)
Pre-Frame Desired State

in *first perceptual position* (seeing the world from your eyes, ears, and skin) and get caught up with the content of everyday life, you forget to use your meta-powers. Then you see, hear, and feel things from out of your own eyes and ears without any awareness of your state or frames of mind.

Stepping aside from this enables you to notice your thinking, notice your emoting, notice how you are responding. You have moved to a meta-level. You have gone meta to where the adventure begins. If you step aside and imagine things from the point-of-view of another person, you take *second position* (imagining the world from his or her point-of-view)—another meta-state. This expands your awareness enabling you to become wiser. It broadens your understandings. When you step aside to a *third perceptual position* (seeing the interactive system and context within which both of us operate), then notice all of that and more, which of course further enriches your perceptual world.

This description identifies how the *Perceptual Positions* represents a basic and valuable meta-stating process. Doing this develops *an observational* or *witnessing meta-state*. Korzybski called this the central mechanism for sanity, *consciousness of abstracting*. Now you can observe and witness your own processes and to make choices about how to take charge of your mind and states. As a result, it increases your sense of choice and control.[1]

Albert Einstein put this wiser and expanded perspective succinctly in his classical words:

> "You can't solve a problem from the same space that you created it."

Step aside from the space where you have been thinking and emoting to a new conceptual space.
*   How would you like to feel?
*   How would you like to think?
*   How would you like to respond?
*   What higher state of mind would you like to entertain about a given situation?

Begin with these meta-questions to free up your creative energies as you begin to imagine new and better response patterns that will enrich your life. This will enable you to make some good choices about the magic that you pick.

2) Access
Now you are ready to access a state to apply to your primary state. In NLP, there are two key processes for eliciting states. One involves memory, the other involves imagination. The inductions that grow out of these two pathways involve putting a person back into a remembered experience or in inviting a person to step into a possible experience. From this gives rise to the classical NLP elicitations:
*   *"Think about a time* when you felt . . . confident . . . when you had all your resources present . . . when you felt in love . . ." *"Have you ever experienced* anger, relaxation, aversion, attraction, etc. . . . ?" "Have you ever known someone who can do X and would be a good model?"

•   *"What would it be like . . .* feel like, look like, or sound like *if* you step into a state of wonder, delight, pleasure . . . ?" "If you imagine being the person who is able to do this, and step into his or her skin, what is that like?"

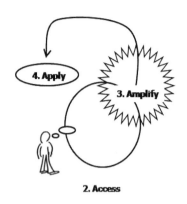

In both *the memory pathway* ("remember when . . .") and in the *imagination pathway* ("imagine what it would be like if . . .") you use your thoughts (sensory-based representations along with words) to construct an internal world of visual, auditory, and kinesthetic stimuli as either snapshots or movies. You can then expect the natural and normal neuro-linguistic processes to take over. In the face of these stimuli, how do you respond? What does it call forth in you? What state do you access?

The power of such elicitations for accessing a state lies in using stimuli that have enough voltage or intensity so that it *evokes* you to experience and feel the reference experiences. For this reason, elicitation power lies in vividness, intensity, strength of image, sound, sensation, smell, taste, etc. This is equally true for the meta-levels as well. The more drama you bring to your internal world as you represent, the more strength and power you give to your elicitations.[2]

Start by simply accessing the state or meta-state with your cognition powers: mind-emotion, imagination, conscience, evaluation, etc. Vividly imagine the meta-level state with much specificity, make it graphically compelling, and amplify it. Once you have a clear and compelling inner image of it—step into it, completely and thoroughly, with honest acceptance of it.

In accessing one state to apply to another state, you use the same elements you use at the primary level: human thought-and-feelings and physiology. These are the mechanisms that drive mind-body states.

What makes meta-stating more complicated and difficult is that you now will also be working with *multiple layers* of awareness. Some meta-states may not only involve one single level of states-about-states, but several levels of states-embedded-in-states. In calling forth a complex of states, there are numerous features to work with:

- Primary states
- States linked together by various kinds of anchors
- Linguistics that encode the states
- A streamlined experience habituated through practiced repetitions of the sequence
- Emergent gestalts
- Coalesced meta-states
- Frames-of-reference embedded in yet higher frames
- Attractors of a self-organizing system
- Feed back and feed forward loops, etc.

To experience any state, you only need to access the thoughts of the state fully and completely, step into it with energy and vigor, and experience it. You can do this for no good reason or for lots of good reasons. You can even do it when nothing external calls it forth in you. You can *just do it*. You have that much freedom within your neuro-linguistics when you know how to use your neuro-linguistic mechanisms.

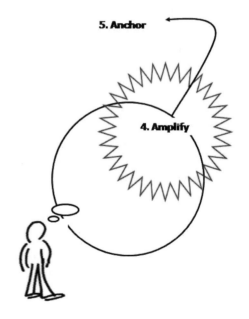

3) Amplify

In the process of applying one state to another, its important that you have enough neurological energy in the state that you put in a meta position to the first state. If you gauge the state from 0 to 10 and the biological, emotional, mental, and personal energy of the state is low (0 to 4), you probably will not have enough energy to set the state as a meta-state or frame over the first state.

States are energy fields. States are mind-body experiences and we need *enough* of a state to "set" it as a frame. We need enough of this energy to embed the first state inside it. If we don't have sufficient energy, the result will be inadequate. We will *know* what to do, what to feel, what to believe, etc., but we will not have *experienced* the higher frame as the meta-state.

The solution is to amplify the state that you'll apply and set as a meta-state. Here you will juice up the state, make more of the state, and add more drama to the state. You can do this turning up the cinematic features or meta-modalities (the so-called sub-modalities) of the presentations. See your images closer, brighter, bigger, etc.; hear your sounds louder, more compelling, richer, etc. Hear more compelling words and step into your movie so that you are— in your mind—fully there.

4) Apply
Now you're ready to make the connection, to link, as you apply one state to another. You can do this by asking a question about the relationship:

> What is it like when you experience X when you are Y-ing?
> What is it like when you feel calmness when you are angry?
> How does X transform Y?
> How does respect for people as sacred beings transform your experience of expressing your anger?

You can do this through anchoring. Once you anchor the desired state of X, you can link that feeling to the target state of Y.

> Notice what happens when you *feel this* [fire the anchor stimulus] when you are in Y state.

You can link in trance by creating an induction into the new state. And given that higher level symbols and linguistics predominantly drive meta-states, finding and creating the empowering words as language inductions enable the new state to cohere. This means you apply one state to another by linguistically gluing the states together.

Applying in this way describes an empowering use of hypnotic language patterns. Language works marvels in creating, evoking, and supporting higher level frames. As you *go meta* and jump logical levels, the resultant meta-states become the governing and enriching experience.

Moving to this level moves you up into trance states and so creates a hypnotic state. The linguistic structures that facilitate this are hypnotic language patterns. Such language is hypnotic precisely because the referents are not "out there" in the world, but inside your mind. To make sense of such language, you have to *transition* from the outside waking state (the uptime state) to an inside process state (downtime), hence, the origin of the term *trance*. Meta-stating uses hypnotic language patterns because it is a hypnotic phenomenon. This gives us another definition of meta-states.

> *Meta-stating is a hypnotic phenomenon. The structure of a meta-state is an induction—a hypnotic induction that builds up and constructs meanings and states.*

Bandler and Grinder modeled hypnosis and hypnotic language patterns after Milton Erickson, the leading pioneer of medical hypnosis at that time. They said that ultimately hypnosis is using vague language precisely, being vaguely precise. So in the meta-stating of *applying* one state to another we precisely use vague language to elicit and structure the higher level states.

An example of this is the language we use in the "magic" of *the Movie Rewind pattern*. This is also called the "Phobia Cure" pattern or the V-K Dissociation pattern.[3] Notice below how the words facilitate the conceptual moves a person makes to meta-positions. These moves enable recoding representations that encourage the development of a comfort zone, use of inner resources, and a re-processing of the old scary movie. In the following induction, I have enumerated the meta-states of this pattern within brackets [].

> "Now as you look at that younger you [1] in that black-and-white snapshot up there on the screen, and recognize how you *feel comfortable* [2] in the tenth row *observing that image* [3], you can now *become aware* of all the things you know now in your adult mind [4] which that younger you did *not know,* but which would have empowered that younger self and made things better [5] . . . And as you float out of your body as you sit in that theater and watch that movie to the projection booth in the back of the auditorium [6], you can now see yourself in row ten watching this old movie and you can *feel the plexiglass*

> on the palm of your hands in front of you [7] as you *look out* at the back of your head in the tenth row *watching with interest* [8] that younger you . . . and when you're ready, just let the movie play out watching it from this safe and powerful place, the control room of your mind [9] and let it play to a scene of comfort, or better, of pleasure that occurred sometime later in your life [10]."[3]

To the extent that you follow and experience these words, you will develop an internal focus and the following congruent states: just observing, observing with comfort, observing two levels back, observing with a sense of safety and control, and so on. To the extent you transition to this experience, you are experiencing "hypnosis." It is hypnosis because you *turn inward* as you see, hear, and experience these words and use them to construct this imagery. Doing so, you *transition* from the outside to the inside.

Because this language is hypnotic, it operates as an *induction* into a particular trance. If you don't like the term "hypnosis," then simply think about this as *meta-stating,* as working methodologically with the content of your higher states of mind to create a more resourceful way to remember and think about the old story. Think about it as a process for setting higher frames-of-reference in your inner world.

This hypnotic languaging facilitates and creates the meta-state of observation and witnessing which, in turn, provides a platform or space for renewing your mind. As it enables you to develop a structured awareness of consciousness, you become more mindful. You might even become aware of how you have created your cognitive constructions as mental maps about the memories. You can also solidify this witnessing perspective, sustain it, and protect it from collapsing back into the primary state. In this way, *the words provide you a new way to represent the old information.* From this new mapping or framing comes new resourceful ways to feel and to respond.

In this example, the primary state is your remembered referent experience. It no longer exists. All that you now have is your fearful memory which is loaded with appropriately scary thoughts, emotions, and neurology. We begin with a memory state where your younger self lacked the necessary resources for coping with some event. The purpose here is to witness the event and to *not* re-experience the event. Re-experiencing it would not help. It would only put you through the trauma one more time. Yet before going through it in a new way, we need to set up a new way to encode the memory so you have access to all of your resources.

The structure and language of this pattern enables the construction of numerous resources, the primary one being that of *psychological distance* from the trauma. When you do this, then you can at least think about it comfortably. *Comfortable thinking* as a meta-state, explicitly enables you to "face the past reality" while remaining centered, feeling safe and able to control the representations. Now you can think about the old movie in a different way. You can just witness it without going into state. This witnessing enables you to now entertain the old fearful memory without re-experiencing the trauma.

Using this pattern to resolve phobias, depotentiate traumas, and nullify semantic-reactions, meta-states the old memory by setting new frames. The pattern invites you to apply several resourceful states to the primary state of hurt, fear, or trauma. Setting all of these new frames outframes the trauma also with numerous implied resources. For example, the process elicits comfort *about* the hurt, *interest and curiosity* in it, *mere observation and witnessing* of it, *broader perspective* about it, etc.

By facilitating this process you to step back from your representations two or three times, you meta-state more distance, more personal control, more perspective, and more wisdom. The pattern then invites you to apply the "going backwards state" to the trauma. That is, you access and apply the feeling of "going backwards" to the fear and hurt movie. Isn't that amazing? What state are you in when you run your memories backwards? What thoughts and feelings do you experience when you see, hear, and feel everything rushing backwards in super-fast rewind? Do you experience disorientation? Confusion? Undoing-ness? The resolving and mastering of phobias, fears, and anxieties works because of all of the new frames.

You set states of observation, calmness, interest, curiosity, etc. and then set a disorientation frame to disrupt things further which helps to deframe your old way of processing information. Along the way you can edit the old movie, add in resources, strengths, self-esteem, etc. All of this provides a whole new reference system for handling such things and it illustrates Bateson's statement about higher levels:

"The higher levels always modulate the lower levels."

When you set a new frame of reference, the frame becomes a new governing influence at a higher level of your mind. When you invite someone to imagine taking a tenth row seat in the theater of the mind, you are inviting the person to adopt *a different perspective* to the traumatic thoughts—as an *observer* rather than participant. Then in inviting the person to step back again from the trauma by floating out of the body and back to the projection booth, you apply more distance to the person's point of view.

All of this is applying witnessing. Then you have a great context for applying other states: relaxation, confidence, compassion, assertiveness, etc. Most people have all of the necessary pieces for constructing a particular empowering state (i.e., proactivity, resilience, self-esteeming, etc.). That's not the problem that most people have. More likely, *the problem is not knowing how to access resourceful states at that point.* Why not? They do not have a particular pattern as a linguistic strategy to tie all of the pieces together in a sequence as a coherent whole. Or, they may not have the pieces automatically linked so that they can easily send their brain-body into that state.

As another example, consider resilience as a meta-state.[4] Almost everybody who has developed a resilient attitude has constructed a language induction that involves such the following things:

1) There is no failure, only feedback.

2) I will not fear failure as if it were fatal.

3) I will not allow hindrances, frustrations, blocks, unpleasant experiences, set-backs, etc. to defeat me.

4) I *can* and *will* learn from these experiences. I am learning how to be smarter and wiser in mastering life's challenges.

5) I will bounce back; I've got bounce in my soul! I shall return. Or, to quote Arnold, "I'll be back!"

This is the language of resilience. Look again at these words. See them from the perspective of questioning the effect they have in you as you experience them. What states do these words access for you? If you consider how each of these conceptual statements construct more resourceful frames about the primary state of getting knocked down or experiencing a set back, what meta-states do they evoke in you? As each of these statements induce a state-about-a-state structure, what new inner game do you create within?

Language induces states and states coalesce through the use of language. No wonder meta-stating an experience, even fear and failure, essentially functions as a hypnotic induction. It explains the value of finding the kind of emotional-laden and value-laden words that provide you a step-by-step instruction for experiencing the gestalts that result whether freedom from trauma or resilience. No wonder memorable, vivid, graphic, and compelling language glues your meta-states and creates an hypnotic induction. These linguistics affect your neurology and program you to carry out the cognitive-experiential construction.[5]

Apply Sequentially
If you have more than one state to apply and set as a frame, you'll be applying the states in a sequence and sometimes the sequence itself is critical.

In the more complex and layered meta-states like resilience you have elements of thoughts and emotions that will require it to be put together in a particular sequence. So specify the representational steps and responses that order the experience. Build *the syntax structure* that formats the layered consciousness that's required for the meta-state.

The difference in this from traditional NLP strategy work is that you have added another direction. Now you not only move out linearly and horizontally, but also vertically. Now you move up and down logical levels. For example, in resilience you start the sequence with the primary state of experiencing some defeat, set-back, or frustration. Within that primary state you specify representational steps—what to see, hear, and feel. *Yet more important than that is what and how you think about the set-back.* What's your frame in thinking-and-feeling about that? This question takes you up a level.

At the first meta-level about the set-back state, do you *accept* the event as something you have to deal with at that moment in time? Resilience involves an acknowledging acceptance that frees you from the fight about what *is,* so that you can begin to find ways to effectively adjust to it and master it.

Then, access the state of self-value and unconditional worth so you can feel a more secure sense of yourself and your dignity. Keep your person separate and distinct from your behaviors, emotions, and experiences while you cope with the set-back. Embedding the everyday experience of step-back within the larger frame of self-esteem you stop personalizing a defeat or using it to dis-esteem yourself.

Next, access a state of vision of your desired outcomes and dreams. This sets the frame of your sense of direction and purpose. In terms of coping with set-backs, this prevents any fall from knocking out your dream. Next, access and apply a state of reality-orientation over the primary state to create an attitude of testing things to discover what you're up against before jumping to conclusions.

In my own meta-state of resilience, as you noticed in chapters four and five, I include another frame —*an optimistic explanatory style.* This provides me with the ability to positively frame things when facing defeats, set-backs, and frustrations. In every highly resilient person that I have modeled, I have found a strong and energetic state of proactivity which plays a significant part in creating that overall sense of an internal "bounce-back." Also, in several people that I modeled I discovered that they had an orientation state *meta* to all of these other meta-states. They had a big picture about the whole bounce-back process and where they stood in it at any given time.[4]

With all of the pieces that go into the meta-state of resilience, no wonder meta-state inductions take more time, more repetition, and more honing to get them just right. No wonder they are not typically anchored with a kinesthetic touch. This also explains why *linguistic anchoring as a form of a hypnotic induction* involves finding just the right words—word that fits one's values, visions, principles, beliefs, etc.[5]

5) Appropriate
In this step you *appropriate* the results from your meta-stating to the

context and primary state. That is, you *appropriate* the resources so that the meta-state gestalt comes together.

To appropriate, simply step in and fully experience the state. This implies that you do not have to earn, deserve, or work your way up to the right to experience this state. Just access the state and experience it. After all, a state of mind, of emotion, and of body involves fully experiencing your own thinking-and-feeling within your body. You don't need a license to do that!

You have immediate access to states whenever you want them. Imagine that! At any moment, you can just think about something and as you do so vividly, it calls the state forth. It works like magic. Theology has a special term for this magic—"grace." *Grace* describes gifts that are yours for the asking, given freely, with no conditions. Just access and appropriate it to this needed context.

Meta-stating is your legacy as a human being. You do *not* have to achieve, earn, or deserve this right to meta-state. You have as much right to them as you do to feeling the sunshine on your face and breathing in the air around you. We do not have to pass any State Board of Examiners to have the right to experience empowering states like acceptance, joy, self-esteeming, patience, oneness, inner peace, etc.

What stops some from accessing and appropriating is the limiting belief that they can't just step in and have these states. They think they have to achieve some competency, become a particular kind of person, gain lots of information, etc. to have the right to experience such states. What a limiting and unuseful belief!

To access your potentials, simply imagine the state in all of its richness, step into it fully, and commission your brain and neurology to take it on and to try it out. Appropriate it to your experience as a possibility. Use your reflexive consciousness to appropriate the meta-state as a way of being in the world.

Connirae and Tamara Andreas (1994) have some marvelously phrased meta-questions that facilitate this appropriation:
•   Would you like to have that loving oneness [a meta-state] as a starting point in an ongoing way?

• How does already having loving oneness as a way of being make things different?

• When you already have loving oneness, how does it affect your experience of connecting with lots of different people on lots of different levels?

• What is it like to begin by applying inner peace to being criticized?

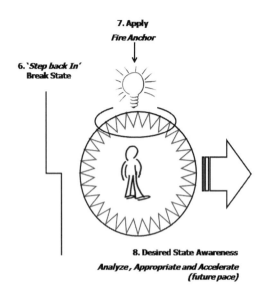

The ability to access and appropriate a state is the gift of your brain and neurology. So use it for all its worth. As you access resourceful states, appropriate them into the contexts where you want to be strong, confident, deserving, centered, loving, passionate, joy, appreciative, etc.

6) Analyze

Now check it out. Analyze the value, benefits, ecology, congruence, etc. of this appropriated meta-state. As you meta-state your primary state, run a *quality control* on what results. If you don't have enough objectivity to do that, then *step back* from the state and evaluate the state. A witnessing meta-state endows you with enough internal distance to run a quality check on the ecology of your thinking patterns, emotional patterns, and response patterns. Frame your viewpoint from any of a multitude of other perspectives, from friends and associates, from geniuses and mentors, from spiritual leaders and writers.

Check to see how well it would serve you as you quality control the experience:

• Is this ecological for my life, relationships, health, career, recreation, etc.?

• Will this meta-state create any limitations for me?

• Will it empower me to take effective actions as I live my life?

• Will it remain productive for me in the long run?

• Would this state create the quality that I want?

Quality controlling the results of your creation expands your awareness making you conscious of your thinking and emoting. Now you are truly in charge. As it is your brain, you can run it as you will, entertain the images that you so choose, and now you can make sure it is serving you well and making things better.

In analyzing, remember that your states are just states—experiences of thoughts-and-emotions—and sometimes they do not serve you well or enhance your well-being. Actually, some of the greatest suffering and dis-empowerment occurs precisely due to unuseful, limiting, and incongruous meta-states.

For a meta-state to truly empower, rather than dis-empower, it must not have any significant conflicting states or levels within it. For it to structure thinking and feeling in a holistically congruent way, you will want to integrate all of the layers of your consciousness. Sometimes this means eliminating built-in conflicts between levels or parts. While you may want to use such patterns as Negotiating Between Parts or Six-Step Reframing, I find that to eliminates most incongruencies, all you need to do is *meta-model the incongruency.*

In a dis-empowering meta-state, the state-about-state structure of your reflexive consciousness harms you or prevents you from responding effectively. For instance, if you are feeling self-conscious about public speaking, that state is what directs your attention away from the people you are speaking to. Worrying about being self-consciousness, or feeling guilt about self-consciousness, etc. is *not* the state for effectively speaking in public. When you feel ashamed of your anger or sexuality, and then condemn or shame yourself for this shame, this does not add to you personal power.

Such meta-level states typically set up *a looping process* so that you loop around a circuit from primary state to meta-state to meta-meta state without an exit. You go round and round. In terms of strategy analysis, this manifests a very poorly designed (although very powerful) strategy. This describes an incredible strategy for making yourself really miserable, stuck in the misery, and then miserable about the misery! In *systems terms*, you have a reinforcing closed system that will spiral out of control until it crashes.

Dilts (1983) in *Roots of NLP* has described this in terms of *oscillation*. "Feedback between different logical types on the same level will result in oscillation."

5. Appropriate
6. Analyze

> "The belief that someone is 'stupid' or 'intelligent' is of a different logical type than that person's actual behavior—the belief is a mental activity while the behavior is physical. The two should have no functional effect on one another. Believing that a chair can dance should not necessarily cause it to dance. Believing that someone is stupid or smart should not affect their intelligence. However, when a feedback system is provided the two may begin to shape each other." (p. 54)

The *feedback* and *feed-forward* information of thoughts-and-emotions in the human system of consciousness here creates "a self-fulfilling prophecy." It operates without an external check or an ecology check to give it an opportunity to pause for thought or to balance its forces.

When you integrate these responses, and run an ecology check on them, quality check the systemic nature of a meta-state structure. To eliminate incongruencies, begin by setting a meta-state of balance, empowermemt, and ecology.[6]

7) Accelerate
Finally you have reached the end of the pattern and it is time to take your new meta-state and accelerate your life and effectiveness. It's time to turn lose and live the new meta-state.

For example, if you use the Movie Rewind pattern for resolving phobic responses, you can now accelerate your own effectiveness in dealing with fears by imagining going into your future with the ability to "just witnessing an upsetting experience" while maintaining psychological distance.

In this stage, you invite the person to take on the new learnings and accelerate it into life. You build a configuration where all of the resources operate as a whole so you use a coherent structure like a story, narrative, metaphor, etc. The pieces do not matter as much as do the construction of this new empowering configuration of thoughts, emotions, values, perceptions, etc. The language will glue the strategy together as a single unit if we experience it as a meaningful whole.

Storytelling and narrative are especially powerful as linguistic structures for organizing meta-experiences. The structure of narrative provides a sequencing that induces, rehearses, and creates various meta-states. Languaging yourself with a story that sequences the domains of knowledge and understanding can powerfully assist you in having easy access to your best meta-states.

7. Accelerate

Summary
- As a human being, you have all the linguistic and neurological equipment you need for inducing yourself into primary and meta-states. The resources are within you as part of the heritage of your nervous system as a class of symbolic life.

- You only need to tap into these resources, use them, develop them, and develop also your ability to manage them well. The process of constructing empowering meta-states makes you conscious about what you naturally do.

- With this explicit process you can *meta-state* yourself and others for fun, profit, growth, and learning.

End Notes:

1. John Grinder grudgingly acknowledges the third perceptual position as a meta-state, but has refused to recognize that the second perceptual position is also a meta-state.   See *Whispering in the Wind* and our debate on this subject on www.neurosematnics.com.

2. One of the unique skills taught in NLP and Neuro-Semantic trainings is the power to elicitation states. In fact, we have made *state induction* as one of the core coaching skills in Meta-Coaching, a skill that we also benchmark as we test for competency.

3. For more about the Movie Rewind pattern and the full steps of the pattern, see *MovieMind* (2001).

4. If you skipped chapters 4 and 5, they are on Resilience. There is also a training manual on Resilience from Neuro-Semantic Publications.

5. For more about hypnotic language and patterns, see the Milton Model in the NLP Practitioner training or in *The User's Manual of the Brain, Volume I*. Also see *Hypnotic Language Patterns* by John Burton and Bob Bodenhamer.

6. There are numerous patterns in Meta-States for eliminating incongruencies and for developing more congruency and integrity, see the patterns of Meta-Alignment, Spinning Icons, the Crucible, etc.

7. In chapter 16 we will more fully explore the Core Transformation model.

PART III:

META-STATES

The Model

and the Theory

Chapter 14

META-STATES

AS A MODEL

The Four Factors of a Model

As a new domain of NLP, based upon the theoretical work of Korzybski and Bateson, *Meta-States introduces a new model for working with consciousness*. It does this by addressing the central uniqueness of human consciousness—self-reflexive consciousness. Previous chapters have enumerated many of the ideas that make up the organizing principles and mechanisms within the Meta-States model. Central to these ideas are:

- A complex and layered state-about-a-state experience
- The psycho-logical levels in consciousness as categories by which we classify things
- Mental contexts as our embedded frames-of-reference
- Mind-body as a neuro-linguistic *system*
- The different kinds and qualities of states
- The non-linear or recursive thinking that spirals around ideas
- The systemic feedback and feed forward loops

How does a set of ideas like these grow up to become a model? For that matter, what do we mean by "model?" What is implied and suggested in the assertion that Meta-States is a model? What are the sufficient and necessary components that make up a model? When is an idea just an idea, or a pattern, and not a full fledged model?

To have an operational model in science at least four sets of components are required:

    1) ***Theory:*** *an explanatory description.*

    2) ***Elements:*** *a set of elements, variables, sequences, etc.*

    3) ***Guidelines:*** *a set of operational principles and guidelines.*

    4) ***Technologies:*** *a set of patterns, processes, and practical tools.*

The Components of a Model

In this chapter we will first explore these facets of a model and apply them to both the NLP communication model and the Meta-States reflexivity model. Then, we will examine some current research in the neuro-sciences, the field of Meta-Cognition, and Cognitive Psychology. This will include an overview of Holland's work in the cognitive-emotional experience of "interpreting literature" and Nelson and Naren's model of meta-memory. Both of these offer a model regarding how meta-levels operate as systemic processes that control and modulate the flow of information.

1) *An Explanatory Theory*

A model involves much more than just an idea. It involves a set of ideas that explain how some process works, the patterns involved, the mechanisms that drive the experience, and *the conceptual understandings about why it works.* In this way a model contains a hypothesis as a thesis or premise that presents a structural outline about the dynamic processes involved. As this theoretical explanation establishes the foundational basis for the model, it enables us to postulate and test hypotheses that fall out from the theory.

This is valuable because it enables us to work out the ideas as concepts so we can then test them to validate or to falsify them. If we construct a system wherein the governing hypothesis cannot be tested, and where the ideas that we have about something cannot be falsified, then we have formatted a system that cannot be questioned or refined. Such a system is closed and self-contained, and as such it can neither be proved or disproved. And that means it can only operate through faith in its premises and presuppositions. By contrast, a true model is testable. We can put our ideas to the test to see if they work, and to see if our hypotheses are valid. All of this underscores the importance of operationalizing our terms and procedures.

- What is the thesis or premise of the idea?
- What is the hypothesis that we could test for?

2) *A Set of Elements, Variables, Sequences, etc.*

To have a model we need a list of component parts that come together to create a process. These parts make up the elements of the system. In this system, we will have dependent and independent variables and, as we detail the relationships between the variables, we can then test our hypothesis.

- What are the pieces and parts that make up the model?
- What are the necessary and sufficient elements that we must have to have a full description of the model.
- How do they fit together?

3) *A Set of Operational Principles and Guidelines*

The principles of a model provide an understanding about how to use the mechanisms that govern the operation of the system. It also provides a set of processes, *procedures,* or instructions, that specify how to use the model as a model, when, where, with whom, in what way, etc. These guidelines do not explain or theorize; they direct and control the use of the model. They provide formulaic instructions, performatives, "Do this first (X), then this other thing (Y), the result will be this (Z)." When we do not have specific procedures like these, we default to more general guidelines or heuristics.

- What are the basic guidelines for working with this model?
- What procedures does the model lead to which enable us to use it for a prescribed purpose?
- What are some of the heuristics of the model?
- When do we not use a particular process?
- What constraints should we be aware of in using this model?

4) *A Set of Technologies*

As we use a guiding theory in the form of a set of procedures that enables us to experiment, test, and play with the various elements, *techniques* emerge—techniques that allow us to do things. These show up as patterns, tools, recipes, formulas, etc. Techniques make a model practical so that it provides specific maps and directions to some creation, products, or experiences.

- What can we do with the model?
- What tools, processes, and interventions can we use the model

> for?
- What are the step-by-step procedures for using the model to accomplish X?

NLP as a *Model*

Like the General Semantics model, the Transformational Grammar model, Bateson's model of the Levels of Learning, NLP arose as a model about *the form and structure* of how we humans communicate in our embodied psychology to create our maps of reality and our inner subjective experiences. At its core, *NLP is essentially a communication model.* Developed from the competencies of three world-class communicators, Bandler and

> **The Four Components of a Model**
>
> 1) **Theory:** *an explanatory description*
> 2) **Elements:** *a set of elements, variables, sequences, etc.*
> 3) **Guidelines:** *a set of operational principles and guidelines.*
> 4) **Technologies:** *a set of patterns, processes, and practical tools.*

Grinder used the formulations of Transformational Grammar to detail how we communicate to ourselves about the world. It specifies the languages and grammar of the mind and how this inner communication affects our emotions, skills, responses, and states.

From this central model, sub-models in NLP were developed. These include models about interpersonal communication, therapy, state management, "running one's own brain," hypnosis, reframing, etc. We can now analyze the NLP Communication model using these four factors of a complete model. Doing so will provide a basis for understanding *Meta-States* as a model.

Elements of the NLP Model

We begin by recognizing that NLP provides us the ability to make many valuable distinctions which we would otherwise miss. Among the central component elements of NLP are the following:

` 1) "Thought" as coded in representational systems: visual, auditory, kinesthetic, olfactory, words, etc.

2) Levels of representing: sensory-based, evaluation based. The representation systems: VAK, words, and symbols.

3) The mapping processes: deletion, generalization, distortion

4) The higher levels of representation: language, meta-programs and meta-states

5) The cinematic qualities, features, and distinctions of our inner movies or VAK systems, the so-called "sub-modalities" that describe the way we structure or frame our images, sounds, and sensations.

6) The NLP algorithm getting descriptions of one's present state and desired state. The SCORE model: symptoms, cause, outcome, resources, effects.

7) Mind-and-body, as a system that interacts and interfaces with each other and not as separate elements.

8) Linguistic distinctions that enable us to challenge ill-formedness (the Meta-Model) and those that enable us to use ill-formedness to hypnotize (the Milton Model).

9) "Time" is represented by lines, circles, and other metaphorical configurations to give us the time zones of past, present, future, atemporal.

10) Meta-Programs as the attentional filters that governs how we pay attention and sort for information.

11) Perceptual positions for taking multiple perspectives and creating a synergy for a greater wisdom.

The Theory of the NLP Model

The primary *explanatory theory* that supports NLP and the original Meta-Model (1975) rests in the Cognitive Psychology model of Miller, Galanter, and Pribram, and Chomsky's Transformational Grammar. John Grinder contributed these pieces having written his doctoral dissertation in the field of Transformational Grammar on "Nominalizations." He co-authored a *Guide to Transformational Grammar* with Elgin (1973). This book was a prelude to the Meta-Model. Other sub-strands of theoretic support for NLP came from Korzybski's General Semantics (his map/territory distinction, sensory-based description of representations, and levels of abstraction), Lakoff's Generative Semantics, Vailinger's *Philosophy of 'As If'* (1924), Bateson's meta-levels in his levels of Learning and Change, Watzlawick's work in meaning construction and reframing, Walzlawick, Weakland and Risch's book on reframing and "problem formation and resolution" *Change* (1974), etc.

The structure of the first NLP model about communication consisted of a list of 12 linguistic distinctions in three categories (deletions, generalizations, distortions). For each linguistic distinction there was a set of twelve questions used to challenge a person's surface statement. The guideline of the model invited a person to probe the surface sentence distinction to elicit in a speaker a fuller deep structure representation of their inner communication and awareness. As a presentation, some charts diagram it in three columns: linguistic distinctions, questions, anticipated results.

NLP Model Guidelines

Among the *set of operational principles or procedures*, the Meta-Model simply prescribed step-by-step procedures:
1) Listen for a surface sentence,
2) Detect ill-formedness in that sentence,
3) Question the person until you obtain a fuller description.
4) Note if this evokes new clarity, resources, and more positive states for handling the situation.

The NLP Communication Model

Theory: Self-Actualization Psychology, people are good and seek positive intentions for themselves, operate as mind-body-emotion systems, create mental maps for navigating reality, experience emotions and skills according to their maps, communicate via sensory representations and language, etc.

Elements: Sensory systems, languages, predicates, eye access cues, states, anchoring, cinematic features, meta-programs, etc.

Guidelines: Listen for predicates, determine favored representation system, distinguish linguistic patterns, ask Meta-Model questions, calibrate to person's state, etc.

Processes: Movie Rewind pattern, State Induction, Swish, Set Anchors, Collapse Anchors, etc.

More specific guidelines occur with each linguistic distinction. To detect a surface level nominalization, the wheelbarrow test was created. "Imagine putting the referent in a wheelbarrow, can you do that?" You can put a true noun in the wheelbarrow—a person, place, or thing, but not pseudo-nouns like an idea. In the basic theory of the Meta-Model, specificity questioning evokes people to engage in a trans-deriviation search. This means it evokes the person to go "inside" to his or her stored internal references by which the person has created associations and meanings at the level of the deep structure.

The Importance of Theory
In business, benchmarking has become popular as a way to quickly adapt new processes without the need to understand the theory behind the processes. While the two processes of benchmarking and modeling are not the same, there are numerous similarities between them. In benchmarking, a manager finds the *best practice or performance* within a given domain (e.g., sales call, customer service response, inventory management, etc.) and uses it as a benchmark or standard for everybody else. People can then copy or mimic the processes of this best practice.

In this description, benchmarking does not require a theoretical basis. The focus is simply to get the response that management wants. Driven by practicality, getting one's desired results is all that matters. This approach fulfils the basic business mantra, "Do whatever works."

Edwards Deming, who almost single-handedly initiated the Quality Movement in business, criticizes benchmarking precisely for this reason—its lack of theory. He argues that it promotes doing anything that works without any controls or constraints. He describes this as an undisciplined mentality of the premise that, "The end justifies the means."

In *Thinking About Quality: Progress, Wisdom, and the Deming Philosophy*, Lloyd Dobyns and Clare Crawford-Mason write,
> "Unless you know *why* something works, knowing that it works in a particular circumstance is of limited value. 'An example teaches nothing,' Deming said, 'unless studied with the aid of theory; otherwise people merely copy. They get into trouble . . . because they did not understand *why* something was good or

why something as bad." (pp. 130-131)

For these individuals, a theory provides a powerful tool and mechanism for developing excellence. When we firmly hold in mind *why* we are gathering information and *what* use we will make of it, our theory gives us something against which to test information and experience. This allows real life experiences to refine and develop our ideas as our conceptual explanations so that we can make them more accurate and useful.

In the scientific mind-set and orientation, we use theories, test them against actual practice, refine them, test them again, etc. By this never-ending process we are able to plan, test, study the results, re-fine our ideas, and cycle back through the process. That's why we need a core philosophy, or guiding theory, to test new ideas, to keep refining processes, and to let the model continue to evolve.

In a similar line of thinking, Korzybski wrote,

> "Theories are relational or structural verbal schemes, built by a process of high abstractions from many lower abstractions, which are produced not only by ourselves but by others (time-binding). Theories, therefore, represent the shortest, simplest structural summaries and generalizations, or the highest abstractions from individual experience and through symbolism of racial past experiences.
>
> "Not one of us, even when profoundly 'mentally' ill, is free from theories. The only selection we can make is between antiquated, often primitive-made, theories, and modern theories . . .
>
> Whenever *any one* says *anything*, he is indulging in theories. A similar statement is true of writing or 'thinking'. We *must* use terms, and the very selection of our terms and the structure of the language selected reflect their structure on the subject under discussion.
>
> "It is very harmful to sanity to teach a disregard for theories or doctrines and theoretical work, as we can never get away from them as long as we are humans." (p. 279)

The critical value of *a theory within any system* is that conscious understanding of a theory enables us to examine it and refine it. If we want to organize a system so that it continues to develop increasing quality, we need a theory. Without theory, we lack what Deming calls *profound knowledge,* that is, no central philosophy, core values, or vision that guides the model. And without a guiding theory, we will typically default to adapt pragmatism for its own sake. Then the guiding vision becomes, "Whatever works makes it valid."

The "NLP is a Model, not a Theory" Myth

Now suppose that you have a great theory, but you lack a structured form of that theory to give it a clear and succinct representation. Typically this will leave you in the lurch about how to even comprehend the model, let alone communicate it effectively.   I write this to highlight a design flaw of NLP. From the beginning, Bandler and Grinder attempted to pretend that they had no theory, that they were just modelers, and that NLP is "just a model." In actual fact, however, NLP has a theory. Its theory has long been hidden in the NLP Presuppositions.   And that has made the theory ill-formed and untestable.

> "When you mix experience together with theories and wrap them all up in a package, that's a psychotheology. What has developed in psychology is different religious belief systems with very powerful evangelists from all of these differing orientations." (*Frogs into Princes,* 1979, p. 6)

The Form of a Model

What other structured forms of expression can we use for a model and theory? We can use diagrams, flow charts, formulas, checklists, and other formats put into our hands a practical and hands-on way of thinking about the model. The popularity of Transactional Analysis (TA) in the 1970s, as a simplified version of Psychoanalysis, rested on the easy to diagram pictures of three circles that stood for the three ego-states (Parent, Adult and Child).

In this, the form of a theoretical model plays a critical role in communicating it and using it with skill and effectively. Modelers describe a model's *elegance* as that which has the fewest distinctions necessary to work with it and make a difference. To some extent this identifies one of the chief problems in General Semantics.

In *Science and Sanity* (1933/1994) Korzybski delineated a tremendous theoretical foundation for "neuro-linguistic training" and "human design engineering." He extensively enumerated the component elements, specified a great many mechanisms and guidelines, and even came up with a few useful technologies. Yet the form of his model left much to be desired since it was formulated mostly in mathematical terms and diagrams.

Operational Principles

For the next step, imagine a great theory with an easy-to-understand diagrams, yet a model that has no practical *operating principles*. In that case, you would have a marvelous theory, but would lack the know-how practicality for using it.

The "flow" model of Mihalyi Csikszentmihalyi to explain the experience of happiness perhaps exemplifies this. The model posits "flow" as a function of two factors, challenge and competency. He detailed each of the factors, created a "flow" channel, and identified what happens outside of the flow channel. But seeing the diagram and reading the descriptions does not give us any a specific process for what to do. And why? Martin Seligman in *Authentic Happiness* (2002) has provided one answer as he wrote this about Mihalyi:

> "Csikszentmihalyi has been very careful to avoid writing 'self-improvement' books such as this one. . . . His reticence is partly because he comes from a European descriptive tradition, rather than from the American interventionist one. Thus he hopes that by describing flow eloquently and then stepping aside, the creative reader will invent his own ways to build more flow into his life." (p. 121)

Yet we need the kind of knowledge that we call *practical know-how knowledge*. Obviously, there are different kinds of knowledge. Some knowledge is theoretical—declarative, conceptual, and abstract knowledge. Then there is operational knowledge—practical, pragmatic, procedural, and actionable knowledge. It is the operating principles of a model that gives us practical principles and guidelines which include specific instructions about *how to* actually use it, *when* to use it, *with what* to do, *where*, etc.

* When do we use the reframing processes?
* When do we utilize our skills in anchoring?
* How do we decide about using time-line processes?

Finally, a model not only has a great theory, specific pieces and components, and guiding principles, but a complete model also has specific techniques. In NLP, we have a great many techniques —human technologies for actually running the brain, modeling excellence, transforming personality, etc. How many do we have? I honestly don't know. I doubt if anyone does. Undoubtedly there are hundreds. In *The Sourcebook of Magic* (1998) I collected 77 of the most central patterns. Together, guidelines and techniques provide us specific step by step instructions about the sequence and syntax of the processes.

Guidelines
Since a model needs a set of principles or governing guidelines that enable us to use the mechanisms within the system, *what are the principles in the NLP system?* What guidelines assist us in using the component parts of this system? Among them we have—

• Listen for ill-formedness in linguistic constructions and ask questions to gather the deleted, distorted, and generalized portions. This will elicit a more well-formed construction.

• Representationally track the words you hear without contaminating them with hallucinations. See if you can represent the see-hear-feel referents. If not, then inquire about what's missing.

• Keep asking systemic questions about the welfare, ecology, balance, etc. of the entire system.

• Listen with a third-ear to the meta-programs that must be operating for a person to filter and sort things as he or she does.

When you recognize that all of this operates from some theoretical base, you can explore the NLP presuppositions and the assumed beliefs of Perls, Satir, Erickson, Bateson, etc. Yet though hidden, there is a theory along with various postulates and assumptions.[1]

Meta-States as a *Model*
I map out this overview of NLP to show how NLP is a full fledged model. Now I'll do the same thing with Meta-States.

Elements of the Meta-States Model
Let's begin with the component elements of the Meta-State model:
    1) *Levels of abstracting* or mapping. These include perceptual,

representational, conceptual, etc. and first-order, second-order, etc.

2) *Layers of states*. These include levels and layers of states: primary states, meta-states, gestalt states.

3) *Reflexivity*. The mechanism of self reflectivity as consciousness reflects back onto itself.

4) *Two royal paths*. The two roads to a neuro-linguistic mind-body state: internal representations and physiology

5) *Logical levels*. Every layer of thought-and-emotion on another level moves us to a higher logical level. Each level *transcends* one level of awareness and *includes* it within itself. This makes the higher level about the lower level. It transforms the lower level into a member of the class of the higher category as it transforms the higher level as a frame-of-reference for the lower.

6) *Psycho-logics*. Our "reasoning" or "logic" that makes sense of things as we set frames that categorize and create classes that become our psycho-logics.

7) *The coalescing of levels*. Repetition and habituation leading to the levels merging and coalescing into each other. Doing this makes room for more meta-moves. It textures and qualifies the lower level with the higher level.

8) *Recursiveness*. The recursiveness about thought and feeling initiates non-linear feedback loops and feed forward loops that allow us to control lower levels by higher levels (in an open system), or that can initiate vicious spirals into ever increasing depths of pain (in closed systems).

9) *Attractors*. Each level operates as an attractor in a neuro-linguistic holistic system. The thoughts "on our mind" is our conscious awareness and the thoughts "in the back of our mind" is what's outside-of-consciousness. The higher unconscious levels sets the bias of the system and so "attracts" to us what we are prepared to see and experience.

10) *Iteration*. Because the "going meta" process is an infinite process, it has no end point. That means that if we get stuck in some concept, principle, idea, belief, etc, we can always take another step.

The Theory of the Meta-States Model
Is there a theory behind Meta-States? What are the theoretical

frameworks of Meta-States as a model?

The theory starts with the same theory behind NLP, namely, constructionism as indicated in the statement, "The map is not the territory." What we construct in our minds-and-bodies is just a map of reality. We are a symbolic or semantic class of life (Korzybski) that live in and relate to the world indirectly through our maps. As we sense the things and activities that exist "out there," and detect patterns, we create neurological and linguistic maps to navigate those experiences.

Given the nature of our bodies (protoplasm and our nervous systems), we begin this process at the neurological level using our sense receptors. This gives us our sensory-based maps of the world which we experience this as perceptions (e.g., visual, auditory, kinesthetic). So we perceive sights, sounds, sensations, smells, etc. which, of course, does not exist "out there," but are *constructs* that arise from the interaction of our nervous system with energy manifestations in the world. Our perceptual mapping is only "real" inside as a facsimile of what our nervous system constructs.

The theoretical framework for Meta-States also includes the levels of reflective thinking and feeling. We map things out neurologically, then perceptually, then representationally, then conceptually, etc. Our special kind of self-reflective consciousness endows us with this ability. This reflecting on our reflections occurs due to representational constancy, a cognitive development that occurs in the second and third years. By being able to *hold our representations constant in our mind* we can then think about them and that leads to manipulating them with other ideas. Theoretically this is what leads to meta-cognition, meta-feeling, and all of the other complex meta-reflexiveness.

This theory of mind is constructivism—we construct our internal model of reality. Because we make and use symbols as we construct our realities, understanding "mind" requires the ability to track and model our symbolic map-making processes. Then, recognizing our own thinking and feeling as maps, we can change our mappings whenever they do not serve us well.

The theory is also phenomenological. While we experience reality as filtered through our maps, our maps as constructed symbols and symbolic systems sends messages to our body which then, in turn, seeks to make it real. The neurology of our bodies is designed to *realize,* or make actual, the ideas as signals that we have constructed. Our life and mind and conceptual understandings is an embodied reality. Our mental maps as beliefs, decisions, intentions, etc. send signals to our body to commission our neurology to make the ideas real.

Figure 14:1

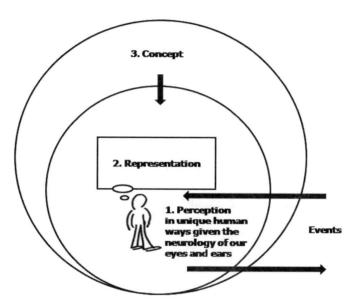

One premise from this theory is: *All of our maps work.* Every idea, belief, understanding in our mental maps sends messages to our body and thereby programs us to feel, see, and act. Schizophrenic maps work perfectly well to create a schizophrenic reality. Such maps typically do not accomplish the things most of us want, and they don't make for an expansive, successful, or happy life. But they work. There's neuro-logical and psycho-logical structure within the schizophrenic's mapping that systematically creates a certain programming. But whether we would want such a program, such a navigational system—that's another question.

There's another premise: *Every experience is a result of some map.*

The map metaphor here undercuts moralizing about whether a map is good or evil. Our maps are not matters of morality, but of information coding. While maps are not evil, they are often ineffective and dysfunctional, and they can be toxic. So we quality control our maps and their effectiveness in the outside world.
* Does this map work well to accomplish my goals?
* Does this map empower me as a person?
* Does it enable me to develop new skills?
* Is it useful, practical, productive, and ecological?

Other premises:
> *A map is only as good as it gets us to our desired outcomes.*
> *We are more than our maps.*

The theoretical framework behind meta-states concerns the mechanism by which we create the levels of our thoughts. And that mechanisms is our reflexive recursiveness. The iteration process of repeatedly bringing thoughts to our feelings and feelings to our thoughts creates a basic recursiveness in our thinking and emoting.

The theory behind this also says, *Our neuro-semantic mapping is holistic.* By mapping we create holistic mind-and-body states of experiences. We do not just "think" in our heads, but throughout all of our bodies and more than that, we encode our maps somatically. As we construct conceptual maps, we evoke bodily emotions and this makes them both neuro-semantic and neuro-somatic. In this way we *embody* our "thoughts" and internal "knowledge." That's why we can "know" things in our bodies, in our muscle-memory. We metabolize words as we digest ideas, making them our somatic reality. This ideo-dynamic processes establishes the mind-muscle connection.

Guidelines of the Meta-States Model
What guidelines do we employ as we use the Meta-States model? There are many, among them are the following:
> 1) Notice the about-ness of your referencing. Are you in reference to something "out there" in the world that can be empirically seen, heard, felt, smelt, tasted, etc.? Or are you in reference to another thought, experience, state?
> 2) When the about-ness changes, so does the state.
> 3) When meta-stating, use small and simple referents so that you can get as pure or discreet a state as possible. It is the

feeling that counts in the meta-stating process.

4) When meta-stating, hold the primary state in place while you apply another state to it.

5) Make sure you have sufficient neurological energy in the state that you are applying to set a higher state or frame.

6) If a process doesn't work, first suspect that there are some higher frames-by-implication nullifying or dampening things.

7) To flush out the meta-levels of an experience, use meta-questions repeatedly.

8) Keep distinguishing frames of the state (meta-states) and expressions of the state — the neurological energy that wants to express things in speech and action.

9) Keep noticing when a person shifts from what's "on the mind" (attention) and what's "in the back of the mind" (intention).

10) Because energy flows where attention goes as directed by intention, access and use intentionality. Then align attention to your highest intention.

11) The problem is never the person, it is always the frame.

12) Always avoid turning negative states of thoughts and emotions against oneself. That creates "dragon" states.

Techniques of the Meta-States Model

In terms of meta-state patterns, there are a great many of these. I published 140 patterns in *Sourcebook of Magic, Volume II* (2005) which probably means that there are 170 to 200 meta-state patterns that provide a way to design a numerous higher level states.

Supporting Research

Norman Holland (1988) has written a provocative work designed to provide a model for understanding literature using the current research in brain neurology and Cognitive Psychology. He describes his model as one that manages higher levels of thought and consciousness by the design of *higher feedback loops governing lower level loops.*

In explaining how we use higher levels to understand and interpret literature, Holland has traversed a similar pathway to myself and has constructed a model that closely replicates the structure of the Meta-States model. While Holland's work represents a scholarly and theoretical approach to understanding the mechanism in the higher levels of mind, he ultimately is seeking to model the working of the mind. To that end he speaks about how higher logical levels emerge in the process of thinking and understanding, and then control the lower levels.

In the book, *The Brain of Robert Frost,* Holland begins with the following idea:

> " . . . human experimental psychology takes as its proper goal *modeling what the mind knows and how it knows*" (p. 9, italics added)

From this Holland focuses on the task of exploring *how* we create, interpret, and transfer knowledge in the process of reading literature. In doing this, he launched out on a massive task. He touched upon the current state of knowledge in the neuro-sciences about the brain, Chomsky's work about language (p. 9), Lakoff and Johnson's work about language and metaphor (p. 112ff), Minsky's introduction of the term "frame" (p. 10), systems thinking (feedback systems, cybernetics, Bateson), schools of literature, psychoanalysis, and cognitive psychology, the TOTE model of Miller, et al. (p. 88), and William Powers' hierarchical model of mind of a loop controlling a loop (p. 94).

Holland especially explores how language works in interaction with human consciousness at various levels in his theorizing to explain the everyday task of understanding literature. The intriguing phrase that he used for the book's title, "the brain of Robert Frost," that phrase stands for every person's brain as we understand language, create language, and interpret language. From this research, he formulated a model that looks very similar to *Meta-States model.* He speaks about a meta-state in the following quotation in terms of an expectational "set" that we apply to our expectations and about feedback loops:

> "As we change our 'set' [expectational set], we bring to bear on our world different expectations. We therefore change the hypotheses we test against our world. The general principle is: We prepare for stimuli and actively search our environment for them." (p. 76)
>
> "It is a fundamental principle of today's neuroscience that the brain operates by means of feedbacks and, specifically, a hierarchy of feedbacks." (p. 178)

Holland (1988) postulated that first comes the stimuli in the world to which we respond—the stimuli in "the events of the world." We then act upon, and to, that stimulus. In doing so, we develop perceptions about the things out there. Holland locates this at the bottom in his diagram (Figure 14:2), rather than over to the right as I typically sketch it.

He says that we then use this perception as we *compare* it with what we *expected* (our internalized model of the world). In the Meta-States diagram, I represent the stimulus first "out there," and then as an inner representation as we bring it within and represent it on the screen of our mind. Then in response to that we apply our evaluation and so create the next level.

After Holland's first level of responding, we then take the results of our comparison and act upon the stimulus. This is *feed forwarding* our thoughts and ideas from our model of the world *onto* the world as we experience it. And, of course, from that, the next set of responses then generates more feedback, which loops back to our updated expectations for more comparisons, and so on it goes (p. 99).

Figure 14:2
Holland's Model
Meta-Levels Governing Lower Levels

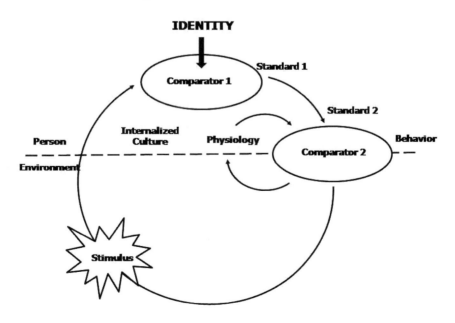

Holland describes the processes and mechanisms in the following quotation using the term "identity" for a higher level meta-state. This is the state which operates as "a central organizing principle."

> "There is the *feeding back* of the output (my behavior) through its consequences to something I perceive, a sensory input. This is what gives feedback its name. . . . There is the *comparison* between what I perceive and the standard I set, between what I want to see and what I in fact see." (p. 77)
> "Brain scientists continue to confirm the general idea of a central organizing principle (i.e., 'identity') that guides feedbacks towards ends that satisfy that identity. . . . At every one of these levels, the creative purpose of a higher level directs the working of lower levels . . . " (p. 93)
> "In general, a higher loop controls a lower one by setting its standard. . . . The higher processes in [the] brain that seeks themes or recognizes characters *govern* the lower processes . . . " (pp. 95-96)

This leads to his meta-level model of consciousness in "reading and writing literature." The *Identity Level* governing and directing a *Comparison Level* that governs a lower *Comparison* that governs the person as he or she perceives and acts. "Feedback controlling feedback" illustrates a hierarchy of feedback loops (p. 99).

What Holland labels "identity" is the highest levels in a hierarchy of feedback loops. This is what is meant by his use of the term "identity" as you can detect in the following:

> "All levels ultimately serve identity, yet at every level feedback operates. Identity is the top-down agency that applies hypotheses. I put trials of meaning and context and syntax out into the text, and the text rewards my good hypotheses and defeats my poor ones, until I arrive at a total reading." (p. 110)
> "The idea of identity governing a hierarchy of feedbacks offers us a manageable picture, a working hypothesis against which to hear claims about reading and writing and Robert Frost and brains. With this picture I can visualize how 'subjectivity' enters the literary process alongside 'objectivity.' I can realize the relation between fixed cultural codes and the mutable canons we learn in school for reading poems. I can imagine how feelings guide our cognitive responses or how the physical

text relates to the emotional experience we have. The picture of an identity governing a hierarchy of feedbacks lets me pose such questions and at least begin to answer them." (p. 111)

How about that? "Identity," as the highest meta-state, "governs a hierarchy of feedbacks" as a "top-down agency." Obviously, Holland has many rich insights into the meta-level structure of how our feedback understandings and knowledge subsequently then governs our perceptions and how this applies to the working of the mind.

    "For me the initial delight is in the surprise of remembering something I didn't know I knew." (p. 47)

Meta-Cognitive Devices as Models

Another work speaks to the subject of mapping and managing our executive meta-states. The following work may become one of the classics presenting formal research supporting the Meta-States model.

The authors and editors of *Metacognition: Knowing About Knowing* (1995), have created a groundbreaking work in the domain of higher level cognitions. In this work Metacalfe and Shimamura, have gathered together the most current researchers in this field to rigorously present the current knowledge of the field. Most of the book addresses the meta-cognition involved in memory, the meta-cognitive devices, processes, and tools for the everyday experience of self-monitoring our memory, for our meta-level beliefs about self-efficacy, "memory's knowledge of its own knowledge," meta-cognitive development in adulthood, etc. Here you will find chapters regarding research on *The Neuropsychology of Metacognition, The Role of Metacognition in Problem Solving,* and even a chapter on *Viewing Eyewitness Research from a Metacognitive Perspective.*

The opening chapter in this book comes from the hands of Thomas Nelson and Louis Narsens which they entitled, *Why Investigate Metacognition?* Quoting Kuhn (1962) on paradigms and crises in "normal science," Miller, Galanter, and Pribram (1960) on the TOTE model (that gave birth to NLP's Strategy Model), and Bateson (1972) on systems thinking and control processes, they generated a model that bears close similarity to the Meta-States model.

Figure **14:3**

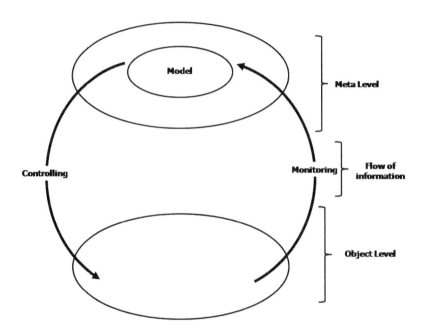

> "Nelson and Naren's (1990) formulation of a meta-level/
> object-level theoretical mechanism consisting of two structures
> (meta-level and object-level) and two relations in terms of the
> direction of the flow of information between the two levels.
> (Note: The meta-level contains an imperfect model of the
> object-level.)" (p. 11)

In explaining this model, the authors note what they mean by "control"
at a higher level:

> " . . . the meta-level *modifies* the object-level, but not vice
> versa. The information flowing from the meta-level to the
> object-level either changes the state of the object-level process
> or changes the object-level process itself."

Conversely, "the meta-level *is informed by* the object-level. This
changes the state of the meta-level's model of the situation." (p. 12).
This sounds very familiar to how the dynamic structures and processes
in the Meta-States model. And it fits precisely with the guiding

principles which Bateson set forth regarding how one level interacts with another level, namely, the higher meta-states govern the lower states.

In meta-cognition, there are several meta-state structures that are highlighted. These include *introspection of introspection.* When we pay attention to, and examine, our introspecting to take into account its characteristics and "systematic deviations" (distortions), we have a way to methodologically improve our introspecting (p. 18). Korzybski described this evaluation of evaluation as the scientific mindset that allows us to create meta-disciplines, to study studying, to learn about learning, to gain knowledge about how we know things (epistemology), etc.

The feeling of knowing is the state of believing that we can retrieve a piece of information. William James (1890) described this as "the tip of the tongue" phenomenon. It involves a sense of awareness of having certain knowledge, while at the same time experiencing a momentarily gap at this point (pp. 47-48).

So at a given point of time we both know and cannot access what we know. We know that we know, but cannot *say* what we know, yet we *feel* it. And the strange thing is that we *feel* this knowing in a particular part of our body—in our tongue. We "know" something that we cannot quite express verbally and yet we almost can. That which we know has become part of our muscle memory. And while we still "know" it, we only feel it, feel it on the tip of our tongue, as if our tongue knows it and is ready to say it, but not quite. And the strange thing is that if we leave it alone, it will usually come to us. The feeling of that meta-cognitive knowledge is embodied in muscle memory.

In this work on meta-cognition, researchers call in question the old idea that older adults do not remember as well as younger adults. They suggest that the actual problem is two-fold. First, those who do not remember as well as they used to are probably using some inadequate meta-cognitive strategies. Second, they have some governing beliefs that are limiting and disabling. That is, they are meta-stating their experience of aging with the idea (and state) that "people lose mental acumen in mid-life." When you set that as your frame of reference, it will thereafter govern the effects that will occur on one's thinking and remembering.

"Uncritical adaption of the stereotype of decline could lead individuals to believe their memory has declined, irrespective of any age-related changes in actual frequency of memory success or failures. Moreover, beliefs of inevitable memory decline may make incidents of forgetting more salient, and bias older adults to attribute memory failures to age-related loss of effective functioning." (p. 240)

"High self-efficacy beliefs limit the experience of concurrent negative affect (depression and anxiety),whereas low self-efficacy beliefs led to increased levels of performance anxiety in the testing situation." (p. 241)

Summary

*   As a *model*, both NLP and Meta-States involve numerous component elements that operate according to specific operating principles and guidelines to create specific patterns and techniques for modeling human expertise and managing one's best states. These all operate out of a theoretical explanatory thesis. Togther these four factors give us a full fledge model.

*   A fully articulated model gives us an explicit theoretical basis of the model that we can test. In testing, applying, and working with it we can then continue to refine the model, working out the bugs.

*   Two other models about meta-levels from the field of the Cognitive sciences and Meta-Cognition support the systemic nature of *Meta-States* as feedback loops that govern and control lower level feedback loops. These models similarly diagram the working of consciousness in a flow chart format that shows the reflexive nature of information in the system.

End Notes;

1. And where did Perls, Satir, Erickson, Bateson and the others get these ideas? These are the "bright side of human nature" paradigm and the ideas that launched the Human Potential Movement of the 1960s and 1970s. For more about this, see *Unleashed* (2007) and *Self-Actualization Psychology* (2008).

Chapter 15

NLP PRECURSORS

OF META-STATES

Meta-States in early NLP Literature

- How does Meta-States contribute to and enrich NLP?
- How was Meta-States presupposed in NLP from the beginning?
- How does the Meta-States model outframe NLP embedding it inside of a larger and more extensive framework?

The *Meta-States* model begins with the recognition that all states are not the same. Primary states differ from higher meta-level states. Mind-and-emotion states take on new qualities, traits, and functions as our cognitive/emotive processes move up the levels and layer thoughts-and-emotions upon each other. This leads to new complexities and gives rise to new emergent properties of the entire neuro-linguistic system.

All of this opens up a new model and domain. It opens up new distinctions about subjective experiences, the role of reflexivity in human states, and meta-level distinctions. The primary state/ meta-state distinction enables you to sort through and separate the classic NLP methods and technologies that have all been lumped together into one pile. *You can now distinguish primary level methods and processes from meta-level technologies.* New possibilities for exploration and development open up with these distinctions of the Meta-States model.

As you take levels of consciousness into account, the Meta-States model directs your attention to *larger level meaning attributions and abstractions that are structured, and hidden, above and beyond primary states.*

This model directs you to the place where the role of frames dominate (e.g., frames-of-reference, frames-of-meaning). And these formulate what are more commonly referred to as beliefs, values, stories (narratives), poetry, presuppositions, etc. Focusing on frames as meta-level structures, and how they ultimately govern your life, also gives you a new lease on how to work with yourself and others at meta-levels.

Given this pervasive nature of meta-states, I have written this chapter to explore the relationship of the Meta-States model and NLP. One of the first reviewers of *Meta-States*, Dr. Graham Dawes, commented that Meta-States may very well become "the model that eats up NLP." By this he meant that the power of meta-states to outframe— to set higher frames that embrace all of the facets of NLP.[1]

Others also have noted the outframing power of Meta-States for subsuming and unifying the many facets of NLP and bringing them together into a more cohesive format. For this reason, today many NLP Training Centers now incorporate Meta-States in the practitioner training. I have also done this with Bob Bodenhamer in the extensive NLP Practitioner manual that we co-authored, *The User's Manual For the Brain, Volume I.* In Volume II of *User's* we fully integrated *Meta-States* into the heart of the Master Practitioner training.[2]

The questions to be addressed in this chapter include the following:
- How does Meta-States represent the next step of development in the NLP model?
- Where does Meta-States fit into the history of NLP?
- What facets and pieces of NLP does the Meta-States model include and embrace?
- Is it possible that the Meta-States model completely outframes NLP?

States Distinctions: Primary State Methods and Processes
If a basic and important difference exists between primary states and
meta-states, and if these differences involve the very nature and quality
of consciousness as well as the operating mechanisms and principles,
then *it will enhance your skills to distinguish primary-state from meta-
state technologies within NLP.*
- Are there techniques and processes for working with, altering,
  transforming, and managing primary states?
- Do these technologies differ from those that more appropriately
  work with states at meta-levels?

The answer is *yes*. Some the NLP technology relates best to primary
states. Central to these is sensory-based anchoring. Anchoring
represents a very basic, primary, and even primitive process—
Pavlovian conditioning. It involves a more "animalistic" (Korzybski's
terminology) use of the human nervous system. Anchoring uses a
primordial process of basic stimulus-response patterning which does
not necessarily involve consciousness. In anchoring, things simply get
connected as a conditioning response.

Anchoring works as a primary state pattern and mechanism. Get
anyone into a state (positive or negative, resourceful or unresourceful),
amplify it until it vibrates with neurological energy ("emotion" or
somatic sensations) and *you can link that state with just about
anything*. As this Pavlovian classical conditional creates associations,
it creates the first level of meanings—associative meanings.

"What does X mean?" is a question that we all ask dozens of times a
day. To answer we first search for the anchored associations that we
have created over time. If anchoring is the prototype primary state
pattern and technology, this gives us a clue for recognizing *the NLP
patterns that are examples of primary state technologies.*[3]
- The Collapsing of Anchors
- State Accessing and Eliciting
- State Amplification
- Swishing from one association to another and anchoring it
- "Sub-Modality" mapping across
- Contrastive Analysis between states

Primary state technologies put into your hands the tools which allow
you to easily control and modulate your states. Typically your states

respond quickly to these interventions, which, in turn, explains the traditional focus on the speed of change in NLP. These processes work quickly. They work quickly because they do not depend on conscious awareness and because they simply link things into a stimulus–response patterning. Frequently we can run these processes with little, or even no, need for the person to even be aware of the process. Anchoring works when you don't know what's happening and even when you do. Although there are times when consciousness could interfere with the process.

Usually, mere representational shifts easily manages and transforms primary states. After all, perceptual and representational maps drive primary states. This explains why a great many kinds of modality and "sub-modality" (cinematic) shifts have such pervasive influence. Turning up or down the tone, volume, pitch, brightness, closeness, etc. (the features and distinctions within the visual, auditory, and kinesthetic modalities) can recode subjective reality that completely reorganizes it.

Of course, here we begin sliding into Meta-State processes. The self-reflexive thinking that generates meta-levels involves permeable boundaries. These processes refer to our nested networks of thoughts and feelings and the holarchy of our states. So when we recode a representation, we simultaneously set a new frame as a meta-state. This shows the fluidity of these levels and why when we unmask "sub-modalities;" we find meta-levels frames (*Sub-Modalities Going Meta*, 1999/ 2006).

Via primary state technologies you can kinesthetically anchor and manage various experiences or states in dramatic ways. This technique empowers you to anchor, swish brains to new referents, and even de-frame old limiting constructions by simple recodings. No wonder you experience these kinds of state changes as intense and powerful!

Meta-modality shifting and recoding (sub-modalities), which involves things like turning up or down the brightness of a picture, the volume of a voice, bringing images closer or farther, etc., can critically impact primary states. This explains why the Swish pattern can radically affect an unresourceful habit—it alters a basic stimulus-response pattern. This is also true when running a *Contrastive Analysis* between two primary states. Doing so gives stimulates insight between running a limiting unresourceful state and a more empowering state. From that you can simply map over the coding of one to the other. This works wonders for transforming timidity to confidence, frustration to perseverance, kind-of-motivated to fetish level compulsion, etc.

Meta-Cognitive Processes

Now while NLP has a good many primary state technologies, *most of the powerful change technology in NLP actually involve Meta-State processes.* And no wonder. After all, NLP is a meta-discipline—a discipline about other disciplines: communication, therapy, psychology, human functioning, information processing, systems, General Semantics, Transformational Grammar, hypnosis, etc. Don't forget that the first model in NLP was the Meta-Model. It is *the meta-function* (i.e., going meta, stepping back to access meta-cognitive understandings about structure) that gives NLP processes its power and pizzazz. And this is what creates the magic of change and transformation.

The Meta-States model more fully explains how NLP's technology actually works through the setting of frames, deframing other frames, exchanging one frame for another (reframes), setting new frames *over* frames (outframing), etc. Why do so many of the techniques in NLP succeed so spectacularly? They do so because within them are processes that generate meta-level frames that reorder the codes at a higher level.

The Meta-States model provides an explanatory understanding of this technology concerning the processes and mechanisms. It explains why some states become unstable and transitory, why they constantly shift, and why yet other states become lasting, durable, and stable. Ultimately, these qualities and features of our experienced states go back to the operating frames-of-reference.

Meta-State patterns involve moving to, creating, or assuming *a meta position* to other states, beliefs, frames, etc. When you do this, you develop a higher level of mind—a "consciousness of abstracting" that puts you at choice point. This higher quality of awareness governs both human sanity and science. Your meta-cognitive abilities play that much of a role in your self-actualization and resourcefulness.

This shows the importance in distinguishing levels and to sorting out levels within states. Then you can use the mechanisms that govern the primary and meta-state technologies at different levels.

Meta-State Technologies

Going Meta. When you first step back from an experience and just witness it, just observe it, you experience a meta-level state of consciousness of mindfulness that gives you "psychological distance." This internal mind-body experience gives a sense and a feeling of distance because you no longer feel *locked inside* the experience and overwhelmed by it. You feel outside of it, with sufficient distance to be able to face it. This enables you to apply your adult thinking and resources to the primary state. Using the resource of your self-reflexive consciousness, and going meta to the first state, *you step out of the problematic experience* and observe it from a different frame of mind. You see it in a way that enables you to apply resources and find better solutions.

Framing and Reframing. When you think beyond mere representation and engage in conceptual thinking you think in terms of concepts—conceptual frames of reference. You now use frames to establish your conceptual reference point. *Your frames govern your meaning-making.* Frames establish the structure of your neuro-semantics. From this comes reframing—the changing of frames, the replacing of one frame-of-reference with another. In reframing you make a meta-level move to the level of the frame where you can shift side to side, from one *frame* to another *frame*.[4]

> "This event does not mean X, it means Y."
> "John's laying around on the couch watching TV doesn't mean that he is lazy, it means that he really knows how to relax."

The Phobia Cure. This pattern works as you step back from your thinking, from the things that you internally entertain on the theater of your mind, and think about those images, sights, sounds, sensations, etc. using the meta-function of observing and witnessing your own processes. This witnessing meta-state describes the essence of the V-K Dissociation pattern for curing phobias and taking the emotional charge out of strong negative states.

By stepping aside from, or out of, old memories and representations of trauma you adopt a higher state of mind—a meta-level awareness. From that second-level or third-level awareness you step out of the distressing, aversive, and fear-inducing emotions that the original frame creates and into more resourceful states.

In Neuro-Semantics we describe this as *stepping back* or *stepping aside from an experience,* and do not use the term "dissociate" or "dissociative." The idea of dissociation was another design flaw in traditional NLP. Neither Richard Bandler nor John Grinder were therapists or psychologists and so they were not aware of the error of describing this as "dissociation."

Actually, the term "dissociate" is just a metaphorical and conceptual way of speaking. We do not do this literally—*we do not literally step out of our bodies.* There is no *actual* dis-embodiment! In using the term "dissociation" we refer to the *felt* sense of no longer being inside a painful memory. Yet we are still inside of our bodies when we experience this *feeling* of "dissociation." I mention this due to some of the over-literalization that some theorists, psychologists, and NLP practitioners have fallen victim to assuming that the "dissociation" label is the territory or at least describes a real thing. It's just a way of talking about a shift in feeling.

Here's another NLP myth. Moving to a meta-level this does *not* equate to being "dissociated." Actually, many higher meta-states, far from being bereft of feeling, involve even more feelings—*joyful* learning, *excitement* about falling in love, *anticipation* of feeling confident, etc. We often experience more emotion when we move to meta-levels. Consider the negative meta-states of self-contempting, self-despising, unforgiveness, and personalizing and the intensity of emotion these involve.

Associating and dissociating are relative terms. They speak about *stepping into* an experience and *stepping out* of another. In fact, every time we associate into one state, we thereby "dissociate" from another. And every "dissociation" implies an "association."

Taking a meta-level position so that you process and re-process the old trauma, phobia, or negative event from a meta-position, gives you psychological distance. It enables you to experience the wisdom and resourcefulness of a broader and more objective perspective as well as the ability to apply new and better thinking. You can then transform the trauma, phobia, or hurt using these higher level resources. You can apply humor, love, compassion, firmness, understanding, forgiveness, confrontation, etc. to your memories. Meta-stating your "memories" with these resources brings closure, and finishes the gestalt of our need to end the old business.

Future Pacing. When you think about the conceptual state of "the future," you engage in a meta-stating process. Future pacing refers to taking the feelings, understandings, and other resources that you attain by accessing an enhancing state and then using these as your frame when you imagine how it will work out and transform "the future." That is, how you will think, feel, speak, and act in the coming days and weeks. As you go meta to the "now" you use the meta-function to plot a future course. From that meta-level, you then apply your imaginative resources to a future "then." In this way you transcend the "time" dimension to making it a higher level dimension to the sensory level.

Time-Lines. The methods and processes of Time-Line patterns are meta-states and operate as meta-level processes. When you ask someone to visually or kinesthetically generate an image or feeling to represent his or her abstraction of "time," you are working at a conceptual level regarding temporal concepts (i.e., "the past," "the future," "timelessness," etc.). To do this you move to a meta-level of awareness. In some time-line maneuvers, a person has to attain two and three levels of abstraction and hold these levels in mind while doing Change History or the Decision Destroyer NLP pattern. As such these patterns also involve meta-state processes.

Meta-levels of consciousness operate in other NLP patterns: Creating New Parts, Negotiating Between Parts, and Designing and Installing Strategies. What is the creative genius of the NLP model in these patterns? *It is precisely in the use of meta-cognition levels for stepping outside of the experience to generate new and better programs for thinking, feeling, experiencing, speaking, and behaving.*

Meta-Level Resourcing
These examples of meta-level patterns within the arsenal of NLP technology highlight that most transformations involve meta-level

interventions.

There are instances where this is not true. For example, the resources needed to move from feeling unsure to feeling confident involve primary resources. You can elicit immediate sensory experience, anchor it, and then bridge over using representational tracking to "swish" your brain from the external trigger to the resource state of confidence.

By way of contrast, to move from the meta-state of self-contempting to self-esteeming requires some meta-resources. In the process of ungluing these static nominalized states you discover that these involve meta-level structures of linguistic judgments, evaluations, and definitions. The strategy for coaching a person to esteem oneself involves generating an enhancing criteria list and the meta-awareness that separates *doing* (achievements, status, looks, money, etc.) from *being*.

The resources needed to transverse the distance from present state to desired state typically involve meta-resources. If your desired state involves a meta-state, then the bridging process for reaching your desired state will not involve a simple primary state pathway. By definition, it will involve two or more higher states that have to be established as referent structures for your thinking and emoting. Building up a meta-state like resilience, proactivity, self-esteeming, etc., involves accessing and correlating various cognitive, emotive, and conative components.

An Explanation of NLP Failures
From time to time reports arise of someone who "tried NLP" but it failed. How do we explain such failures? How can such powerful change technology fail? How can it go wrong or be misused?

One answer is provided by the Meta-States model. The "failures" result from failing to distinguish primary and meta-states. By failing to distinguish the methodologies and processes of primary states and meta-states, the person confuses simple states with layered and systemic states.

To access an enhancing and empowering primary state is a fairly direct and easy process. All you need to do is to think about a referent stimulus that will call it forth. Almost any piece of anchoring and swishing can accomplish this. But constructing a state-about-a-state, a higher, executive state of consciousness, involves more finesse and skill.

I have a theory about those who have "tried NLP and found it wanting," and who have become negative and critical about NLP for changing state or altering subjective experiences. My hypothesis is this:

> In "trying NLP," they failed because they sought to access, anchor, swish to, etc. a meta-level structure using processes appropriate for primary states.

Perhaps they sought to access, build, and install layered meta-states as proactivity, self-esteem, assertiveness, and forgiveness by simply accessing and anchoring.

> "Think about a time when you were really proactive . . . good, now as you *feel it fully,* you can *feel this* whenever you feel this also [touching the shoulder]."

Later when they attempted to "fire" off this kinesthetic touch anchor, they were not able to re-elicit the proactive state. And, if they didn't know the difference between primary and meta-states, they could easily jump to the fallacious conclusion, "NLP just doesn't work" and then dismiss the model.

So what really happens in that scenario? Why could they not "fire off" a kinesthetic or visual anchor and get someone to re-experience state like "self-esteem?" In that instance the error is the failure to distinguish levels of states. The error is using a primary state method when they needed to construct a meta-state experience.

This is further complicated if the person does not operate with the right spirit or attitude as exemplified in the NLP presuppositions. No wonder the process doesn't work! These inadequacies characterize most of the more formal experiments that I've read about where experimenters have tested the NLP model. So, when the experimenters did not get the response that they wanted or expected, they just quit and did not even consider their attitude a variable in the experiment. Nor did they operate from the NLP guideline: *When what you are doing isn't working, do something different.* They immediately assumed that the model was the problem and did not use the feedback to improve their understanding and skill in using the model.

Meta-States Implied in NLP
From time to time in Meta-State Trainings, people have asked, "Did the original NLP developers know about Meta-States?"

The short answer is "No, they did not." At least they did not know it explicitly. They certainly knew and spoke about the meta-function. They spoke about meta-parts, going meta, the meta-move, the meta-function, meta-rules, meta-representational system, etc.[5] But they never spoke about meta-states as such and therefore were not aware of the structure of nested states within states as a recursive system.

The first use of that term "meta-states" that I have found occurred in Wyatt Woodsmall's (1988) spiral notebook, *Metaprograms*. There he listed as potential new meta-program: "states: regular, meta."

Yet the first NLP developers did *implicitly* describe meta-states. I'll substantiate that by highlighting some of the precursors of Meta-States in the first scholarly book on NLP and strategies, Dilts, et al., *Neuro-Linguistic Programming, Volume I* (1980). We will see that the NLP co-founders alluded to states-about-states without making this structure explicit. And because they did not punctuate it, they also did not explore these structures or realize their potential or place in the structure of subjectivity.

For example, in the context of strategy notation, elicitation, and explanation, the authors (1980) wrote:
> "A *meta* response is defined as a response *about* the step before it, rather than a continuation or reversal of the representation. *These responses are more abstracted and disassociated from the representations preceding them.* Getting feelings *about* the image (feeling that something may have been left out of the picture, for instance) that the individual had made of what it would look like to be swimming, rather than indirect response to the content of that image, would constitute a meta response in our example. ... We will notate the meta response modifier as

an arrow between the steps with "m" beneath it, "→ₘ"." (p. 90, italics added)

Note that I italicized the second sentence in the above quotation to highlight the misunderstanding and myth they here launched about meta-levels. Now while it is true that moving up the levels moves into experiences that are generally more abstract (until they coalesce), only occasionally in special instances do they create a "disassociated" state. This has created a tremendous misunderstanding of the higher levels. *Meta does not mean, and is not equated with, disassociation.* As noted previously, when we move to higher levels, often we experience more emotions and emotions more intensely. *Joyful* curiosity and *fear* of fear as meta-states increase the emotionality of the experience.

Later, they wrote out a strategy for a person who expresses the following:

> "I know that I should do it . . . and I really feel that it's the right thing to do, but at the same time I keep looking at all the times I've tried before and haven't been able to . . . it's really a struggle."

In unpacking the strategy and notating it, the co-founders of NLP came up with two versions both comprised of a linear and sequential formula. They noted:

> "Both of these show that there are two responses to the verbal proposal of the behavior. The final kinesthetic response is about the conflict of the two responses preceding it." (1980, p. 95)

Figure 15:1

$$A_d \; \rightarrow \; K^{i+} / V^{i-} \; \rightarrow \; _m \rightarrow \; K^i$$

Figure 15:2

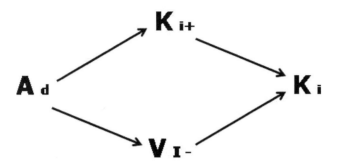

The Meta-States model notations gives us a new way to diagram the structure of this experience, a way that takes into account the fluidity of logical levels (which operate in a systemic and holoarchical way). It departs from a strict horizontal, linear, and sequential process of strategy. It adds the vertical and holistic process of state. To read this notation, begin at the bottom with the primary state and move up and then horizontal.

Figure 15:3

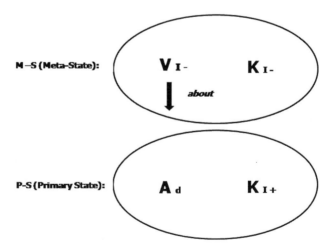

You will find a similar discussion by Dilts (1980) about *meta-responses* regarding a creativity strategy where a business executive began his strategy by looking externally at the significant components in the situation (V^c).

> "He would then begin to *talk to himself about* [words indicating a meta-state] the object or components (A_d); how they operate together; asking what kind of resources may be required for the situation . . . As he talks he gets a feeling *about* [meta-state indicator] each of the verbalizations (K^i) . . . " (Italics added, pp. 109-110)

A central problem arises with using linear and sequential strategy notation language in handling aspects of human subjectivity operating dynamically at meta-levels. *It confuses logical levels.* It confuses the primary sensory-based neurological level (where primary states operate) with the secondary, etc. evaluative level of abstraction where language operates. These represent not only different logical levels, but different "worlds" of existence, and different levels of abstractions. Meta-States provides a way of maintaining this distinction.

Dilts' "Meta-Experience" Model
Early in the development of NLP, Robert Dilts described a set of levels that closely outlined the basic structure of the Meta-States Model. In *Roots of NLP* (1983), Robert separated three different logical types of experiences. He then organized it into three graduated levels in the following way.

1) First level experience.
> Immediate sensory experience which involves perception at the sensory level.

2) Experience of experience.
> The next level which involves "the mental maps or models we make to organize and respond to our immediate sensory perceptions. Neurologically these are representations resulting from the stimulation of networks of cortical cells and neurons . . . " (p. 15)
> This level also involves consciousness and language—"a symbolic representation of our sensory representations; 'meta' representation so to speak." (p.16)

3) Experience about experience.

This level "deals with the forms and patterns governing its own processes . . . the representation of how experience is represented." (p. 19)

Suppose Robert had used the word *states* in this passage rather than *experience*. If he had, he would have written about state, states *of* states, and then states *about* states. If he had, he could have perhaps created a model of meta-states for NLP in 1977. Yet, even though the term was not used, Robert was alluding to some of the distinctions that today informs and governs the Meta-States model.

Where did Robert get his ideas? Interestingly enough he provided the basis for this level of experiences. Quoting from E. Roy John's work, *A Model of Consciousness* (1975), Robert found that John had earlier sorted out three experiential levels. The bottom level, as a primary state, begins with kinesthetics.

> "Sensations are the spatio-temporal patterns of information arriving in the central nervous system because of excitation of exteroreceptive and interoceptive organs. They are a product of the irritability of living matter and constitute *first order information* . . . sensations can elicit reflex responses adjusting the organism to its environment." (Italics added)

This distinguishes a *primary state*—a state that we can quickly and effectively anchor with sensory based stimuli. Next comes the visual-auditory sensory modalities.

> "Perceptions constitute *second order information* . . . " (Italic added)

About this Robert Dilts wrote this following which sets up three levels of states.

> "John defines a third level which he calls *consciousness* where perceptions become the variables and form a 'unified multidimensional representation of the state of the system and environment, integrated with stored information generation emotional reactions and programs of behavior for adjustment.'" (pp. 51-52)

In these writings, as Robert Dilts intellectually played around with the levels of experiences, he was very, very close to discovering Meta-States. Very close.

Logical Levels

From the beginning, "logical levels" were introduced into NLP from Gregory Bateson's influence on its developers. From his use and writings about logical levels in *Steps to an Ecology of Mind*, NLP incorporated several different expressions. Logical levels show up in Grinder and DeLozier's work on the focus or genius state (what they called the "demon" state). They show up in Dilts' Neuro-Logical Levels, and in the early use of "chunking" in NLP.

The idea of "chunking" was derived from computer science and the language of moving up a scale from specificity to generality. "Chunking up and down" then came into NLP as the *global/specific* or general/detail meta-program as an attentional pattern governing how we sort and pay attention to information.

"Chunking" in NLP refers to the size of information that we process. Higher chunks are at the top of the scale signifying more generality. Smaller chunks are at the bottom of the scale signifying specificity. Depending on the size of information that a person feels most comfortable with, this leads to two different kinds of thinking and reasoning, *inductive and deductive*. It also alludes to the logical levels within meta-levels. As we move from details to higher and higher levels of generalization (gestalt configurations) we "chunk up." Thus chunking up can describe working with increasing levels of abstraction.

To chunk up, we have to ask meta questions about the information, to elicit the meaningful patterns that structures the data.
• What pattern does this indicate or reveal?
• What relationships exist between this and this other thing?
• What can I conclude from these facts or details?

To chunk down, we have to ask the specificity questions of the Meta-Model:
• What specifically?
• Who specifically?
• Where specifically?
• Which specifically?
• How specifically?
Answering specificity questions sends our thinking-and-feeling awareness to lower levels. We move down as we extensionalize the

precise details of the experience.

When we model meta-states in a person and write out the strategy language, we include these distinctions in our encoding. In abstracting we create new thoughts and feelings as we "chunk up" to higher levels. That is, we jump a logical level by generalizing to a higher category. This creates more complex conceptualizations about life which we code in beliefs, decisions, values, understandings, and paradigms. When we meta-model abstract language, we de-abstract. We "chunk down" to identify the members that make up the class of the higher category.

Meta-States Elicitation Questions

The Meta-State model articulates more fully one of the languaging patterns of Virginia Satir. Bandler and Grinder (1979) mentioned this briefly in *Frogs Into Princes*. In quoting a therapeutic conversation between a father and his daughter, Virginia first separated the father's *intent* in yelling at his daughter from his actual *behavior* of yelling.

> "Do you yell at everyone like that? You don't yell at the paper boy? Are you trying to tell her that you care about what she does? Is that what this anger is about?"

Once she reframes the "yelling" as a "caring message," she then asks a question that presupposes a meta-state.

> "Well, how do you feel *about* knowing that now?"

Regarding the linguistic form of this question, the co-authors comment:

> "That's a weird sentence; it doesn't actually have any meaning. But it works!" (p. 171)

What an amazing comment! And with it Richard and John completely dismissed the power of the meta-level jump within this question. "It doesn't actually have any meaning"!? You've got to be kidding!

Actually, earlier in their writings, even they *thought* that it did mean something. Notice how close they came to the Meta-States model in the following quotation from *The Structure of Magic, Vol. I*:

> "When you ask questions like, 'How do you feel *about* that?' (Whatever *that* might be) you are, in fact, asking your client for a fuller representation (than even Deep Structure) of your

client's experience of the world. And what you are doing by asking this particular question is asking for what you know is a necessary component of the client's reference structure." (p. 160)

The question, "How do you feel *about* that?" *is a meta question* that takes a person upward to the next higher logical level as it asks about the person's thoughts-and-feelings at that next level. As such it flushes out the higher level frame that the feelings are embedded within. From the perspective of the Meta-States model we recognize that it elicits the person's frame-of-reference—*the conceptual or semantic state governing and creating the experience.* But the founders of NLP didn't recognize that.

> "The new question, which is characteristic of Satir's work, is: 'How do you feel *about* your feelings *about* what is happening?' Consider this question in the light of the Meta-Model. This is essentially a request . . . for the client to say how he feels about his reference structure—his model of the world." (p. 161)

Here they tell us of the source of this meta question—it came from Virginia Satir. And here they seem to believe that the question did mean something; it referred to and equated with the person's model of the world.

Again Bandler and Grinder *almost* stumbled upon Meta-States in *The Structure of Magic,* Volume II, in the section "The Meta-Question."

> "This question [How do you feel about feeling angry?] is extensively used by Virginia Satir in her dynamic therapy—she describes this question as an excellent way to tap the client's self-esteem (the client's feelings about his feelings)—a part of the client closely connected with his ability to copy. . . . the client shifts . . . to the next higher logical level" (p. 57)

Here we learn what prevented them from recognizing and inventing the Meta-States domain—they blindly accepted Satir's erroneous explanation that the "reference structure" elicited "was the client's self-esteem." (p. 161). They unquestioningly accepted that complex equivalence. "Referent structure" = "self-esteem."

Later, in integrating incongruities, they speak about assisting a client
        ". . . in achieving *meta-position* with respect to his polarities
. . . A person has achieved meta-position with respect to his polarities
(parts) when he has choices in his behavior . . . To achieve integration
and, therefore, meta-position . . ." (pages 77, 86)

To integrate parts we build an integrating meta-state of awareness and
observation. Let's now go back to the statement they made as their
conclusions, ". . . it doesn't actually have any meaning. But it works!"
(p. 171). It works? *How does it work?*

It works because it first elicited and formulated a new state. To answer
the question, people have to step out of their awareness of the yelling,
and to entertain ideas about how the yelling could be interpreted as a
caring message. This creates the new frame and a new awareness. It
elicits and sets a whole new category. Both the father and the daughter
are now invited to see and frame the *yelling* as a member of the class
of *caring*. The question then invites the person to *go meta* to this new
understanding and explore how one feels about yelling as a category of
caring.
        "How do you feel *about* your feelings *about* what is
        happening?"

Developing "Meta-Parts"
Another early development in NLP was the idea Richard Bandler and
John Grinder (1982) described when they talked about *building a meta-
part*. You can find this in the chapter "Creating a New Part"
(*Reframing*, pp. 71-72). Since that time, there has been little use made
of this as NLP moved on to other things. Yet with the Meta-States
model, we now have a way to more fully articulate the idea of building
and installing a meta-part, or as we say in Neuro-Semantics, a higher
frame of mind.

Bandler and Grinder presented it as a way to step outside of a system
to think about the system. They conceptualized it as a —
        ". . . meta-part that temporarily dissociates and takes an
        observer position and says, 'Hey, what's going on here right
        now?'"
They offered it as a way to "get you out of loops."
        "The meta-part is only operational at certain times, and the

contextual cue that triggers its functioning is usually based on how other parts are functioning. For example, it could be a part that comes into play only when you feel stuck, dissatisfied, or doubtful." (p. 49)

In *Meta-States* we talk about this as the ability to step back as you access a meta-state of observing and step into that pure witnessing state.

> "A meta-part is kind of *like an amnesia state* waiting in the wings to be fired off. Within the meta-part is a program, a formal set of procedures, that comes out linearly. It's like a computer sub-routine more than anything else. 'If parts disagree, then do X.' The meta-part operates and modifies the disagreeing parts. It operates *on* the other parts, but is only functional in response to a cue . . . There are lots and lots of possibilities for what a meta-part can do."
>
> "With a couple, you can build a part in one of them that operates only when they argue. This part recognizes that the reason they argue is because they want things to be better . . . [a higher meta-state with the intention of making things better] it recognizes that they are now making themselves feel bad *because* they want to feel good. What they want is fine, but the way they are going about it stinks . . . "
>
> "The meta-part goes into some way of generating alternatives: it provides ways for them to get what they really want. At specific times it says, 'Go in and change your behavior and get out of this loop; you've been here before and it has never worked.'" (pp. 71-72)

What Bandler and Grinder here called a meta-part obviously is *a state of awareness of one's larger goals above the state of arguing*. From that higher state of observation the couple can gain distance, perspective, and insight with this new resource for monitoring how they talk to each other when there's a disagreement. This higher state functions as a state about their primary state. This higher perspective empowers them to quality control their arguing. This new meta-state provides a place for them so they can see the larger picture of their relationship and make better choices about how to communicate and work through the differences.

Summary

- The bottom line is that while Meta-States is new to NLP as an explicit model, it has also been implied within NLP all along. It has been presupposed in NLP from the beginning.

- *Meta-States* have been inherent within NLP from the beginning without being explicitly named or described. The original developers, however, did speak about meta-parts, meta-functions, going meta, meta-experiences, etc.

- Using the *primary/ meta-state distinction* now allows you to recognize that there are particular processes, mechanisms, and hence technologies that belong to each domain. This results in *primary state* and *meta-state technologies.*

- Recognizing these distinctions enable you to work more effectively and knowledgeably with each domain so that you know when to use the methodologies and processes of each.

- *Meta-States* provides an outframing influence on the NLP model itself by providing a frame-of-reference that provides more exquisite distinctions about states, levels, reflexivity, complexity of layering, systemic modeling, etc.

- The Meta-States model adds to NLP as it incorporates logical levels and self-reflexivity. Mind inevitably jumps levels to create and set new higher frames-of-reference, frames of mind.

End Notes:

1. The reviews by Dr. Graham Dawes were published in *Anchor Point* and *NLP World* in 1995 and 1996.

2. The Practitioner and Master Practitioner content of NLP is now within the textbooks, *User's Manual of the Brain, Volume I and II.*

3. The basic NLP books with these and other patterns, see *The Sourcebook of Magic* (1997), *Using Your Brain for a Change* (1985), *Introducing NLP,* and *NLP For Dummies.*

4. To explore the structure and the art of conversational reframing, see *Mind-Lines: Lines for Changing Minds* (2005).

5. With all of these terms with *meta* in them, John Grinder is really in no position to criticize or mock me for my constant use of the term. In *Whispering in the Wind*, he challenged me to write a single paragraph without using the term *meta*. You can see the exchange I had with John Grinder on www.neurosemantics.com under the articles, Critiques of NLP.

Chapter 16

TRANSCENDING TO

HIGHER "CORE" STATES

Meta-States and Core Transformation

Because of the structure of meta-states as states about other states, *transcendence is a built-in feature of meta-states.* In meta-states you always and inevitably transcend to higher levels. What does this mean and what explains this?

What explains transcendence is the higher level of mind that arises from our power to abstract as we make self-reflexive moves. Then, as we layer one set of thoughts-and-feelings about other thoughts-and-feelings, these unite and merge as a set of related states. As this matrix of states develop, it interacts with itself systemically. Then something special results from all of this—we create and experience higher executive meta-states.

Now as already noted, your higher executive states do *not* refer to things "out there," but things inside—to your states of consciousness. This, in turn, changes your experiences. It creates your inner game, your attractor frames, your focus and attention, your way of being in the world, and your conceptual and semantic states. It creates your highest transcendental states that define and govern your identity, direction, destiny, personality, and style.

These highest transcending meta-states correlates to the "core" states as enumerated by Andreas and Andreas (1994, *Core Transformation*). To a certain extent then, the Core Transformation model and the *Meta-States* model have similar yet unique processes for working with the highest states. In some ways they reflect similar attempts to model the same territory, yet in other ways, they reflect very different approaches. This chapter correlates these processes to identify some of these similarities and differences.

Core Transformation

The Andreases describe their work in *Core Transformation* (1994) as originating from using the first three steps of the Six-Step Reframing pattern.[1] As a pattern for accessing and utilizing core states, the process involves creating layers of meta-states through the meta-stating process of outframing with positive intentions. By repeatedly asking one meta-question, the Core Transformation pattern invites a person to elicit a series of embedded outcome-of-outcome states. This pattern then results in a list of "core" states (which, of course, mixes metaphors). In *Meta-States*, these are our highest intentional states within our Intentional matrix.[2]

Core Transformation begins with the traditional NLP process of Six-Step Reframing. First, you identify a limitation, a disliked part, or some "dark" behavior.

> "Think about a behavior or response that you create which no longer serves you very well and which you'd like to transform so that you do something else."

With the limitation or disliked behavior in mind, you then elicit the positive intention of that problem.

> "What does this part seek to achieve or do that's of value and importance for you? How does this serve you? What do you get from it?"

Then, unlike six-step reframing, this process sets up a recursive loop at this point using *the positive intentional frame and continues to outframe every response with a new level of an even higher positive intention.* So rather than stopping after the first positive intent of the limiting behavior, the pattern leads you to specify an ascending list of higher positive intentions. The process elicits more and more layers of outcomes and outcomes-of-outcome, etc. To initiate this meta-stating, a meta-question is used to facilitate the looping:

> "If you obtain this desired outcome, fully and completely, and you find yourself fully experiencing it in just the way you desire, *what do you want* to experience, through this resource, which is something even more important and deeper?"

Did the term "deeper" jar you? This term switches metaphors mid-stream. Here you go *up* to the next highest level, to the intentional frame-of-reference that governs the behavior, then you are told to go "down" deeper.

This differs from the approach in Meta-States. The Andreases use the word "deeper," as well as the depth metaphor throughout their work. Yet the question they ask and its effect go in the opposite direction, up instead of down. So in the end you move up and identify *a series of meta-states of intention that creates an ultimate meta-outcome.* This use of formatting the pattern with the "depth" metaphor is a central difference between Core Transformation and the way we think and visualize using the Meta-States model.

The Core pattern operates by inquiring of your intentions, "What do you want . . . ?" It then does this repeatedly, "And by having that fully and completely, what do you want through this that you deem more important?" If you follow this process, it invites you to move upward to higher and higher levels. In *Meta-States,* we graph this process as moving our thinking-feeling states to higher and higher levels of awareness. So we go *up,* not down. We create transcending states, not "core" states, as we *transcend* the lower and *include* it in the next highest state.

In the Core pattern, as in Meta-States, *this questioning ultimately results in an outcome chain.* Through this process you begin with a behavior, emotion, or habit that you produce while in some limiting state. The Andreases illustrate this with the limiting emotional behavior of nervousness—a primary state. By exploring its intended outcome or purpose, you come to a meta-level—"to do a good job." The next intended outcome identifies the next meta-level—"to relax," and then another—"to be creative," and another—"a sense of freedom," and finally—"to feel connected with people" (1994, p. 36).

Figure 16:1

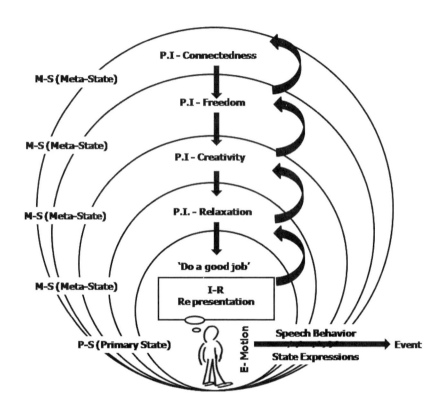

Core states are "strong inner states" (p. 136) which the process describes, elicits, and accesses. They are not, and do not function as, primary states. Why not? Simple. They do not relate to the world of events "out there," they relate to the internal world. They relate to a person's purpose, goals, destiny, value, belief, etc. Yet because they set a higher frame of mind, they establish "a way of being in the world." That is, you take your ideas, concepts, beliefs, etc. and use these meta-states to direct your way of being in the world.

The Andreases note that these higher states are more "spiritual," that they are more about your *being*. And why not? After all, they are your highest values, qualities, traits, and meanings. This means that the outcome questioning and the meta-questioning is a process that endows your life with meaningfulness and inspiration, creating your personal version of "spirituality."

The Andreases say they have found five core states which "usually emerge through the Core Transformation Process" (pp. 20-24).

Beingness: presence
Inner peace: deep sense of serenity or acceptance
Love: a neutral unconditional agape-love
Okayness: deep sense of worthiness, intrinsic value
Oneness: connection, grace, oneness with God.

These highly desired transcendent states occur at a meta-level to sensory experience and arise from the capacity to abstract reflexively and recursively. As your highest intentional states, they function also as your presuppositional states which set and create the larger level frame of reference for your orientation in the world. Standing in a *meta* position to your primary states, *these transcendent states of intentionality operate as self-organizing attractors in your mind-body system.*

This means that as you stabilize these states as your higher executive states, they continuously influence and govern your perceptions, emotions, behaviors, etc. Unlike primary states which come and go and which depend on circumstances, these meta-level states form and solidify your predispositional attitude about yourself, others, and life.

In a state of anger, you think-and-feel and respond with anger toward some specific object that you believe violates your values. But in the meta-state of *respect for the dignity of life*, you respond with this attitude toward all of life. So now, when you feel anger, it is anger-within-the-frame-of-respect-for-persons. This gives you the new gestalted meta-state of *respectful* anger.

What is the structure of these core spiritual states? By now it is undoubtedly obvious that they are made up of layers of meta-states in a rising hierarchy in your mind as you move up to higher concepts about life, origin, self, destiny, purpose, etc. They allow you to operationally define your form of "spirituality." "Spirituality" here refers to the total gestalt of all of your higher states of intention, belief, and understanding frames which creates your passions and inspirations in life. These "core" states give specific definition to your governing attitude or spirit and consequently to the disposition that arises from your beliefs, understandings, abstractions, values, etc.

- What do you believe in?
- What inspires you and evokes a sense of inspiration about human possibilities?
- What are your highest intentions for how you want to live your life?
- What do you believe is your purpose in this world?

There's something else. Because these "core" states are your highest meta-levels of intentionality, *they are your executive states*. And this explains why they create such pervasive transformations. As your highest frames of meaning and intention, they not only influence and modulate your lower states, they set the bias for your mind-body system.

As you now develop more ready access to these transcendental *being* states, you empower yourself to actually use and experience the higher meta-states of acceptance, forgiveness, connectedness, harmony, love, defenselessness, self-valuation, etc. All of this facilitates the process of getting these conceptual states into your muscles. Accessing your highest semantic states enriches your self-definition and self-experiences in handling difficulties and traumas in life and relationships. It makes you more "spiritual," that is, living above mere survival and other lower "animal" needs.

Within their pattern the Andreases include a premise that goes against all of cultural norms, namely, that a person has to earn, create, and work to reach this higher level of human development. They note that when we strive to achieve "core" states, it backfires. The implication that we have to "earn" the right to experience these states makes them performance-based rather than experience-based. Positing that you have to earn the right to access your "wellspring of wholeness" only adds another stressor. So they say that these highest states are unconditional.

When you make the higher spiritual states *conditional,* you set the legalistic frame that you have to work for them, you have to do "good works" and then you are allowed to experience them. This means that you can only allow yourself access to these states after achieving certain conditions. This actually creates a taboo against starting from your best, it means you cannot use them as resources. Of course, none of this helps or enriches life.

The alternative is to imagine that *your higher states are unconditional gifts and possibilities* simply because they are just states.

> "Just begin by *having* inner peace rather than working to have it . . . this way you aren't leaving something that important up to other people. It's a lot nicer than going to all that effort and work to get others to respect you first." (p. 90)
>
> "Somehow our inner parts get the idea [a cognitive misbelief from our cultures] that in order to experience core states of being, they first have to go through a whole series of Intended Outcomes. Unfortunately, this doesn't work very well. We don't experience our Core States very often when we go about it that way, because a core state of beingness is not something that is possible to earn or to get through actions. The way to experience a Core State is just to step into it and have it." (pp. 116-117)

This reflects the frame that Maslow initiated about the basic goodness of human nature which was the basic premise of his Third Force psychology and human potential movement. An expression of this premise is the idea that "Behind every behavior is a positive intention." Treating your highest meta-states as unconditional, unearned, undeserved, unmerited, etc. also recaptures the original idea in various theologies of *grace* which is defined as unmerited "love, grace, and kindness." Compare these "core" states with the list of states in such texts as "spiritual" states: love, joy, peace, longsuffering, gentleness, goodness, faithfulness, meekness, and self-control (Galatians 5:22-23).

> "You don't have to work at Core States, you just have them . . . . work doesn't bring about Core States. Just stepping into those states and having them, on the unconscious level, brings about Core States." (p. 92)

Discovering Your Highest Spiritual States

The Core pattern begins at the primary level where you feel stuck. In some way or another you experience a limitation, pain, distress, etc. Then, assuming positive intentions, you move to a higher state about the problem that enables you to feel and think more resourcefully.

> "What are you seeking to achieve that's positive and valuable?"

This question sets the structural frame for this pattern. So as you repeat this question several times, you'll create a whole series of embedded nests of positive intentions. As you experience the positive intentions premise, you move beyond the lower levels of hurtful and ineffective behaviors and step progressively into higher meta-states.

This belief will also enable you to more effectively navigate interpersonal reality. After all, you generally do whatever you do, however thoughtless, mindless, stupid, or cruel the behavior, because you're trying to make things better for yourself. Typically, you are *not* trying to be evil, an idiot, an asshole, a tyrant, or a demon. If on occasion you do get into a really unresourceful state and do intend to hurt someone, you usually are doing so in order to make things right, protect yourself, or make something painful or hurtful to evil go away. So even then, your intention is good. What sucks is your choice of behavior and the low level of your intention.

The search for positive intentions, and then positive intentions of positive intentions, discovers and creates these higher states. Doing this first sets the frame of positive intentions which you then *foreground*. As this assumes and sets the frame of value and usefulness, you bring this into your focal awareness. You meta-state yourself with positive intentions until you have a whole matrix of positive and inspiring intentionality.

In doing this, you befriend those behaviors, emotions, communications, and somatizations that you might otherwise hate, despise, condemn, and not understand or validate. This transforms what would otherwise be a dragon state of judging, blaming, condemning, accusing, and demonizing. It enables you to turn undesirable states into allies. It creates a whole new direction for transformation.

- What can I appreciate about this negative or unpleasant state?
- What positive intention can I find or invent that explains this behavior?
- How can I reorient myself to more effectively obtain that desired outcome?

Figure 16:2

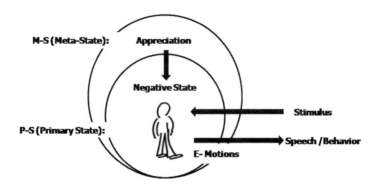

Identify a negative state you experience at times, and over which you want more choice and management. Go inside and ask yourself:

> What positive value am I seeking to achieve by generating this response? What do I want that's of value or importance?

When you get an answer, meta-question it again.

> If I have the experience of X (i.e., feeling relaxed, safe, assertive, confident, loved, etc.), fully and completely, what do I want, through this experience, that I would find of even more value and importance? If I get this X experience, by experiencing X fully and completely, what will I then want that I would deem of even more value?

As you meta-question your states, and the parts of your mind in this way, you generate a chain or sequence of outcomes — desired outcomes all the way up to your highest meta-levels. They take you up into your richest semantic and spiritual meta-states. Suppose, for example, you frequently get into a nervous and anxious state when you try to want to speak up to someone that you care about.

Question: What is your positive intent behind this state of nervousness? Why do you generate such feelings? What do you want?

> *You:* "To do my best, to come across well, to not mess up."

Question: What would you want by doing your best and coming across well that you consider of even more value and importance?

> *You:* "To express my thoughts and feelings."

This is the meta-state you desire from the primary state. And what is the valued outcome of that?

"To connect, to feel validated."

Good! That's yet another, and higher, meta-state. And what is the desired outcome of that?

"To experience love and bonding."

What is the desired outcome of that?

"To know myself as a loveable person."

Figure 16:3

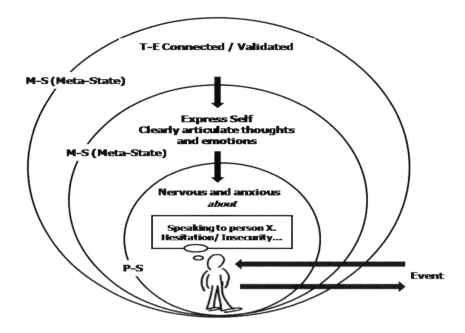

This set of desired outcome states flushes out (or creates) specific meta-frames driving your intentionality. *This is what you're living for.* You do what you do, think and feel as you do, to experience these transcendent states. These ultimate frames encapsulate your highest spiritual maps about being fully yourself. If you want to know the kind of spirituality ultimately governing your life, you only have to look here. This is your personal teleology governing your theology.

To give more power to this spirituality, begin with these transcendent meta-states by *allowing yourself to step into them fully.* Step into them and imagine using them as your resources for *being.* Access them as you do the primary states using the formulas "Think of a time when . . . " and "What would it be like if . . . ?" You no longer have to worry about the legalistic "earning it" approach. You can just accept them. Treat them as gifts.

> *As you step into* that transcendent state of recognizing and feeling yourself as a loveable person, *how does this empower you* to experience a state of love and bonding?
>
> And if you experience yourself as a loveable person, fully and completely, and in just the way you want it, how does that enhance your feelings of validation?
>
> And what does this meta-state do that enriches your experience of expressing yourself to someone else?
>
> And as you start with the meta-state of loveability, how does that make it even easier to interact, listen, speak up, do your best, make a good impression, etc.?

Starting with your ultimate outcome states, *you can now allow yourself to experience them as your way of being in the world.* As you do this, notice how it affects and transforms you and how you experience others. Let its transforming energy ripple down through and into all of your other states as you appreciate and enjoy this higher level mind.

The Height and Depth Metaphors

Obviously, one difference between *Core Transformation* and *Meta-States* is their organizing metaphors. Core uses *depth*, Meta-States uses *height*.

Consider first the depth metaphor and all of the words talking about "going down," "to the core," "deeper," etc. Consider what this metaphor does, what it suggests, and how it works. When you begin by picturing "personality" as having depths, then you go inside and imagine yourself going down deeper and deeper and deeper until you get to your core. This evokes images of things that are *down* and *deep:* a pit, basement, celler, cave, etc. By implication it suggests:

narrowness, smallness, darkness, constriction, descending, etc. The entailments of this metaphor makes it less desirable and useful for most people.

Personally, I just don't like where these entailments of the metaphor take me. And I say that even though I grew up in southern Indiana where I belonged to a spelunking club as a teenager and engaged in spelunking throughout my youth. And while I thoroughly enjoyed caving, as a psychological metaphor, going down inside myself carries undesirable implications of narrowness, darkness, smallness, tightness, etc.

By way of contrast, the *height* metaphor has a very different effect as it works on your mind, emotions, attitude, etc. When you picture yourself going inside and then *upward* to higher and higher levels, you have a sense of transcending thought, emotion, time, concepts, etc. You rise above previous frames and move to the largest frames so that you can look over all of your other frames. This rising above and beyond the other frames broadens and widens our perspective giving you more light, more openness, more possibilities.

> "Once we have discovered the Core State our inner part wants [your best and highest meta-states], we are in a position to transform the basis of our inner life. Now the process guides us in literally turning our old pattern around. We can *begin* by having what we were hoping we could somehow get to if we worked hard enough at it. We can *begin* with the Core State—the wellspring within. We invite the part of ourselves . . . to step into its Core State and have it. Then we invite our inner part to notice *how already having the Core State as a way of being in the world* transforms each of our Intended Outcomes." (p. 37)

Going Meta with Dante

All of this reminds me of my graduate studies in Dante. Did you know that seven centuries ago, an Italian poet single-handedly created the Italian language? He did so, in part, by penning a three-volume piece of poetry about a journey through the three domains of the after-life. These domains dominated medieval Europe at that time. Using the Ptolemaic cosmology (the universe as geocentric or earth-centered) which was in vogue then, Dante envisioned the pit of *the Inferno* beginning at Jerusalem and going down, down, down and down into the deeper and deeper circles of hell. He portrayed it as an ever-narrowing pit of darkness, foul smells, torture, gloom, hopelessness, etc. It wasn't a very nice place, not even to visit.

This portrait of "the hellish state" involved deeper levels of blindness, irresponsibility, stupidity, distress, and pain until you got to the bottom of it— where a giant satan stood immobile in a frozen lake (i.e., the freezing over of hell!).

The second realm stood on the opposite end of the planet from Jerusalem, *Mount Purgatory,* a seven-layered mountain (half the size of the planet) that ascended up and up and up toward the earthly paradise of Eden. Unlike the Inferno where people hardly moved since they couldn't leave their domain, those who began the ascent up Mt. Purgatory continually move upward and so continually experience greater vision, understanding, learnings, renewal, and rejuvenation. At the end of each terrace an Angel of Blessing would meet them and flap his wings to blow away the wounds that the traveler had just purged on each given level. This blessing freed them for the next level until finally they would reach the top, where the Garden of Eden was—the earthly paradise.

From there Dante began his space travels into *Paradise.* As he would look upon the radiant and glowing face of the beautiful and lovely Beatrice (his symbol for grace and love), he would find himself immediately transported to higher and higher realms of light and glory. [It was Dante's fourteenth century version of being beamed up.] He was first beamed up to the circle of the moon, then to Mars, Venus, Jupiter, and on up through the cosmos of Ptolemy until he reached the Empyrean. This was the place where "the unmoved Mover of the Universe" lived.

And with each ascension to the greater heights, Dante would look back and down to "the small threshingfloor of the earth" having gained so much more perspective, insight, and light. Each state offered a higher state of love-consciousness. So that each meta-position he moved to gave him a greater sense of expansiveness—and so he felt more loving, more wise, more understanding. What an image!

In the same way, when you go meta up through the higher levels of mind using various meta-stating processes, you also continue to rise up to ever-new meta-levels of resourcefulness. This uplifting process itself empowers you to move up and out of self-imprisonment to your own darkness. It empowers you to experience more self-transcendence into the realm of love and wholeness. If that sounds like the structure of a peak experience, then give it a try.

Summary

- The higher level meta-states of intention describe your "core" transcendent states. These states take you to the qualities that we call "spiritual" as they specify your beliefs about the outcome of your existence.

- Both *Core Transformation* and *Meta-States* tracks and models the human experience of "spirituality." Both does so by eliciting outcome levels, the second adds the layers of meanings involved in those intentions.

- One way these two models differ is in the metaphors that each use. In Meta-States, you move *up* and set higher executive frames, in the Core Transformation you go *down* into *core* states.

- Here's another difference: *Meta-States* not only includes those wonderfully positive spiritual states, but the negatively destructive states as well. The later do not serve your spirit very well, yet may comprise the higher levels of belief, attitude, understanding, and intentionality: to prove yourself or your group superior, to dominate, to vindicate injustices, to condemn errors, etc. If you apply sick and toxic intentions to yourself, you create sick and toxic meta-frames: self-contempt, self-doubt, paranoia, morbid guilt, denial, self-righteousness, etc. These then become higher level torturous states infecting your spirit.

End Notes:

1. Several years ago, NLP trainer Roye Fraser told me that Core Transformation is partly derived from his work on the Generative Imprinting Model (1983). I have not seen any documented evidence of this, but then again, most early NLP development didn't document things.

2. See *The Matrix Model* (2002) for the Intentional Matrix.

Chapter 17

META-STATES

EPISTEMOLOGY

"The word 'know' is not merely ambiguous
in covering both *connaitre* (to know through the senses,
to recognize or perceive)
and *savoir* (to know in the mind), but varies—actively shifts—
in meaning for basic systemic reasons.
That which we know through the senses
can *become* knowledge in the mind."
Gregory Bateson (1972, p. 134)

Using your self-reflexive consciousness enables you to do something very magical. It enables you to *step back* from your experiences of thinking, emoting, and acting and consider these experiences through a meta-lens. You can now consider your mental and emotional experiences through the lens of, or in terms of, whatever *idea* or *concept* that you choose. And there's no end to the kinds of conceptual ideas that you can use to view or frame your experiences.

What does this magic of reflexively stepping back from yourself enable you to do?

> *You are now able to apply conceptual frames to your experiences and embed them within all kinds of meaning structures . Meaning now is truly at your command.*

As a symbolic-class of life, you can look at your experiences through the lens of effectiveness and productivity, morality and ethics, cultural conformity and sameness, adventure and differences, self-esteem and other-esteem, and a thousand other conceptual frames-of-reference.

Isn't that wild? Imagine what this means. You can enter into the world of communication, ideas, and concepts to such an extent that you can now actually experience the world in an entirely new and different way because *you can experience it in terms of the ideas you apply to it*.

If you don't get it yet, then what this means is that *the symbols you use* for your thinking, perceiving, feeling, etc. *will form, filter, govern, direct, control, and modulate your experiences* in the world of events. This framing, via your reflexivity and meta-stating, creates structures in your lives that work in ways that can seem utterly "magical."

As a conceptual creature who creates meaning, you can access and apply *concepts* to your experiences. We commonly call these concepts beliefs, ideas, understandings, decisions, intentions, permissions, identities, etc. This results in several things. On the first level, you create your conceptual or neuro-semantic states. On the next level, as you map things, so you create higher logical levels of classifications and categories that can change everything. It can elevate you to a level of consciousness determined by your beliefs. Now, consciously and unconsciously, you live in the semantic states of your belief and beliefs-about-beliefs. At this higher level, your states are now created, influenced, and operated by the "things in the mind."

This explains why doing this generates an entirely new epistemology in your life. From this point onward, what you know and *how you know what you know* (epistemology) *takes on new qualities and properties*. You begin operating at a different and higher level—and by different principles of consciousness.

The "Mind" that Creates States and Meta-States
In this model, "mind" or more accurately, your *mind-body-emotion system,* plays a central and formative role in your experiences. States are, after all, preeminently states of mind, that is, states of meaning. And, as a neuro-linguistic and neuro-semantic being, you generate your states by means of how and how you think-and-feel, as well as what

you do.

Every state of consciousness you have ever experienced, or ever will experience, arises from your *embodied thinking*. The systemic fact is that your linguistics and semantics (meanings) do not operate apart from your neurology. For that reason, Korzybski used a hyphen and created the terms neuro-linguistic and neuro-semantic.

*   What do we mean by *thinking?*
*   What does the nominalization *mind* mean*?*
*   What is a mind and where is it located?
*   How does mind relate to the physiology of brain events?

Gregory Bateson's classic works, *Steps to An Ecology of Mind* (1972), and *Mind and Nature* (1979), address *mind* as an emergent quality in the mind-body system. Bateson identified his working model of an operational definition of mind by generating six "criteria of mind." He also provided many pages of explanation (1979, chapter 4. Criteria of Mental Process, p. 97). While I have addressed some of this extensively in *Languaging* (1996), I do want to mention these in passing as I move on to a facet about this kind of a mind, namely its epistemology, because this is the epistemology of meta-states.

As I mention Bateson, I issue this warning. Bateson is not for the fainthearted! As an anthropologist, linguist, and communication expert, he represented one of the foremost thinkers of the twentieth century.[1] The following criterion of "mind" summarizes how he thought about mind and the kind of mind that we have.

Bateson's Criteria of "Mind"

1. A mind is an aggregate of *interacting parts* or components.

2. The interaction between parts of mind is *triggered by difference,* and difference is a nonsubstantial phenomenon not located in space or time; difference is related to negentropy and entropy rather than to energy.

3. Mental process requires *collateral energy*.

4. Mental process requires *circular* (or more complex) *chains* of determination.

5. In mental process, *the effects of difference are* to be regarded as *transforms* (i.e. coded versions) *of events* which preceded them. The rules of such transformation must be comparatively stable (i.e., more stable than the content) but as themselves subject to transformation.

6. The description and classification of these processes of transformation disclose *a hierarchy of logical types* immanent in the phenomena.

Notice the last criteria here—mental processes reveal "a hierarchy of logical types." Bateson used this to create several of his models, his model of the double-bind theory of schizophrenia, his analysis of humor, play, aesthetics, and the logical levels of learning.

Bateson's structured his Learning Model beginning with Zero Learning, then Learning I, learning II (learning about learning, or deutro-learning model), and Learning III.[2] Regarding schizophrenia, Bateson and associates developed the "so-called double bind theory of schizophrenia" pointing out that the meta-bind which creates the schizophrenic suffering. This makes sense of the strange responses.

Bateson said that the traditional meaning of "logic" as direct and linear cause and effect statements inadequately accounts for things in a system. We need to distinguish several kinds of logics (1979, p. 61). From systems theory and cybernetics he noted the role of "time" in a system. He noted that events within an open system with feedback circuits will "over time" create a different kind of system, a system which will govern and modulate from a higher level. As a system operates over time, later events can operate at a higher logical level to first level responses.

There's far more richness in Bateson's work than I can explicate here. At this point I only want to focus on his *levels or logical types* for "mind" and relate them to the Meta-States model

Logical Types and the Coding of Messages
As a linguist, Bateson constantly addressed the nature of language as a description and evaluation of experience (a map *of* the territory). His work with schizophrenics, dolphins, dogs, etc. led him to think about

the coding of messages, and specifically to the confusion of messages when messages comprised different logical types.

Accepting the Korzybski's map / territory distinction, Bateson (1979) wrote:

> ". . . no messages, under any circumstances, *is* that which precipitated it. There is always a partly predictable and therefore rather regular relation between message and referent, that relation indeed never being direct or simple." (p. 123)

At the first or primary level then, there are messages about X. As such, the symbols *stands for* and *points to* some referent event. This involves learning the relationship between a specific stimulus and a specific response. For example, a dog learns to sit when he hears the word "sit." A dolphin learns to jump at the sound of a whistle. A rat learns that putting his nose in box X will result in an electrical shock.

Next in the coding of messages are those *messages that refer to a previous message*, meta-messages. These involve a higher level generalization.

These messages offer a "double description" as in the case of your binocular vision that generates your experience of depth perception. The layering of messages (information from right eye; information from left eye) then creates a synergism of information that contains something "more than the sum of the parts." Bateson (1979) wrote,

> "In more formal language, the *difference* between the information provided by the one retina and that provided by the other is itself information of *a different logical type*. From this new sort of information, the seer adds an extra *dimension* to seeing." (pp. 73-4)

Meta-messages create a new dimension. By meta-messages, you transcend the first level as you rise to a new level. You make new and more comprehensive abstractions about the lower level abstractions and so extend your knowledge and understanding. These meta-messages may arise through the process of generating new generalizations as you mentally compare the information about one set of particulars with those of another set of particulars, or compare information over time. In this way, you make a meta move to a higher level.

When Dolphins Jump Logical Levels

Bateson illustrated the "generalizations after sets of particulars" from his work with dolphins. He said that the dolphin trainer could easily condition these quick learning dolphins to discriminate about the desired behavior by rewarding them when they produced some desired response.

But when the trainer would repeatedly invite a dolphin into the water tank *and not* reinforce their behaviors, this created a new and strange context for the dolphins. It created confusion. If the trainer had always picked out some behavior and rewarded it, the dolphin lived, as it were, in that world. So when the trainer *changed that world* in relation to the dolphin by repeatedly *not* rewarding or reinforcing that behavior, or worse yet, *any* behavior, the dolphin would experience the state of "being wrong." The dolphin's world no longer worked. In this, the dolphin was made wrong existentially. The dolphin's inner maps about the world of trainers, conditioning, rewards, etc., no longer working, was now wrong.

Given this new context, the dolphin no longer knew her world. Having always been rewarded via the previous conditioning, the dolphins didn't seem to know what to make of things. It was as if the dolphins were thinking about that change of context:

> "The behaviors that I have learned to produce are *not* working. In fact, the very structure of the world that I have always known, 'do behavior and get reward,' is no longer working. Where's my anticipated reward? Something is wrong with my world! But, what? What is wrong?"

What now results in the dolphin, as in us, when we are "made wrong" is *anxiety*. So in the tanks the dolphins became highly agitated. Bateson reasoned that the mental map of the dolphins, the internalized model of the world regarding the learning situation and about what the trainer wanted from them, had failed. It was as if the dolphins were suffering from a non-functioning mental mapping. What they had mapped as a generalization about their world was now failing to produce results. Their dolphin-thoughts about the context of the relationship to the trainer was no longer providing them guidance in this world, how to understand it, and what to do. Their old mapping about their situation, relationship with the trainer, etc. not only made them "wrong," it was completely silent about what to do. It offered no next step for any solution.

So as this disordering of the dolphin's mental mapping made them "wrong" it initiated in them a high energy state. The same happens to us. We also become emotional, creative, disruptive, and reactive when we are made wrong and/or when the world we map no longer works.[3] Yet out of that agitation, something new emerges.

> "Between the fourteenth and fifteen sessions, the dolphin appeared to be much excited; and when she came onstage for the fifteenth session, she put on an elaborate performance that included eight conspicuous pieces of behavior of which four were new and never before observed in this species of animal. From the animal's point of view, there is a jump, a discontinuity, between the logical types. . . . The step from one logical type to the next higher is a step from information about an event to information *about a class of events . . .* " (1979, p. 132)

From this series of events the dolphin somehow jumped to a new level of discrimination. As she went meta to the series of individual learnings, she shifted levels, and at a higher level she learned something new. *She learned something about the overall context.* It is as if she discerned a new level of regularity and pattern. Our conclusion is that she transcended the learning of particulars (the detail of specific behaviors that call forth rewards) and formulated a meta-principle. She moved to a new meta-state of awareness as she "learned" about her previous learnings and so expanded her epistemology.

And what did she learn? She learned that the trainer did not want a specific behavior already learned, but wanted brand new behaviors, different from what had already been learned. She learned,

> "Do something different. The game of doing what you already know is over."

When "Mind" is Made Wrong
We also live our lives according to our meta-levels of frames of

understandings about ourselves, others, the world, etc. And, we do not like being wrong. "Being wrong," in fact, seems to be one of the most disturbing, upsetting, and semantically distressing experiences that we humans can suffer. Give many people the choice between being wrong and suffering a beating, or loss of income, end of a marriage, and many will take anything other than being wrong (!).

This makes perfect sense given that it is your mental mapping that connects you to reality. So when you experience a map *not* succeeding in helping you to properly orient to your environment and *not* enabling you to navigate to where you want to go, you experience tremendous inner disorientation. And you register that disorientation as "threat" which you experience as fear, anger, loss, anxiety, confusion, etc.

Yet something good can come out of this. The context of being made wrong actually gives you an opportunity to use your *meta-function* to jump levels and experience a higher level of awareness of your contexts. This, in turn, allows you to set higher frames that empower you in new ways. You can create expanded understandings for enabling you to navigate the territory in new ways.

Non-Linear Causation

In a system that goes round and round a circuit, the generalizations that you make operate at different "logical levels." To illustrate how you make generalizations over time, Bateson described the cybernetic system of circular causation in a machine. He began with a basic description of "information" passing around the system of fuel to cylinder to flywheel to governor to fuel, etc. With the second, third, etc. "times" around this circuit *linear cause-effect descriptions no longer works as an adequate explanatory model.* When every part in the system effects every other part, *emergent properties* will arise in that system.

Why is this? Because the information processing within the system now begins to reference its previous levels of data and information processing. That is, the next generalization is about previous generalizations; it is information about information.

There's also another factor involved. Because "the whole process occurs in time," complex, layered, and meta processes begin to transpire.

> "At some time, 1, the load was encountered. The change in the speed of the flywheel *followed* time 1. The changes in the governor followed still later. Finally, the corrective message reached the flywheel at some time 2, later than time 1. But the amount of the correction was determined by the amount of deviation at time 1. By time 2, the deviation will have changed." (1979, pp. 112-114)

This means that in systems, events may not occur linearly. Yes in our conceptualizing and languaging, we separate events linearly, but we can only do so conceptually as our mental process for understanding. We do this so we can discuss the processes we're observing and formulating. Yet our conversation, made up of linear words, do not reflect the same structure as the systemic reality. So while events in systems function recursively and all at once (simultaneously) throughout the system, we are severely limited in being able to talk and map things out that way. The nature of our language and our thinking prevents this.

What are we to do? The beginning place is to remind ourselves of this difference and that *we are dealing with a system*. We can also create system maps of multiple processes occurring simultaneously. This gives us a picture not only of a thousand words, but of a thousand words simultaneously in different parts of the system. We can also learn to value the importance of thinking in circles, loops, and spirals. When we apply this to personality as we meta-state, we move to the next higher loop in the system and this frequently generates a brand new gestalt.

> "Not caring about all of the apprehensions, worries, and 'what ifs' about a project" may initiate the gestalt of "courage."

If we then really like and appreciate, and even get excited about this boldness to move forward on a project, we may then become "passionate." As we go round and round, each level of thinking-and-feeling *about* the previous level adds new textures and qualities to it. With each loop we create new frames embedded within higher frames that will stabilize the experience as a new system.

Meta-Stating Meta-Contextual Information
Bateson (1979) summarized one of his most insightful realizations and discoveries about the power to classify information in a system in the following way.

> "A function, an effect, of the meta-message is in fact to *classify* the messages that occur within its context." (p. 124)

What does this means? *It means that you have to go meta to a system to step outside that system.* This process enables you to then think, reason, perceive, understand, feel, and respond to that system *as a system*. This corresponds to the quote from Einstein that you cannot solve a problem from the same space within which you created the problem. You must step outside the problem to another space—a higher space.

Ascending logical levels as going to higher meta-states describes how you generalize, classify, and language your next level awareness about an experience. By transcending primary experiencing in this way you step up into meta-states where you experience conceptual states and semantic states that actualize your highest and best—your fullest humanity, spirituality, meaningfulness, and self-actualization.

It is at these meta-levels of experience that you experience those phenomena that characterize human nature and personality at its best. Bateson describes *multiple typing* as essential to human communication (p. 124), for humor (p. 124), paradox (p. 125), abstraction (p. 126), perception of contexts and context markers (p. 128), evaluations (or nominalizations, "discrimination, exploration, dependency, crime, etc.) (p. 130), sense of rightness/wrongness (p. 131), play (pp. 133-4), etc.

Paradoxically, it is also at meta-levels that phenomena of human pain arise. This occurs due to errors in logical typing. *It is an error in logical typing.* In this error we misread, mis-evaluate, and misunderstand signals due to our interpretative frames. An example is schizophrenia—"the outcome of maltreatments of logical typing" (p. 134). Another example is the general pain, anxiety, and terror that many experience as they over-value logic for mapping out causation (pp. 134ff). Here we experience meta-pathologies (Maslow), morbid states (Korzybski), or what I've described as dragon states.

Bateson emphasized that the emergence of *mind* in all of its forms in the neuro-linguistic and neuro-semantic system functions "by 'maps,' never by territory" (p. 136). If it functions by our maps, then all of our experiences are always modulated by our thinking—our generalizations. Experience by itself has little ability to effect us. What forms us and what transforms us are our interpretations of our experiences—our frames and perceptions. That's why our most wonderful human capacity involves moving to meta-levels and creating the concepts that will endow us with the most empowering explanatory style.

Our Higher Conceptual States
As the meta-stating process inevitably takes us higher, we therefore inevitably generate transcendent states of experiential phenomena —our *being* states. Yet with the emergence of these peak experiences or higher level states, we enter into the "spiritual" realm of those states that seem to bring out our highest transcendental nature of being loving, considerate, fair, kind, forgiving, caring, etc.

Regarding exploration, play, crime, type-A behavior, etc., Bateson (1979) wrote:
>   "... all these are not categories of behavior; they are *categories of contextual organization of behavior*." (p. 144)

Now you might think Bateson that would have known better than to tie together a string of nominalizations like that, "categories of contextual organization." Give me a break. So what did he mean by that phrase? To find out, let's denominalize the fluff of that statement.

In that statement Bateson makes a distinction between different kinds of behaviors. There are behaviors, and then there are things which are not strictly "behaviors" as such, but *ways that we mentally organize our conceptual categories about behaviors*.

An example is the category of "play." We can put lots of specific behaviors into this category. Hide and seek, tag, chess, football, foreplay, betting on the stock market, etc. "Play," in itself, is not a sensory-based term. "Play" does not occur on the primary level. You can't see, hear, feel, taste, or smell "play." The word "play" refers to an understanding, generalization, and interpretation that we make about certain activities. *"Play" is a conceptual category.* To make this as shocking as possible, let me put it starkly.

> *The concept of play only exists in the mind of the person doing*
> *the categorizing.*

We use the unspecified verb "play" to establish a category of behaviors or as Bateson said, "categories of contextual organization of behaviors." Ah, that's a meta-state! Why didn't Bateson say so?

Similar to this analysis of play as a category of mind are many other things that we regularly confuse as behaviors: "exploration," "crime," "kindness," "being rude," etc. None of these are behaviors! They don't exist in the real world. They operate at a higher logical level as "categories of contextual organization of behavior."   They are classifications. This explains how and why in your everyday life, you have to operate with an awareness of contexts. This means that when you think about and engage in the behaviors such as "exploration," "play," "crime," etc., you are actually operating from, and living within, a higher level. You are now seeing and experiencing the world *not as it is, but through the lens of our mental frames.*

At this point your concepts are creating your felt experience out of some raw data. The epistemology of your "knowing" what you are experiencing at that point arises not from the world, but from your mind *about* the world. Of course, it doesn't seem or feel that way. It feels real. It also feels permanent, stable, obvious, intuitive, etc.

The Stability of Characterological States
Once you build up your personal epistemology of felt concepts via your meta-stating and live in them for some time, they become your personality and your character. And when you meta-state a concept to this degree, these kinds of experiences "are difficult to extinguish."

Bateson noted and illustrated this by describing a rat learning to *not* put his nose into a particular box because it contained electric shocks. In this situation the rat is quickly conditioned to learn the particular response of not putting his nose in the box. About this Bateson then wrote, "It is not desirable that he learn the general lesson," namely, "Exploration is not desirable; it is dangerous; don't do it." If the rat generalizes and makes *that* learning about the category of *"exploration"*—it will undermine his ability to survive. He will stop investigating his environment and not be able to find food.

From this data Bateson said that trying to extinguish the rat's "characterological state" would demand a "paradigmatic change," a change in epistemology (1979, p. 133). Now a characterological state" was Bateson's term for *higher conceptual meta-states*. So by way of comparison, while it is relatively easy to change specific behaviors, it is more difficult to change a meta-level category that classifies behaviors in a particular way. If your inner mental world of categorizing or framing makes up your inner epistemology, then to change that we will need another process.

This means several things for us. This explains the difference in the stability of meta-states over the ever-in-flux nature of primary states. No wonder it is easy to anchor and alter primary states. And conversely, no wonder it is typically a more demanding and difficult process to elicit and anchor meta-states, especially *gestalt* meta-states.

When you build the abstractions that you code linguistically as nominalizations, which include your *value* words, and then abstractions of abstractions (more nominalizations of your beliefs and belief systems) and abstractions of those abstractions (paradigms, models of the world, etc.), you move to the highest meta-dimension wherein you operate from your "categories of contextual organization of behavior." As these higher states lose more and more of their emotional feel, they become your "reality strategy"—your frame of reference about what's real. When that happens, the only *affective feel* left is that of "matter-of-factness."[4]

I noted in chapter 15 that one of the myths in NLP is that it is not a theory, but a model. From the beginning, Richard and John were known to say,

> "We don't have a theory; we're not into that, we only have a model about how something works."
> "We have no theory about *why* things work, we just noticed that when we start with these assumptions, we end up experiencing more of a sense of choice, flexibility, and resourcefulness."

Yet they did have a theory. It was only later that many of us discovered the mythology and realized that their epistemology was hidden away in "the NLP presuppositions." Not only was their theory hid in those premises, but by setting these frames as workable assumptions for greater effectiveness regardless of whether they are true or not, they were able to create epistemological change in people's lives.

Epistemological Change
To change epistemology necessitates a change of higher logical levels. *And in changing highest logical levels, we are changing our epistemology.* This means we are changing our mental paradigms that operate as our "model of the world." Here we do not merely change a primary level map about something, here we change our meta-maps regarding *how we know what we know* (our epistemology) regarding our maps and our mapping.

- Is this possible? And if it is, how does it work?
- How is it possible to change a person's highest level maps and thus their epistemological maps that govern how they know what they know.
- How do you do this?

First, destabilize the current epistemology. Set the stage for epistemological change by de-stabilizing a conceptual system by using the indexing questions of the Meta-Model. The Meta-Model challenges those constructions and frames of references. It does so by evoking a person to index the specific situations and experiences from which the original mapping was created. This meta-level awareness of consciousness deframes and de-stabilizes the system making you aware of ill-formed constructions and conclusions in your maps.

Second, anticipate a state of anxiety. Destabilizing a person's epistemology will almost inevitably make the person anxious. As you become aware of how your maps have been or are wrong and erroneous to the territory, experientially you will feel "wrong." By anticipating this, you can then get excited about the anxiety and if you then stay with that anxiety, you'll eventually jump another level.

Third, distinguish map and territory. Facilitate this epistemological change by setting the map/territory epistemology frame as a governing frame. This will meta-state your conceptual understanding with a mapping qualification and make it your perceptual lens through which you then experience the world. This will facilitate your ability to step back from all of your models and epistemologically, you will then recognize their essence as just *maps*.[5]

Fourth, quality control your frames. To leverage epistemological change, once you have stepped back, check the quality of your meaning frames, *and out-frame every map that doesn't enhance and empower you.* The stepping back and evaluating your mental mapping and previous evaluations, checks the ecology of your inner games and "models of the world." Doing this puts you at choice point for choosing your frames of mind. As a way to do this, Bateson provided a mathematical way of thinking about this kind of framing.

Mathematizing Meta-State "Magic"

The following comes from a wonderfully provocative piece, *The Group Dynamics of Schizophrenia,* where Gregory Bateson described "the world of communication" and how it radically differs from the world of physics and forces. The "world of physics," he said, innately involves the cause-effect processes of Newtonian dynamics. In this world, actions and things are energized by the transference of energy from other actions and things. Here billiard balls move entirely and exclusively according to the physics of impact and gravity. You hit the ball with your cue stick and the ball moves according to the energy transfer of that force.

An entirely different set of "dynamics" occurs in the world of communication. When we kick a dog, the movement of the dog in response to your kick is only partially explained by a "Newtonian trajectory." To predict the trajectory of the dog, the intensity of his response, etc. not only involves the amount of force applied by the kick, but also by the dog's own metabolism, internal energy system, learning history, relationship to the kicker (!), and so on. In a word, it depends on the dog's inner psycho-logics (the meaning of the person kicking to the dog).

Bateson (1972) commented that while we may use the word "dynamics" when referring to psychological processes, we must remember that we use it in a different sense from the way physicists use the word in the domain of physics. In distinguishing these two realms, Bateson wrote,

> "This, I think, is what people mean by *magic*. The realm of phenomena in which we are interested [psychological, mental, communicational, etc.] is always characterized by the fact that *'ideas' may influence events.*" (p. 229, italics added)

In so introducing the word "magic" into realm of communication, Bateson may have unknowingly provided some of the inspiration for Bandler and Grinder's book, "*The Structure of Magic*" (1975).[6] If we inquire as to what precisely Bateson meant by using the term "magic," and keep it within the Batesonian context, we come to this statement:

> "It might well be sufficiently confusing to be told, that according to the conventions of communication in use at the moment, *anything can stand for anything else.* But this realm of magic is not that simple." (p. 230, italic added)

"Magic," in the Batesonian context refers to the realm of communication, to the cognitive-neurological understanding about *how ideas may influence events.* In the realm of symbolization, Bateson contented that words and language is sometimes so plastic that "anything can stand for anything else." Yet as he noted, it is not that extreme. It just feels that way sometimes. Yet this does describe the fluid and complex arena inside the human nervous system that transcends the laws of physics.

Where do these ponderings take us with regard to epistemology and to the ability to create epistemological change? One more quotation and I will offer a practical application. Bateson (1972) noted this about the "dynamic" of communication:

> "All communication has this characteristic—*it can be magically modified by accompanying communication.*" (230, italics added)

Question:
> How can we magically modify one communicational message or set of representations?

Answer:
> By nesting it inside of another communication message so that the second message classifies the first. Whenever we put a message within a higher level message, the higher level can

always change, alter, and even transform the first message.

As evidence, Bateson illustrated by using the example of speaking with one's fingers crossed behind one's back. The meaning of that symbolic representation qualifies and modifies the lower-level message of whatever the speaker verbalizes with his words. In the structure of humor, the "punch line" exists at a different logical level than the syntax of the joke set-up which predisposes a person to expect. The sudden shift in logical levels jars consciousness to produces humor.

These examples show how *the role of meta-communicational signals* plays out in such ways that the meta-message modifies or qualifies the lower-level message "magically." To use mathematical symbols to convey this understanding, the meta-messages can operate as a plus **(+),** a minus **(-),** as a multiplication or times **(X),** or as a division **(÷)** *signals* of the original state.

Bateson (1972) asserted that this means that "the world of communication is a Berkeleyan world" (p. 250). In other words, in the world of communication (representations), no true "things" exist —only *messages*. Things and events cannot enter into this world. "I" as a material object (p. 251) cannot enter it, only "I" as a message, or as part of the syntax of my experience. External objects only enter into "the communicational world" by representation (mapping) them (correctly or distortedly) in the communication system that comprises and drives that world.

In this way, mapping can function in "magical" ways. This provides the basis for the "word magic" and the languaging "wizardry" that we can do with ourselves and others. This creates the unique psycho-logics (Korzybski) that govern our experiences.[7]

The Magic of Linguistic Bracketing
What's fascinating about these ideas is how messages and messages-about-messages structurally operate in mathematical relationships to each other. When I first read Bateson's comment that communication signals can operate as either pluses (+), minuses (-) or multiplication (X) or even division (÷) processes, I did not realize the power or usefulness within this. It wasn't until the *Meta-States* model awakened me to realize the powerful significance this could have for creating

transformations.

In describing how messages can interact with each other mathematically, Bateson wrote:

> "All messages and parts of messages are like phrases or segments of equations which a mathematician puts in brackets. Outside the brackets there may always be a qualifier or multiplier which will alter the whole tenor of the phrase." (p. 232)

That's powerful, is it not? *"A qualifier or multiplier ... will alter the whole tenor of the phrase."* To illustrate how the way we can sequence and bracket messages at different logical levels, imagine a little boy growing up experiencing some very unpleasant interactions with his dad. Figure 17:1 shows the overall formula of bracketing the messages. Read from the inside bracket outward.

Figure 17:1

$$\mathbf{M_6} \; (\; \mathbf{M_5} \quad [\; message_1 + message_2 + message_3 + message_4 \;)$$

In Figure 17:2, the inside messages (1 through 4) act upon by the meta-message 5 and then all of those messages by meta-message 6.

Figure 17:2

$$\mathbf{M_6} \; (\; \mathbf{M_5} \quad [\; message_1 + message_2 + message_3 + message_4 \;)$$

↓	↓	↓	↓
#1	#2	#3	#4
Painful experiences with dad	I'm not good at anything!	People are painful.	Life sucks!

↓

M_5: If you have a painful childhood it will plague you for the
rest of your life and determine your future

↓

M_6: These old messages all involve misbeliefs.
The best thing that you could pull off at that age,
but still only the thinking and
mental mapping of an eight-year-old.

Begin with messages #1 through #4—these occur at the first level of experience. These primary states operate linearly, indicating one experience after another. Here the boy experiences each of them as *additions* of pain, each one *adding* to the previous pain. Message after message (each existing as a primary state of distress and negative emotions) also adds to the overall content message from the original experience. Addictively each one increases the boy's mental-emotional pain. So in the first bracket of the first four messages, the structure is that of "addition"—the adding of one state to another.

However, message number #5 is a meta-message and functions in a completely different way from the addition of #1–4. As a message-about-the other messages, it provides communication and representation of a another painful message, yet it does this at a meta-level. In this case, it does not merely add to the boy's personal misery, it *multiplies* that misery. *It multiplies the primary messages and states (#1–#4).*

So just as the first messages were messages of pain, message #5 is a message of pain, but a higher level pain. Structurally its syntax introduces a different kind of pain—one that amplifies the pain exponently. It amplifies and intensifies the lower-level messages by multiplying them.

In Message #6, the same process occurs yet another time; it is yet another meta-message. Yet its effect sends things in the opposite direction. Message #6 multiplies all of the lower messages. Yet instead of increasing pain, it has the effect of *negating* the personal distress. Structurally, its message about all of the messages at lower levels *reverses the sign* from - (minus) to + (plus). Then multiplying all of the lower states with the message that negates nullifies events and so effects a transformational reversal.

About messages within us, Bateson explains,
> "What exists today are only messages about the past which we call memories, and these messages can always be framed and modulated from moment to moment." (p. 233)

Here Bateson establishes an essential principle about meta-levels: *Meta-messages modify lower-level messages.* It does this because the higher message relates to, and frames the lower. What results from this may be positive or negative.

Meta-messages operate in a way similar to the procedural and introduction parts of a fax message. Such procedural messages index for the recipient meta-information about:
- Source
- Sender
- Recipient
- Date
- Time

All of these "messages" in the text communicate *about* the text and so modify the text. Or we may say that they frame the text. They create *the context of meaning* for the text. This can best be seen if you examine an unlabeled fax. When you receive a fax that has no framing, you certainly get a message with particular contents, but something is missing. You don't know who sent it, from where, who it is for, or why.

Meta-State Epistemological Change
All of this demonstrates how a higher level qualifier (a state, frame, concept, etc.) can alter the whole tenor of an experience. If all that exists of the "past" or the "future" or any other construct of meaning in the "messages" that we set and send within our mind-body system, then *changing the qualifiers creates epistemological change.*

The helping profession of psychotherapy involves a context of multi-level communications (Bateson, p. 224). We can say the same thing about consulting, coaching, problem-solving, and communication in general. Every time we meet and communicate with each other, we are exchanging messages of meaning on multi-levels. On the first level we exchange meanings about specific content and details. Above that, our exchanging of meanings occur via the theories that we operate from, the presuppositions of the language that we use, the assumptions of the cultures we live in, etc.

Figure 17:3

Message[6]

These old messages all involve misbeliefs. The best thing that you could pull off at that age, but still only the thinking and mental mapping of an eight-year-old.

↓

Message[5]

If you have a painful childhood it will plague you for the rest of your life and determine your future

↓

Messages[#1-#4]

#1	#2	#3	#4
Painful experiences with dad	I'm not good at anything	People are painful.	Life sucks!

Figure 17:4

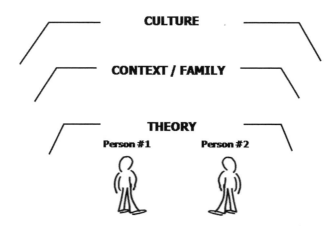

Summary

- There is an epistemology within us about how we know what we know—an epistemology made out of our levels of the meanings and messages that we create, send, and receive.

- Taking these messages, which are at different logical levels, into account and noting how messages at higher levels affect the lower messages gives us a way to more systematically deal with the complexity of our meanings and experiences.

- The multiple levels of Meta-States gives us *an explanatory model* regarding the "magic" we can perform using meta-levels in our communications. It enables us to mindfully create generative and transformative change.

- This model of epistemological change enables us to do all kinds of "magical" things: we can *negate* old messages that create pain, *divide* old childhood pains in half and then half again, *multiply* into our representational equations new resources, *subtract* hurtful and irrational beliefs that serve no useful function.

- *There's magic in the higher levels.* With this analysis of the structure of magic shows how words can work magically at various levels. With Meta-States we bring into play logical levels, self-reflexive thinking, and the syntax of meta-levels on lower levels.

• *Our meta-states creates our personal and individual epistemology setting up the psycho-logics of how we know what we know.* In this way, the Meta-States model enables us to classify or categorize lower levels as we apply our concepts to our primary states.

End Notes:

1. I have been and continue to be absolutely amazed and impressed by Bateson, for more about Bateson's contribution to NLP and Neuro-Semantics, see *The Bateson Report* (2002), *NLP Going Meta* (2001) the entire seventh chapter is on Bateson and his logical levels of learning.

2. You can find a fuller description of these levels of learning and change in *Coaching Change, Meta-Coaching, Volume I.*

3. See *The Structure of Personality: Ordering and Disordering Personality* (2001). This also fits the theory of Self-Actualization Psychology that "neurosis" is a deficiency problem. The problem is not that there's something wrong with people; the problem lies in our mapping, our frames.

4. The Meta-Dimensions was a new development in Neuro-Semantics in 2007. See chapter 20 for a description of these dimensions.

5. Recognizing that all of our internal thinking and emoting is *framing* initiates the higher level awareness that makes for *frame game mastery* in Neuro-Semantics (see Appendix C: Winning the Inner Game).

6. Bateson also used other such phrases as: "the realm of magic," "the magical realm of communication" (1976, p. 231).

7. In *Mind-Lines: Lines for Changing Minds* (2005) I played with the word "magic" to create the "magic box" that describes the magical way our words and language can change our sense of reality.

Chapter 18

META-STATING

AS FRAMING

How to Win Your Inner Games

"To say anything significant,
one simply has to rise above that level,
and the higher above it one can rise
the more significant one's remarks become—
provided the steps taken in rising, so to speak,
are taken in an orderly fashion
and can be readily traced back to the level of factual data."
Wendell Johnson
(*People in Quandaries*, p. 114)

Throughout these pages I often treat *meta-stating* as synonymous with *framing*. I hope you notice that. If so, have you wondered how they are synonymous? Since our focus has been on modeling consciousness in how it reflects back onto itself, we have been exploring reflexivity, logical levels, and meaning-making. So how is all of this related to, or connected to, framing?

This chapter is devoted to the idea of *framing*—what that means and how it fits into the Meta-States model. The questions addressed here are these:

- How does meta-stating and framing refer to the same process?
- How does a meta-state differ from a meta-program?

• How can we use the meta-stating process to set new frames and transform our outer games?

• What are some of the best *frame games* to play?

Framing Meta-Programs
Meta-Programs as Solidified Meta-States
If we start with a state of mind or emotion as a primary state, *how* we think or feel in reference to something, describes our thinking pattern. And it is this thinking pattern that gives birth to the next higher state of mind.

To illustrate, here are three parenting scenarios. In each, notice how the speaker invites a child to a particular way of viewing things:

• Look at that forest . . . it has so many trees. That's a National Forest. Look at the immensity of it— it stretches on for a hundred miles in that direction. [*visual, global*]

• Do you hear what I'm saying? This fits precisely with what I told you earlier would happen. [*auditory, matching, future time*]

• You need to stop treating people that way. It will only come back to make things a lot worse. Do you understand or do I have to spank you again? [*away from*]

The implicit thinking patterns in these examples are indicated by the *italicized* words that follow in the brackets. The content of the information reflects what the speaker is processing, yet simultaneously *at a higher level of computation and data processing,* the speaker is using a particular style or pattern of thinking. Consequently, those receiving these statements are invited to experience and learn something else. Above and beyond the content, there is an implied frame about how to structure consciousness as an interpretative schema.

In the first one, the person is being invited (frame by implication) to learn to focus on the visual aspects of the environment and to do so by taking it all in at a single glance generally in a global way. The second person is learning a different focus and emphasis—on matching the things that she is hearing with what has already been said and to project them into the future.   The implication for the person in the third scenario is to structure his awareness in terms of moving *away from* the consequences as his behavior.

Let's now fast forward our movie of these individuals twenty years and as we do, let's suppose that these children have received this kind of training repeatedly thousands of times during the intervening years. If they had received an abundance of these kinds of experiences, what would they have most likely created?

*   What effects will that have on the way they will come to perceive and think as adults?
*   What would be the probability that they will structure their consciousness with those formats as their meta-programs?

If we repeatedly access a certain state of mind and emotion (whether a global or specific state, whether a matching or mismatching state, whether a visual or auditory state) and then *reflexively use that state on more occasions, on more things, on ourselves, on our other states— eventually it will solidify into a meta-program.*

This describes how a *state* becomes *a meta-state* and then a *meta-program.* It will then become your typical and standardized way of mentally perceptually filtering the world that you see and live in. These "programs" for how to think will then operate at a meta-level as your *attentional filters* and so govern how you input, output, and process information.

In NLP, *meta-programs* refer to your mental filters by which you develop our processing style. How many meta-programs are there? In the book, *Figuring Out People: Reading People Using Meta-Programs* (1997 / 2006) I set out 60 meta-programs. Common ones include:

Optimistic/ Pessimistic	Self/ Other attention
Global/ Specific	Sensing/ Intuiting
Match/ Mismatch	Options/ Procedures
Toward/ Away From	Internal/ External authority
Perceiving / Judging	Stepping in/ Stepping Out

In *Figuring Out People,* Bob Bodenhamer and I designated some meta-programs as *driver* meta-programs. These are the meta-programs that *drive* perceiving in an emotionally intense way in multiple contexts. So strong and intense are these meta-programs that they both empower a person with a way of looking at things and limit from seeing the world from the opposite of that program. If you meta-state them with belief and value, then your belief in them, value of their significance, and repetition makes them your only lens. Of course, this intense perceptual experience then evokes within you filters that correspond to your emotional states and meta-states.

Driver meta-programs typically create your best personality strengths. In them we find the skills and abilities that you excel at. And ironically, within your driver meta-programs are also your weaknesses, limitations, and sometimes your character flaws. The solution is not to change your meta-program, but to expand it so that you have full range of consciousness and perception with it.[1]

What is a meta-program? A meta-programs is a cognitive-emotional program for perceiving, noticing, and orienting yourself in life. These structured ways of thinking and perceiving describe the mental-emotional patterns that you use for processing information, emotionally responding, and choosing as you interact with people and things. A meta-program is your lens for seeing.

Where do they come from? Well, first and foremost, they arise as your generalizations as you navigate reality. For example, the *away-from* meta-programs arise from a primary state of avoidance. Whereas the *judger* or *perceiver* meta-programs arise from a corresponding primary state of judgment/evaluation (judger) or from a merely witnessing with accepting way of perceiving (perceiver).

What starts out at the primary level as a way of thinking and feeling eventually moves to a meta-level and operates there as *a program for mentally structuring perceptions*. What explains this? *Reflexivity.* As you turn your ways of thinking and emoting on yourself, and apply them to more and more contexts, this process gives birth to your meta-programs.

Suppose you *judge* yourself for operating from a *judger* filter. You thereby create and induce yourself into a meta-state of judgment about your concept of self, about your experience of judging, and about any other state that you might bring it against—your anger, fear, joy, sexuality, etc. What will this give rise to? Probably the mental-emotional connotations of self-condemnation, and non-self-acceptance. Do this long enough and you'll also make the judger meta-program a driver.

No wonder your reflexivity requires careful handling. Meta-programs set frames—frames for how you think and perceive. And meta-states about those meta-programs can turn these against you as hurtful experiences. By it you can build programs that you may later regret. Of course, by it you can also completely reframe things, even outframe ourselves to transform your experiences for a more enhancing way to live. The bottom line is that when you meta-state yourself with your primarily level experiences of thinking, you establish frames for perceiving, sorting, attending—meta-programs.

Framing Higher Designer States
Korzybski initiated the vision of engineering human experiences. And no wonder, he was an engineer. He talked about designing and redesigning the very structure of experiences. To that end he created neuro-linguistic models: the levels of abstraction, the structural differential, his theory of multi-ordinality, etc.

The *Meta-States* model facilitates this kind of designing or engineering more directly to create new states, higher states, and experiences of excellence as we work with our self-reflexive consciousness.

What enables this is understanding the structure of our meta-levels. This is what enables us to engineer various kinds of layered states of consciousness. Because meta-states incorporate Korzybskian levels of abstracting, self-reflective consciousness, and analysis of the meta-levels of mind, we can create higher level *executive states* as self-organizing frames.

It is the systemic complexity of your recursiveness that enables you to build executive states as high intentional frames. Now you can establish these higher levels of mind as *self-organizing attractors*—a neuro-linguistic energy field that will *self-organize* our mental, emotional, and neurological powers. Setting up a self-organizing dynamic on this order enables your higher executive mind to run the show so you don't need to micromanage the process. The frame will run the show. The frame will govern what you see, how you respond to things, and what you are inwardly organized to experience.

So in terms of design, pick your magic. You can set meta-level states so that you can, with precision, determine the interface effect of one state upon another state. In this way you can engineer structures that will intensify a state, reduce a state, negate it, distort it, interrupt, confuse, create paradox, create psychological distance for a sense of safety, etc.

This will also facilitate your frames awareness. It encourages you to quality control your meta-states. And then, the sky is the limit. Within your higher states of mind, you have a tremendous range of choices and options for formatting resources and orientations.

Meta-States in Action
If a friend approaches you and says, "I feel really bad." Respond by asking, "About what?" This will enable you to discover if the person is operating from of a primary state or a meta-state. Test it.

> "I feel bad about getting so embarrassed the other night. I can't believe I got so embarrassed and upset just because I got caught off-guard at the surprised party the other night."

Figure 18:1

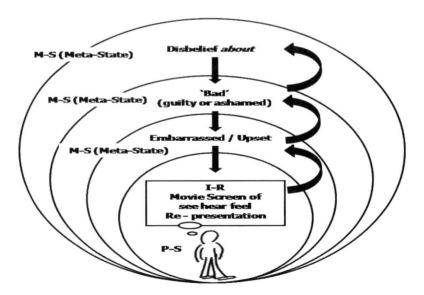

Do you immediately recognized your friend's primary state? He feels surprised having been caught off guard at the surprise party. Did you also recognize his meta-state? Did you also immediately hear that *above* the primary state, he felt embarrassed by getting caught off-guard and then he felt "bad" about feeling embarrassed and upset? Your friend jumped a two logical levels, accessing a yet higher level of disbelief about the experience. Whatever it meant to him, his frame generated "feeling bad." Quite a complex experience comprised of many layers of consciousness about consciousness in just a short sentence!

How can you facilitate your own, or another's, meta-awareness of this layered structure of subjectivity and catch what you do to yourself as you jump logical levels? One way is by asking good meta-questions. By meta-questioning you can flush out the reflexive vertical thinking by which you move up logical levels to set your frames. To do this, first pace the reality, "So your friends really surprised you and caught you off guard!"

Then make the meta-level distinction. "And after you did that, what did you think-and-feel *about* those first feelings?"
    "Yes, I felt so embarrassed and kind of upset."

Since validation and pacing are so important, be sure to do that abundantly,
        "How fascinating. Your first thoughts-and-emotions as you respond to that event, to the surprise party, was that you reflected back onto yourself and responded to your sense of surprise in a negative way. Is that right?"

Reflecting back precisely what a person says enables him to hear himself and to become aware of what he said. It's as if he gets to see himself in a mirror. He gets straight feedback. Doing this also facilitates the development of a *meta-witnessing state* from which he can become aware of his states without judgment. Other meta-questions further assist him in becoming more objective about his states.
        "How intense did you find your embarrassment thought-feelings *about* your surprise? How pleasant?"

For the person to answer these questions, he has to step back again and access a witnessing space.

> "Then, to your embarrassment you accessed another state—which sounded like a judgment state which you called 'bad.'"
> Answer: "Well, yes I felt ashamed of myself."

You can then ask an ecology question for quality controlling the experience. Doing this will invite him to access a more thoughtful and reflective meta-state.

> "So how useful did you find it to entertain such thoughts-feelings of shame and badness about your embarrassment about your surprise?"

As this questioning recognizes the difference between primary states and meta-states, it enables a person to recognize the differences between the referent and his responses. This discerns external stimuli in the world and some abstraction involving other thoughts, feelings, awareness, etc. Primary states involve primary emotions (e.g., mad, glad, sad, and fear) that are directed to the world, others, events, actions, tasks, etc. Primary states cope with the world and reflect thinking-emoting responses to the world.

Meta-states take you into the internal world where your self-reflexive conscious creates mental maps about yourself. A great many meta-states refer to what Gregory Bateson called "the biggest nominalization of them all" —I or your "self." Your identity and sense of self usually involves multiple layers of consciousness which are then turned into static nominalizations. This creates all kinds of self-states: self-contempt, self-acceptance, self-rejection, self-nurturing, self-as-masculine, self-as-feminine, self-as-worker, self-as-role, self-as-having-moral-nature, etc.

Meta-States Framing via Meta-Questioning
A meta-question is a question that elicits or reveals a higher level meta-states. Earlier I mentioned the meta-question of Virginia Satir which captured the attention of Bandler and Grinder, but which they didn't understand or know how to understand (chapter 15). I'm referring to Virginia's therapeutic conversation between a father and his daughter. First, she separated out the father's intent in his yelling behavior from his behavior of yelling.

"Do you yell at everyone like that? You don't yell at the paper boy?"

Her question here distinguishes contexts as to when and where the father yells which implies that he has control over his yelling. Then she set a higher level frame by simply asking another meta-question. With this question she took the behavior and classified it as a primary state detail and then put it into a new category.

"Are you trying to tell her that you care about what she does? Is that what this anger is about?"

What a magical move! In this maneuver she offered a new frame. By identifying and reframing yelling in this way she put it into the class of *"caring messages."* Virginia then asked yet another meta-question to presupposed, and thereby create, yet another higher state of mind:

"Well, how do you feel about knowing that now?" (*Frogs Into Princes*, p. 171)

This meta-question elicited in the father a new state—a meta-state of evaluation about the invented category that Virginia suggested as a new frame. To respond to that question he had to step back from his state with all of his neurology of yelling and try on the new frame-of-reference *about* yelling at his daughter—and view it as a caring message.

Virginia's meta-questions invited him to set a whole new frame. In this way she graciously prescribed a new meaning—a meta-state of loving concern about his relationship with his daughter. It invited him to go meta to *"know that"* loving message *"now"* (a hypnotic embedding of a command) and then develop the next higher meta-state of evaluation *about* that knowing.

Richard and John recognized that this sentence worked. They acknowledged that, but they also said they didn't understand how it worked.

"That's a weird sentence; it doesn't actually have any meaning. But it works." (p. 171)

"It doesn't mean anything"!? Really? Well, without understanding how reflexivity of consciousness works to set new states-*about*-states and higher frames of reference for meaning, I would have concluded the same. But using the structure of the Meta-States model we can now recognize what that sentence meant and how it worked at higher levels to create new neuro-semantic frames.

Designing Executive Levels for New Inner Games
Let's apply this to something very practical like the effective management of anger.

Suppose the next time that you get angry about something, you take a deep breath and relax your body and breathe in *a state of calm relaxation* to increasingly allow yourself to think and feel completely relaxed about your anger. Do that and you'll experience *calm* anger. Then suppose, from that calm relaxation about your anger, you adopt a *loving appreciation of yourself* and your ability to appropriately relax yourself and use your emotive power of anger to discover whatever has violated your values.

Figure 18:2

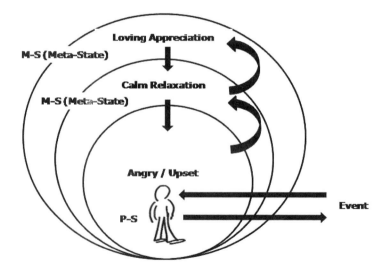

Meta-stating yourself in this way radically and wonderfully *modulates* your primary state of anger—changing it, altering it, and making it something more than you would experience it without the larger level frames surrounding and encapsulating it. When you set higher frames like these for your experience, *you texture your primary state with these resources.*

This applies the meta-level power of "magic" that Bateson described and how that "meta-messages always modify lower-level messages." Meta-states inevitably modify lower states in a variety of ways: intensifying, reducing, negating, interrupting, confusing, paradoxing, dissociating, entrancing, solidifying, loosening, etc.

The Inner Game of Mindfulness
As you learn to recognize and identify the structure of meta-states, you develop a new and higher level of awareness. You recognize and account for the workings of your self-reflexive consciousness. When this happens, you are then able to make meta moves and develop an expanded awareness of the higher levels which operate as your governing frames.

Being consciously mindful of your meta-states then awakens you to the structure and meta-levels meanings that govern your executive states. This is the "red pill" that awakens you to your matrix of frames and truly opens up the realm of choice for you.[2]

While NLP assumed this process from the beginning, it did so without making it central. The confusion comes from the misinformation that *going meta* means being "dissociated." Yet it does not. The problem here is twofold: first the nominalization and second the term dissociation.

While the term "dissociation" gives the impression that we are dealing with *a thing,* we are not. There is no such thing as "dissociation." The relative verbs, "associating" and "dissociating" always involve some set of relationships.

> It means that every time we *associate into* one state of awareness of feeling *we dissociate or step out from* another and every time we *dissociate or step out of* one state, we *step into* another.

These processes always work together. Every "dissociation" involves an "association;" every "association" involves a "dissociation." So we ask two things:

- What idea, feeling, awareness, perception, etc. are you stepping *into*?
- What idea, feeling, awareness, perception, etc. are you stepping *out of*?

To fail to do this invites confusion and misperception. Whenever we *go meta* into a higher level of thought and emotions, we step out of a lower level. This may involve *less* emotion, yet it may also involve *more*. It all depends. Yet it always involves *some* emotion. There is no such thing as being totally and absolutely without emotion. *To be embodied is to have somatic experiences.* We may feel numb, disoriented, unsure, confused, unable to speak the emotion, etc. But we always have an emotion. Mr. Spock and Data of *Star Trek* may offer interesting phenomena of supposed non-emotional beings. Yet even they are not without emotion.

When you make a *meta-move,* your awareness and mindfulness expands. It often gives you more expansive emotions about things. Many of the emotions at meta-levels are more cerebral involving as they do, the evaluations that you make: self-esteem, proactivity, inner peace, etc.

Yet many meta-level feelings are more emotional and somatic: *joyful* curiousity, *celebrative* commitment, *fearful* anger, *guilty* fear, etc. The emotions that we experience at the second perceptual position (empathy, understanding of another, sympathy, concern), third perceptual position (expanded clarity, disinterested objectivity, neutrality, etc.) and at the fourth position (e.g., appreciation of systemic functions, good will for an entire community, family, or group, etc.), extends your mindfulness.

Moving upward into the higher levels of your meta-mind empowers you to structure your mind with a broader and wiser perspective. This move to the higher levels facilitates more ecology, balance, integrity, integration, etc.

Framing an Inner Game of Clarity and Precision
When you can step back and obtain a broader perspective, you can also begin to sort out things that confuse you—things you have fused together in your mind which need to be separated. Getting enough

distance frequently allows the insight and detachment necessary for de-confusion. You can then distinguish the different levels in a layered piece of consciousness and become aware of the syntax of your experience.

Korzybski described this structure by introducing a new linguistic distinction, *multi-ordinal*. Multi-ordinality describes a linguistic pattern from General Semantics which Bandler and Grinder did not bring over to the Meta-Model. That's why I incorporated it into the Meta-Model in *Communication Magic* (2001). In essence, a multi-ordinal term is one that can be applied to itself.

The artful vagueness of *multi-ordinal words* results in terms having broad and general meanings. Because these terms can be applied to many levels of abstraction, we have to use the speaker's context of the word to determine the meaning. The meaning of a given term therefore varies from context to context, and from mental context to mental context, or level to level.

Here's how Korzybski (1933/1994) explained multi-ordinality:
> "The main characteristic of these terms consists of the fact that on different levels or orders of abstractions they may have different meanings, with the result that they have no general meaning; for their meanings are determined solely by the given context . . . " (p. 14)
> "If we reflect upon our languages, we find that at best they must be considered only as maps. A word is not the object it represents; and languages exhibit also this peculiar self-reflexiveness, that we can analyze languages by linguistic means. This self-reflexiveness of languages introduces serious complexities, which *can only be solved by the theory of multi-ordinality . . .* The disregard of these complexities is tragically disastrous in daily life and science." (p. 58, italics added)

For example, consider the nominalization that we use for primary state of unspecified fear—anxiety. Think about a specific anxiety toward a specific trigger, for example, not knowing where your young child is at nine o'clock at night. Within the word, "anxiety" we summarize a great many thoughts and feelings of our experience.

But what happens when you become *anxious* about that *anxiety*? Now you have anxiety^2 *about* anxiety^1. And this layered state refers to an entirely different experience. You no longer focus your anxiety on the child, now your focus is also on your state of anxiety. What if you worry that your anxiety will activate another problem? The term "anxiety" now means something very different.

So with fear^2 of fear^1, enjoyment^2 of enjoyment^1, etc. Each level introduces new complications. Yet as we pull apart the different logical levels that the terms jump, we gain a clearer understanding of the structure and construction of the meta-level experience referred to by these words. These interfaces generates new gestalts.

   Worrying about worrying → hyper-worry
   Thinking about our thinking → meta-thinking
   Hate self for feeling imperfect → self-contempt
   Philosophizing about our philosophy → theory of philosophy
   Reasoning about our reasoning → epistemology
   Satisfied about contrition for error → happiness, growth
   Impressed with my ignorance of reality → awe
   Statements about statements → meta-statements
   Frustrated/angry with being a people-pleaser → self-anger

The quality and nature of self-reflexiveness leads to this kind of multiplicity in abstracting and evaluating, and when that leads to a multiplicity in experiencing, you experience a great many thoughts and feelings about many things. What do you feel? What do you think? No wonder your consciousness is so complex, layered, systemic! It is recursive and "infinite."

These multi-ordinal words which involve multiple meanings change with each change of context. In "normal" language it is challenging enough to determine meanings since words in themselves do not mean anything. Meanings come from the person who creates the meaning and who use words to convey meaning. That's why we have to ask, "What do *you* mean when *you* use that word?"

On the primary level, we can't even know what sensory-based words mean without identifying the context. This is true with a vengeance when we consider nominalizations that are reflexive and can be used at different levels: "science," "knowledge," "love," "hate," etc.

How can you test for multi-ordinality? The test for a multi-ordinal term involves checking to see whether you can *apply the term to itself*. Is the term self-reflexive? Check on the multi-ordinality of the word love:

> Do you love someone?
> Do you love loving them?
> Do you love loving love?

Prejudice:

> Do you have a prejudice?
> What about a prejudice against prejudice?

Facts:

> What facts can we learn about facts?

Inferences:

> What inferences can we make about inferences?

Assumptions:

> What can we assume about assumptions?

Questions:

> How can we question our questions?

When you use a nominalization as a multi-ordinal word in reference to a state, then each time you use the word at every meta-level, you introduce different meanings about the word.

> Love^2 about love^1 is not the same as love.
> "I hate you" represents a very different use (and reference) of "hate" from "I would hate hating you."

This wild and wonderful ability to react^2 to your reactions^1 and then to react^3 to those reactions^2 describes how meta-reactions begin to loop around on themselves.

Vicious Self-Reinforcing Cycles

Because *the frames* that you set about your thinking, emoting, ideas, concepts, responses, etc. establish a self-organizing and governing executive level, *your frames enhance or limit you*. They facilitate personal mastery or a helpless victimization. Frames keep your mapping of reality open, flexible, and sensitive to feedback; or closed, rigid, inflexible, and not open to feedback. The first programs a reality oriented, scientific, and ongoing development. The second programs you for getting stuck in loops without any exit. Which *game* do you play? Which *game* would you like to play?

Sometimes you experience a problem that involves an "attempted solution" which doesn't work, but which you cannot stop from continuing. This is a great description of being stuck in an un-sane operation. Sometimes what you initiated originally as *an attempted solution* becomes a loop without an exit and so continues to operate inside of some limiting belief framework. The belief that holds the attempted solution in place may be, "I know that it once worked." Or it may be, "I believe it *should* work, even though it does not." So, instead of recognizing that it does not achieving its outcome, and trying other choices, options, and experimenting, you get involved in attempting "more of the same" solution. The result is that you amplify the problem so that the more of the attempted solution, the worse the problem becomes. This generates a vicious self-reinforcing cycle.

Insomnia is a great example of this. When you discover that you are not falling asleep, you then *try* to sleep. Yet the more you *try to fall asleep*, the more awake you become. So you try really hard to fall asleep because you have to get your sleep and you'll be a mess tomorrow if you don't.

Figure 18:3

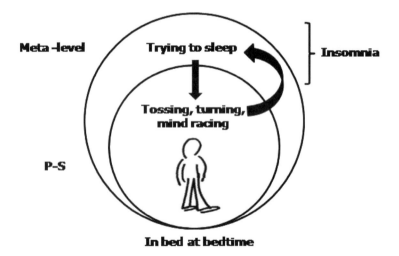

Here the repeated application of a wrong or unsuccessful solution and the meta-level frame that "it should work" locks the difficulty into a self-reinforcing pattern. In many non-productive and harmful meta-states, we are inside of a feedback loop that goes nowhere useful. The first step in interrupting this is to become aware of these dynamics.

This dynamic occurs in the meta-states of self-contempt, self-disgust, self-rejection, etc. The person first experiences some primary state that they find unpleasant, distasteful, painful (e.g., criticism, rejection, failure to accomplish an objective, anger, fear, dread). They then do a most natural thing—they bring a negative emotion or judgment against themselves. They criticize, reject, get angry, fearful, disgusted, etc. with themselves. Of course, this makes things a whole lot worse for themselves. When they experience this negative emotion about their first negative emotional state, they then access another negative emotional state *about* that.

> I feel disgusted *about* getting so angry *about* feeling so helpless to change that situation.
>
> I feel so guilty *for* feeling so upset *about* feeling so rejected by her.

And so they loop round and round. And as a vicious cycle that goes nowhere, it is a dragon state.

Distinguishing "Logic" at Different Levels

As a multi-ordinal term, we can expect the nominalization "logic" to function and operate in different ways at different levels. As a result, primary-state logic that might work "out there" in the world on something will frequently not work when we apply it to various meta-levels. What seems "logical" as a treatment at one level may make things worse at another.

In the context of dating, when John feels "rejected" because Jan says "No!" to an invitation to go out with him—that may be an accurate and useful negative emotion. It could provide direct information about Jan's desires. If John can stay resourceful, he may explore the reasons for the "No!" and use such for self-improvement and/or understanding the kind of person who would say yes to him. Even "upsetness" about "the rejection" would serve a useful function. But consider feeling "upset" at one's self. This expresses a psycho-logic quite different and quite unuseful. And how much more so the logic of feeling "guilty" for feeling upset?

In the context of feeling depressed, meta-level thinking can change the very "logic" of the primary state. This occurs when we try to cheer up a depressed person by attempting to get her to see the positive side of life. The more we try to cheer her up, the more we facilitate an increase in the depression. Why does this happen? How could the person hear a caring and helpful message by feeling worse?

It happens due to the meta-position she takes to the incoming "helpful" communication. "Brenda, you just need to look on the positive side of your life—to the things that you have going for you." About that communication, Brenda thinks, "They really don't understand me at all; nobody does. This is worse than I thought!" When she applies *that* to the communication, the very action meant to bring some alleviation of his then pain, she aggravates it.

Figure 18:4

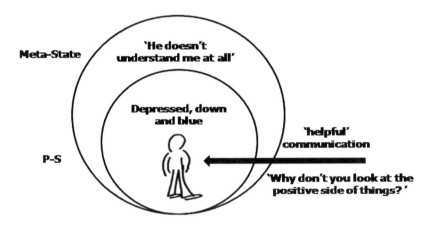

On the primary level, the message makes sense and seems logical. "Why don't you try to look on the positive side of things?" Yet at a meta-level it evokes a negative response, "You really don't understand." That higher thinking will then set a frame that will aggravate the down-feelings even more. "I don't have anyone to turn to. I can't do anything." Then that message is used as another reason to feel bad. If Brenda *discounted* at the primary level, then *discounts* at a meta-level, this could easily begin to spin-out of control.

The solution is to notice when a "cure" makes something worse. Notice it and then outframe it. Meta-states that involve a belief or certainty about your mental maps about a situation or a solution can especially get you into a spinning out-of-control process. Believing in your beliefs generates the gestalt of dogmatic fanaticism, thereby preventing you from "trying something different." The reason for this is because you have fallen into a feedback loop of "believing in your beliefs."

Figure 18:5

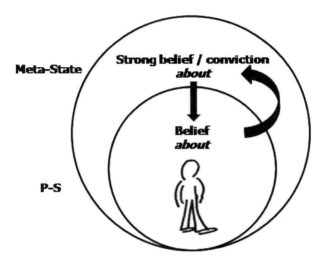

Consider a teenager in a primary state of feeling uncooperative and rebellious to some particular context. When the parents then "solve" the teen's problems with some "advice," a few rules, or a military order, the teen does not hear a solution at the primary state level. He hears and interprets the words as a relationship message at a meta-level. His thoughts and feelings about the "advice," "rules," and "orders" might be, "Why are they speaking down to me? They don't trust me! They think I'm just a child. I can't stand this!" The logic of the primary state level message not only fails to get through, it is completely altered so that the teenager experiences it as an insult.

The chronicity of a primary state interactions which go nowhere occur because people are *not* processing the messages at the primary state, but at meta-levels. They are meta-reacting to each other's messages, feeling more and more misunderstood. Until they get together on the same level, they will not be able to "hear" each other accurately, let alone figure out a win/win solution.

Figure 18:6

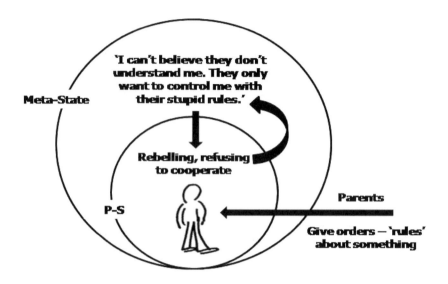

How do we get on the same level—on the same page? The first step is to recognize the levels of your states and at which level you're communicating. "What meanings do you give to my advice? What do you believe about my suggestions?" Only by meta-questioning can you bring some order to your internal syntax of states, meanings, interpretations, emotions, etc. and figures out how the person created his or her psycho-logics. It makes sense to the other person due to the frames used. It always does. So what are those frames?

When you do not clearly differentiate between these levels, *you confuse levels*. You then end up imposing or projecting your inner world onto the outer world. Then you lose the ability to differentiate the constructs that govern your semantic world from the external world that you are attempting to navigate. You end up making the mistake of "the fallacy of misplaced concreteness" (Alfred Whitehead). You assume and equate what you inwardly perceive at meta-levels with what exists "out there." At the next level you confuse your primary and meta-states.

How do you stop the persistence of this meta-muddle? First with awareness of what's occurring. Become mindful that you are operating from a meta-state belief that keeps you persisting in a behavior. It may be an old motto like, "If at first you don't succeed, try, try again!" That idea could keep you persisting at something even if it fails to bring any positive reinforcement. This linguistic construct could cause you to perpetuate a non-functioning attempted solution that never had a chance in the first place.

You can also stop the feedback loop by using *a pattern interrupt*. By interrupting the vicious-cycle, you can prevent the pattern from continuing.

You could also turn the state back onto itself. When you do this you create paradoxical interventions as you prescribe the very symptoms of the problem. For the meta-state of stuttering, for example, we invite the person to intentionally practice non-fluency. The frame by implication is that the stutterer fully accepts the non-fluency and becomes playful with it. when the person does this, he experiences and practices the primary state of acceptance of non-fluency and this prevents stuttering.

Summary

- *In meta-stating you set frames.* You set frames that become your meta-programs, belief systems, motivational structures, your purpose and destiny, etc.

- The meta-state frames that you set establish various *frame games* in your mind as the rules of the games that organizes personality, structures emotions, and sets up self-reinforcing loops.

- Via meta-stating, you are able to design engineer new gestalts, states, structures, and experiences. In this way you can work much more methodically and systematically with your powers of self-reflexivity.

- In all of this, meta-stating advances NLP by integrating insights from General Semantics about the engineering of human excellence. It does this by providing a way to use Korzybski's Theory of Multi-Ordinality to create some virtuous loops.

End Notes:

1. *Figuring Out People,* see Chapter 11 "Changing Meta-Programs," where you will find 7 patterns for expanding a meta-program. This theme of *expanding* meta-programs is also at the heart of self-actualization and one of the key processes for unleashing untapped potentials.

2. In *The Matrix Model* I extensively play with the metaphor of taking the red pill. On the website there are articles of the three Matrix movies.

> "Wake Up, Neo! The Matrix Has You"
> "Do You Need Your Matrix Reloaded?"
> "Matrix Revolutions"
> "Coaches of the Matrix"

Chapter 19

META-STATE

PRINCIPLES — INTERFACES

Designing States for Fun and Profit

"Self-Reflexiveness is not a new idea,
but its explicit, systematic use in therapy and education has just begun."
Kenneth Johnson

There's a wonderful thing about knowing and modeling how something works, knowing the mechanisms that govern its operations, and the principles. *When you know how it works, you can use the model to do things.* You can then create, design, and innovate in that associated domain. With a model to guide your understanding and acting, you can not only fix broken things, tune up things that already work, and model new things that you discover, but you can also actually create and invent completely new things.

This brings me to one of the central values of the Meta-States model. You now have all of the elements to create *designer states* for the experiences you desire that will enrich your world. You can now move to a higher level by specifying the executive states and frames of mind that you want to construct.

To facilitate this I will here make explicit the principles of meta-levels. Then I will introduce 16 of the key interfaces of one state with another so that you can then check the construction of these state-upon-state interfaces. This will enable you to quality control your meta-states. And with that, the design work can begin.

Taking Charge

Prior to learning how to run your own brain, you typically experience your subjective experiences in a passive and chaotic way. States of joy, anger, happiness, passion, stress, fear, aversion, etc. seem to just happen to you. You experience them as thoughts and emotions that come upon you "out of the blue," and seemingly "without rhyme or reason." You experience them as if they operate apart from your choices and your constructions of meaning (your framing).

The journey toward state management begins from the decision to take charge of the contents in your mind. So you increase your awareness of the inner processes of perceiving, coding, attributing meaning, framing, etc. Then you discover how to elicit, access, and anchor the leanings that drive these states. Eventually you discover something truly magical,

> *"It's my brain! I'm doing it. I am the one creating my internal world of sights, sounds, and sensations and all of the higher level frames!"*

This exciting insight then ushers you into the experience of setting your frames, managing the content and form of the information in your brain, and reflexively noting the results you get. This puts you in the designer's chair. Design engineering your own experiences begins as you notice the signals you use to cue your brain with various signals, and begin to experiment with your use of symbols to generate your very best internal mapping.

Meta-State Principles

With the Meta-States model there are some basic principles that you can use to govern the way you create designer states. These principles summarize the key secrets for personal mastery in building up meta-states for new resourceful experiences.

1) *The person is never the problem; the frame is always the problem.*
When you find a "problem" in yourself or another, a problem that prevents a person from being successful, congruent, healthy, or sane, the problem is never the person. The problem is always the frame. And every person is more than his or her frames. The frames are simply the ways the person has learned to think and feel. Yet the frames are the determining factor for the meanings that the person creates and attributes to the facts of life.

2) *Frames are created by meta-stating thoughts and feelings.*
You create your mental and emotional frames of reference as you both absorb the ideas, thoughts, understandings, beliefs, etc. of those around you and invent new ones through your own conclusions and generalizations. You think by using references—references that you encode by representations, language, concepts, etc. As you apply a reference to your thoughts (a meta-stating process) you set frames. After that your reflexivity enables you to set multiple levels of frames. Then, as you frame, so you become.

3) *Change occurs through detecting and changing the frame.*
The frames of meaning that govern your life are the structured information in your mind that work as your interpretative style and framework. These frames are usually outside-of-consciousness and so operate without your awareness. Detecting these puts you at a choice point for choosing the frame that will be most useful, productive, and effective.

4) *Higher logical levels of frames drive, modulate, organize, and control lower levels.*
The layering of frames creates a "logical level" system in your mind body and in this system, the higher levels govern the lower levels. And the highest frames of intentionality, decision, and identity operate as "attractors" in a self-organizing system as we use these processes to set a direction and focus. By meta-stating you set a higher "logical level" which establishes the frame that dominates the lower levels. The interface between higher and lower levels then generates a whole list of interfacing effects (which we'll explore indepth in the next section).

5) *Someone or something always set the frame.*

Given that frames, as human constructs, dominate human perception, meaning, and experience, then someone sets the frame. But who? Who sets, or is setting, the frame? Sometimes the frame occurs by osmosis as you simply breathe it in by living in cultural, linguistic, familial, professional, etc. frames. Living within any environment for long enough will blind you to the context and frames of that environment. On a humorous note, Marshal McLuhen said he didn't know who first discovered water, but he was sure it wasn't the fish.

Meta-level frames are mostly unconscious. Above your normal conscious awareness is your mental atmosphere which you can imagine as a canopy of consciousness that you live in. Meta-states are unconscious frames that mostly operate outside your awareness as your assumptive world. So what are you assuming?

6) *Whoever sets the frame governs the experience.*

Because higher frames govern mind-body experiences, and because somebody sets them, the person who sets the frame will exert the greatest influence. From those frames will come the resulting thoughts, ideas, concepts, beliefs, emotions, behaviors, language, problems, solutions, and experiences. Frames rule due to the self-organizing nature of interactive systems.

7) *Meta-levels holistically operate as a holoarchy.*

The mind-body system works systemically to evoke gestalts of the neuro-linguistics processes. The system that emerges from the meta-levels governing the lower levels will bring about an overall gestalt (or configuration of interactive parts) which, in turn, will define the character of the whole. So the whole emerges from the parts and the whole gestalt in turn determines the parts.

As *holons*, a single meta-state or frame is a whole that's also a part of a greater whole. Your holon states make up the holoarchy of your mind. These wholes which are at the same time parts of a larger whole makes up your embedded states-within-states, the holoarchy of your mind-body system is what we call "personality."

8) *Meta-levels can always be outframed.*

There is a process by which you can step aside from any given frame or state and quality control it. That is the process of identifying frames. Identifying your frames enables you to adjust a frame or to set a whole new frame. This out-framing process can transform everything. This can create meta-level "magic" because with it you can install a new self-organizing attractor in your semantic system of holon states. The frames used in outframing will then operate as an executive level frame. That is, it will set the bias for your mind-body system—your values, standards, and criteria. This is the mathematizing of your inner psycho-logics (chapter 17).

9) Levels of experience need to be distinguished.
All "experience" is not the same. What we call an experience, say "love," "fun," "fear," etc. can differ radically and significantly at each level. In his "levels of abstraction" Korzybski described how the nervous system abstracts at different levels. He called the different experiences as "second-order abstractions," "third-order abstractions," etc. When you use of a same word at the different levels for an experience, that term is a *multi-ordinal term*—this means it only has a general meaning until you specify the level at which you are using the term (chapter 18).

Your "love" of an object or person at the primary level differs from your "love of love" (infatuation) at the second level, and even more from your "love of anger," and "love of loving love" at the third level (romanticism).

10) Reflexivity endows consciousness with systemic processes.
Reflexivity drives your levels of abstracting and your meta-level experiences. Reflexivity describes your special kind of consciousness that reflects back onto itself and its products (e.g., thoughts, emotions, beliefs, values, decisions, specific concepts). As this creates your unique form of consciousness, it sets feed-back and feed-forward processes in motion thereby creating a dynamic circular system. No wonder your mind goes round and round in circles and spirals upward and downward.

11) Misused meta-states create meta-muddles that diminish people.
The general principle is that when you reflexively bring *negative* thought-and-feeling states *against yourself,* or against your thoughts and feelings, you put yourself at odds with yourself. In this way you

create inner conflicts and incongruency. And when you disturb your relationships to yourself in this way, typically you will begin to loop around in vicious downward self-reinforcing cycles. Then as you become increasingly self-disturbed (e.g., self-condemning, self-contempting, self-repressing, self-hating, etc.), your disturbances will disturb your relationships with others. In this, meta-level disorientations and conflicts create living hells. In the end, this will create all sorts of meta-muddles: neurosis, psychosis, personality disorders, character disorders, etc.

12) Meta-solutions are often paradoxical and counter-intuitive.

The solutions at meta-levels that create health, integration, balance, transformation, sanity, empowerment, etc. often seem counter-intuitive. The way to rid yourself of unwanted thoughts, emotions, behaviors, habits, etc. often involves seeming paradoxes. It involves welcoming, accepting, appreciating, and celebrating that very thoughts, emotions, and behaviors that you want to rid yourself of. Welcoming these facets of your responses into consciousness changes your meta-frame. Now you can take counsel of it, reality check it, learn from it, texture it, or apply a wide range of responses to it. The opposite, *not* reckoning with it leads to unuseful suppression, repression, self-rejection, etc.

13) Energy and repetition is required to set a frame.

How do you set a frame or establish a new meta-level state? Merely "thinking" and even "feeling" will not do it. You can think, know, feel, and experience lots of things without that, in itself, establishing a higher level frame.

To set a fully integrated frame within requires that you apply sufficient emotional energy to the meta-relationship between two levels. The formulas for creating a meta-relationship involve one of the following. If X refers to the first state and Y the second state, then do any of the following:
* Apply X to Y
* Bring X to bear upon Y
* Embed Y within X

You can set up this meta-relationship by using drama, repetition, emotional intensification, metaphors, stories, rituals, etc. Any of these processes can link the two states setting one state in a meta-relationship to the other.

14) Identity is a function of frames.

Ultimately all of your frames influence your sense of self, and how you define your identity. Yet those that mostly transform, enrich, and expand your identity are your highest meta-states of intention and self-definition. That's why sometimes to change what you *do* in a pervasive and generative way requires that you change who you *are*. Does your higher frame of self-definition support your desired change? If your behavior is a printout of your operating programs, what new operating programs do you need to set? Who do you need to be and become to do this?

15) Meta-States naturally coalesce to embody the higher ideas.

Meta-levels never stay higher or meta in a heady or intellectual way for long. They are forever coalescing into primary experiences to be experienced as a holistic state. While you can conceptually move up to a higher level and layer your mind with additional thoughts and feelings, normally your mind-body system is designed to integrate those higher levels. So, they will not stay there for long. With repetition, habituation will bring the higher levels and qualities down into the flesh and you will embody the meta-information in your muscles, eyes, breath, posture, face, countenance, etc. This process turns meta-states into meta-programs.

In Neuro-Semantics we explicitly use this process in the Mind-to-Muscle pattern to integrate what we *know* at the highest levels of our mind so that they are incorporated in our *body*. This mind-to-muscle process is an integral part of meta-stating.[1]

16) The sequencing of meta-levels is critical for quality control.

The sequencing of meta-levels makes all the difference in the world for designing experiences and modeling. In structuring the higher levels of consciousness, the order and sequencing (syntax) of how you layer one level of thought-and-feeling upon another critically determines your experience. The syntax of how you meta-state yourself determines the quality of your states. This plays a significant role in the wide range of interface possibilities and in the texturing of your states (chapter 12).

17) The quality of your states is the quality of your meta-states.
The quality of your states is textured by the higher levels that govern them. Because the higher levels inevitably coalesce or percolate down into the lower levels, they set the frames that qualify and texture your states. Flush this out by asking, "What's the *quality* of this state? What's the quality of my anger, my fear, my confidence, my joy, etc.? Does it have the quality and richness that I want? How else do I want to quality this state?"

Meta-Stating Interfaces
One of the principles governing the use of meta-states concerns the phenomenon of meta-state interfaces. Yet merely knowing that the syntax of one state upon another state is critical is not enough. The next step is to have become skillfully competent in working with the order and syntax of meta-states. What kinds of things happen in the meta-stating process? What kind of responses and consequences can you create by using various meta-stating patterns? As you engage in designing your highest states, consider the possible interface effects of the state-upon-state structure that you create. There are many such effects.

1) Reduce painfully intense states.
Some meta-states will reduce the primary state. When you meta-state the state of feeling upset and distressed with relaxation, the state of relaxed upsetness reduces the pain. Examples: ruthlessly meek; insincere arrogance; boldly shy; calmness about anger, doubting doubt, witnessing shame; cautiously and curiously stupid; contentedly enthusiastic.

2) Intensify states.
The effect of the structure of some meta-states amplify the primary state. Examples: worrying about worry, loving the state of learning, feeling anxious about anxiety (hyper-anxiety), loving the state of being in love, feeling calm about calmness, feeling passionate about learning, appreciating the experience of appreciation; persistent self-doubt; honestly honest, ruthlessly honest; shamefully stupid; exuberant joy; irritable impatience; cheerfully romantic; jealously loving.

3) Qualifies experiences.
Because higher levels inevitably affect and govern lower level

experiences, the higher frames qualify and textures the states embedded within it. Examples: joyful learning—> *joy* qualifies and textures the learning; respectful anger—> respect textures anger making it thoughtful; calmly fierce, fierce attention, happy anxiety, tenaciously persistent; playfully serious or seriously playful; joyful embarrassment; grim determination; and honorable humility.

4) *Solidify states and frames.*
Many things can create a strengthening and solidification interface. If you bring confirmation, belief, conviction, valuing, importance, etc. to a belief frame or a state, you will solidify the belief or state. This will make the belief or state stronger. Solidifying a state makes it more stable and enduring. Examples: pride in your belief about your ability to learn; feeling confident about your self-efficacy; proud of your pessimism; optimistically pessimistic, tenaciously audacious; determined joy, committed playfulness; proud confidence.

5) *Loosen states and frames.*
The converse interface of state upon state can loosen and weaken frames, to deframe them, and to cause a state or experience to become unstable. Apply questions, doubt, suspicion, wonder, etc. to a state or frame, and you will loosen or weaken the experience. This can clear the space for change and transformation as it releases the interfering frames and meta-states. Examples: doubting a belief; questioning a conviction; unsure confidence; skeptical belief, worrisome fear that you might be wrong. Do you absolutely and always believe that without a shadow of a doubt? Deliciously terrified: How delicious is your terror?

6) *Exaggerate and distort states.*
If you amplify a state with another strong and intense state, the intensity factor will sometimes create an exaggerated state. This is especially true when you apply a negative state of thinking and feeling to any primary state. *Doing that essentially turns your psychic energies against yourself.* Examples: vengeful anger; loving hatred; fearful fear, hesitating to hesitate (talking non-fluently which creates stuttering); sadness about sadness (depression); mistrust of mistrust; gleefully depressed; congruently insincere; happily insanity; bitterly playful; self-loathing fascination; a bitter readiness to be disappointed; vicious compassion; chronic arrogance about a refusal to release sorrow.

7) Negate a state.

Sometimes when one state interfaces with another it negates or blows out the first state. When you doubt your doubt this typically leads to feeling more sure. When you resist your resistance, you may become cooperative. When you procrastinate about your procrastination, you may take action because you put off the putting off. Other examples: mistrust of mistrust; ashamed of shame; fervently ambivalent; joyful grief; trivial significance; significant triviality; forgetting a realization; wisely stupid; nervously confident; awesome complaining.

8) Interrupt states.

As you have undoubtedly already noticed with some of the previous examples, some interfacing so jars and shifts the first state that it totally interrupts your state. It arrests your current psycho-logical meanings about things. Examples: feeling humorous about being serious; feeling anxious about calmness; feeling calm about anxiety; intentionally panicking; outrageously timid; awe-filled indifference; bewildered certainty.

9) Create confusion.

By getting various thoughts-feelings to collide and "fuse" "with" each other in ways that you do not comprehend will typically induce a state of confusion. When you create a layered state that doesn't make sense and which you have difficulty even processing, you create a state of disorientation. Examples: seriously ridiculous; altruistically selfish; remembering amnesia.

10) Create paradox.

A paradox is a seeming contradiction. It does not make sense or is logical when you view the ideas or components of the paradox on the same level. "Paradox" is created by confusing levels and the paradox vanishes when you separate levels and sort out the seeming contradiction. Bateson (1972) said *paradox* is a contradiction in conclusions that you correctly argue from consistent premises.

In therapy, shifting an experience to a higher level or a different level is offered at the heart of the powerful technique of "paradoxical intention." Watzlawick (1984) explains the confusion of the territory level with the map level:

"Kant recognized that every error of this kind [map/territory confusion error] consists in our taking the way we determine, divide, or deduce concepts for qualities of the things in and of themselves." (p. 215)

Examples of paradox: the "Be spontaneous now" paradox of deliberate spontaneity; try really hard to relax; the title of the book, *"This Book Needs No Title."* (Raymond M. Smallya, 1980); resolutely deciding to never say never.

"Never and always are two words one should always remember never to use."

"I'm absolutely certain that nothing is absolutely certain."

Other examples: cheerful impotence; impeccable sloppiness; euphorically fearful; intentionally panicking; flexibly stubborn; deliberately enjoying the shame and embarrassment of dysfluency or stuttering.

11) *Create dissociation.*

Sometimes in meta-stating we create a state interface of "dissociation" so that we step out of a primary state into what we call a "dissociative" state. If we dissociate dramatically enough, it may result in amnesia as happens when we switch states so rapidly that we lose our reference point and so experience amnesia or other trance phenomena. Examples: distancing from pain; calmly observing an anxiety; witnessing a remembered trauma; amnesia about a resentment.

12) *Initiate a new process.*

Some interfaces initiates the first step of a new experience and allow a new emergent experience to arise. You may not feel capable of accessing the courage to take a certain risk, but suppose you just begin by being willing to feel courage about developing courage? Examples: playfully exploring an uncertainty; learning about how to really learn; gently and respectfully angry; willing to become willing; fabulous shyness; boldly shy with a touch of audacity that pushes just to the edge of embarrassment.

13) *Grab and focus attention for new choices.*

Some interfacing will provoke awareness of new and/or different choices. Some interfaces can arrest attention, overload consciousness, stimulate new thinking, and get you to question axioms, beliefs, reasoning, memory, etc. All of this facilitates the ability to deframe. Examples: feeling calm and relaxed about anger; feeling appreciative about your anger; feeling lovingly gentle about anger; resisting your resistance; absolutely curious about your fearful apprehension of ruthless honesty.

14) *Induce trance and trance phenomena.*
Most people experience third-order and higher levels of abstracting as "trancy." In meta-stating you "go inside," and sometimes you will do so to such an extent that you develop the "inward focus" of trance as you engage, consciously and unconsciously, in an internal search for meaning. Meta-stating is "trance" especially when you shift logical types and sets up double-binds.

> "And now I want you to rebel against thinking about just how comfortable you can feel if you don't close your eyes before you're ready to relax deeper than you ever have before, now . . . I wonder if you're going to fail to succeed at not going into a resourceful trance at exactly your own speed or whether you won't."

15) *Create gestalt states.*
States-about-states frequently generate gestalt experiences so that something new emerges from the process—something that cannot be explained as merely a summation of the parts. Instead new systemic and non-additivity qualities emerge that make the expression something more than "the sum of the parts." Examples: suppressing excitement —> anxiety (Fritz Perls); worrying about what something means—> existential concern; passion about one's responsibility—> courage (see the next section on courage, seeing opportunities, and forgiveness).

16) *Creates humor.*
At times meta-stating interfacing will jolt and jar you so much that it will result in an explosion of humor and you will laugh or giggle. Plato said that humor occurs when you suddenly discover that something is "out of place in time and space without danger." In humor, a conceptual contrast tickles your fancy, delights your consciousness, surprises, amazes, shocks, etc. Examples: meekly sadistic; a momentary experience of chronic arrogance; a sad triumph; deliciously lustful.

To conclude this section about the interfaces, here's some meta-state structures just for your enjoyment:

Perversely refuse to feel happy
Wildly moderate
Ruthless compassion (Graham Richardson)
Gently stern
A voice of velvet steel

Designing Courage as a Rich and Robust Meta-State

To illustrate using these principles and interfaces in meta-stating, let's apply them to the state of courage. What would it take for you to experience the state of courage in response to a situation that holds potentials for reward and danger? What resources would you have to apply to a primary state of fear so that out of that mix, *courage* would emerge for you?

In terms of designing your own meta-state of courage, use these questions. Realizing that there is no one right way to do this, playful experiment with all kinds of possibilities. Try out various mental and emotional resources, as well as behavioral, gestural, and tonal resources? Like a white-coated scientist in a lab, playfully toss in various ingredients and see what concoctions you can invent.

Courage is much more than the sum of the parts. It arises as an emergent property from the "chemical" interactions of various neuro-linguistic states. Think of this as what happens when you combine two poisonous chemicals of sodium and chloride. Suddenly you have table salt! It is out of the combination that something more than the sum of the parts arises.

What's needed to design your customized state of courage? If the primary fear that limits you is that of making a presentation at work about a product or service that you believe could become a big money maker. Suppose you add a big bold vision as the frame you apply to that specific fear. Would that be enough to empower you to courageously face that fear anyway? If so, there you have it. If not, then what else? Suppose you applied the idea, "There's no failure, only feedback."

As you set an experimental frame so that you can play around with various interfaces, you'll be able to do this in a spirit of playfulness. As you access and elicit *playful experimenting* to your presentation, what gestalt state emerges for you? Perhaps you need to set that frame for the others as well.

> "Here's a wild and crazy idea. I don't know if it will lead anywhere in terms of product design, but then again it might just be a real money maker. I'll toss it out and we can massage it for awhile to see what happens."

Sometimes, for some people, applying a state of apathy to the fear blows out the timidity (apathetic fear), and then allows one to apply, "Hell, do it anyway."

> "It just doesn't matter what others think about this idea, what really matters is finding my own voice and sharing my own ideas, and giving success a chance. So, regardless of the responses of others, I'm just going to go for it. I'll use this to learn, grow, and develop even better ideas."

The gestalt of courage starts on the ground level with a fearful and apprehensive state. You then apply that state to ideas, thoughts, feelings, understandings, beliefs, and so on to outframe it.

In terms of gestural and tonal resources, simply ask questions about a wide range of gestures and voice tones. Who do you know in real life or in the movies who has a voice of courage? Think of something that would take courage to say and utter it with the tonality of courage. Refine that voice as a voice coach would. Make it richer, fuller, more rhythmic, louder, quieter, etc.

Designing *the Seeing Opportunities* Meta-State
Entrepreneurs and those who are wealth creators have a gestalt state that drives their passion. If they know anything, they know that opportunities are not seen with the eye, but with the mind. An opportunity, like beauty, self-esteem, wonder, and all other nominalizations, occurs in the meta-mind and the meta-eye of the beholder. That's why a person can live in an environment full of opportunities and never see them, never hear them knocking on the door, and walk away feeling despondent because of their conclusion, "There are no opportunities here."

Entrepreneurs, business people, artists, etc. typically find and make opportunities while all around them others are singing the blues and bemoaning that they never get a break. So we begin with the primary state of everyday life. What governs these experiences? What higher states of mind and emotion do you need to access and apply to *see* and create "opportunities" in the context of everyday life?

Perhaps you might begin by applying thoughts and feelings of *possibility* to your state? If not, do that. "What's possible in this situation? What problems are calling out for a solution? What value needs to be added here?"

Suppose you apply some wild and crazy "what if" questions to the situation. Suppose you meta-state the feeling that "there's an untapped gold mine in every experience." What other resource would you like to access and apply so that the seeing opportunities gestalt emerges?

Designing a Meta-State of Forgiveness
We typically feel deeply hurt when someone mistreats us by betraying a confidence or violating a trust. Suppose we meta-state these wounds with a forgiving spirit. If we decide to keep our heart sweet rather than bitter, gracious rather than resentful, how would we go about eliciting this resourceful response and evoke the gestalt state of forgiveness? Forgiveness supports resilience by freeing us from old hurts, from living in the past, and from defining ourselves as a victim of someone else's bad mood.

The state of forgiveness involves a layered complexity of states so that a kinesthetic anchor will seldom, if ever, work. Because forgiveness is not a primary state, it doesn't function as a simply stimulus —> response process. It's much more complex than that. You will have to orchestrate numerous pieces of awareness and embed numerous layers of semantic understanding, believing, valuing, and deciding.
When someone violates your values or relationship, typically you will link that person with the hurt and conclude that the person is "bad," "horrible," and/or "evil." This, however, puts you in a double-bind. How can you be moral *and* forgive? Would you not be accepting, tolerating, and validating *evil*? If identifying a person-with-his-behavior creates this problem, making it difficult if not impossible to forgive, then what's required is to surgically separate this connection.

As long as you identify someone as being *evil,* you have no choice. You have to hate that person. Mentally attributing evil to someone imprisons you in that frame to the negative thoughts and feelings of anger, hate, disgust, aggression, rage, revenge, bitterness, etc. Talk about a prison to be locked up in! No wonder it is impossible to release the person! The problem is in the psycho-logics of that reasoning: because the person produced the hurtful behavior, that behavior defines that person. From there it is a short step to: "He *is* his behavior." This sabotages forgiveness and locks you into a negative state of hatred and rage. By contrast, forgiveness rages against the evil *behavior* while showing compassion to the *person.*

Only after you separate person and behavior can you set another frame. Only then can you look for and validate the positive intentions behind the hurtful behavior. Forgiveness emerges when you look for positive intentions. "What positive value was this person trying to achieve or create?" Most hurts and violations arise from unresourceful states, poor coping skills, or the misuse of some strength.

Forgiving involves mentally slicing away the wrong from the person who did it. This disengages the *person* from his or her hurtful *act.* And it empowers you to recreate that person in your mind. Prior to doing this, you see the person as, "The one who did me wrong; the evil one." The next moment, you change his or her identity in your mind. You remake the person in your memory.

Now you can apply your anger to the hurtful behavior and fully rage against it. This frees you to properly express your anger and to use your anger to set a boundary between acceptable and unacceptable behavior. After all, some behaviors are totally unacceptable. The problem with anger is, as Aristotle noted, knowing *how* to express anger at the right target in the right way to the right degree for the right purpose at the right time. Now you can.

For forgiveness to emerge, *apply your anger against the wrong* and fully register it as a violation. This will energize you empowering you to now do something constructive about it. After you do that, then you can release it.

Summary

* When you meta-state, you engage in the art of creating designer states for yourself and others—for fun and profit, for exploration and enjoyment, for growth and self-actualization.

* So as the interior decorator of your inner life, you can now design your inner space using the meta-level principles to guide and govern your creativity in state designing.

* Now you can use your reflexive consciousness to engineer new experiences and states and set them as your highest frames. You can layer rich and enhancing thoughts and feelings upon these states to facilitate new emergent properties to arise.

* Similarly, as you recognize the many different kinds of interfaces that can arise from state-*upon*-state arrangements you will be able to playfully experiment with what will work to your highest and best.

End Notes:

1. The focus on embodying what we know in our mind is a central focus in Neuro-Semantics. To explore this area including the Mind-to-Muscle pattern, see *Achieving Peak Performance* (2007, spiral format).

Chapter 20

META-DIMENSIONS

When I began exploring meta-states and meta-levels, I began with the four levels in Robert Dilts model (i.e., beliefs, values, identity, spiritual)[1] and within a very short time, I identified 15 or more levels. Given that these levels were already there, that part was easy. The problem at that point was trying to figure out a way to communicate the multiple distinctions of the levels and *how they relate to each other*. That was harder as noted in the last chapter.

Later, with the *Mind-Lines model,* I took the 14 patterns of NLP (the sleight of mouth patterns) and expanded them to 26 and then using the Meta-States model, I set them up as meta-levels for outframing in persuasive communciation. At the time, I thought that was pretty exhaustive. Later I discovered that while it might have been exhaustive of my mind at that moment in time, it was actually just the beginning of discoveries![2]

Later with the development of Meta-Coaching, I put the meta-level distinctions into the form of *meta-questions* and expanded it to 26. Then I found a couple more, then so did Denis Bridoux. We were then up to 30, a couple months later there were 38. As you will see later, there are now over 100 meta-level distinctions.[3] And that definitely goes beyond the $7^{+/-2}$ distinctions that we can normally handle at a time.

What's a person to do? These questions initiated a new search.

"If I collected and categorized all of the meta-levels and sort them out into a new classification form, what form would that take? How are the levels related? What is the relationship between the scores and scores of words and terms that refer to various meta-phenomena? Are there any layer level classifications, domains, or dimensions above the specific levels?"

This exploration got me interested in mapping out *the dimensions of the mind's meta-levels*. While I had been doing this for years implicitly, I had not done it explicitly. The time had now come to do that.

Metaphors of Meta
First, I revisited the metaphors that we already use in modeling the meta-levels of the mind. What are the metaphors that describe *meta-level phenomena*? Dilts used a *hierarchy* as a metaphor, but I felt that was far too static, staid, and un-dynamic and un-systemic to describe the system interactive nature of the meta-levels. I first used the *height* metaphor of reflexivity and to reflexively applying back to oneself one layer upon another layer of thoughts-and-feelings. That led to the frame games metaphor of *frames embedded in frames* and a framework of personality. Yet this also still involved mostly static images.

Next came the *diamond* metaphor. Here playing off of the idea that each meta-level was but another *facet* of the same subjective experience only with a different view, the image of the *diamond of consciousness* provided a more three-dimensional and dynamic approach. With the *matrix metaphor*, an even more energetic, dynamic, and systemic feel was brought to the meta-levels. That helped considerably. We can now draw pictures and diagrams of an emerging, evolving system.

Within all of the Neuro-Semantic metaphors is the *spiraling and circling metaphor* of a eddy of water or *tornado* that moves both upward with more of the same and then downward. This allows the system dynamics of feed back and feed forward loops to be portrayed with much more clarity. It also allows an image of the ongoing evolution of the system with each layering. In the development of some of the Self-Actualization models the *onion metaphor* has emerged. This enables us to convey that the layering is made out of the same living stuff at each level and that by unpeeling an onion of meaning we can get to the core of things — the original thoughts-and-feelings that created the reflexive system of meaning.

With these metaphors, we had been getting closer to understanding the landscape of our meta-levels. The multiple metaphors enable us to think and talk about the world of reflexively layering thoughts-and-feelings to build up a matrix of our meaning frames and giving us multiple perspectives or facets for entering the system and getting to the heart of things.

Since discovering the reflexivity process within the basic Meta-States model, it has been clear that there's no hierarchy to the meta-levels. Instead it is a holoarchy. *A holoarchy* is a dynamic structure of wholes in parts in such a way that every whole is part of a yet higher and larger whole. As a whole, it is embedded within layers of wholes. This explains why the question, "Which is the highest level?" is a pseudo and irrational question.

When it comes to the meta-levels, no level is higher than another level. [This is in spite of the language, "levels."] That's because we can reflexively always step back and outframe whatever we have experienced with yet another. Do you think *identity* is higher than *belief*. If so, can you have a *belief* about your *identity*? Can you *value* your *spirit*? Your self-reflexive consciousness prevents one level from being higher than another level. It does this because you can always reflect back on any level with another. This is the infinite regress of your self-reflexive conscious. You can always meta-state any level with any other level.

Dimensions of Meta-Levels
So while no one single level is higher than another, what about the existence of different *dimensions* of meta-phenomena? Could there be areas of meta-levels by which we can describe the landscape of various dimensions within the landscape of meta?

Suppose there are some basic *dimensions* that can help with mapping out the meta territory. What would be the difference between a level or a dimension?

>A *level* is any thought or feeling, any distinction that you can layer upon other thoughts and feelings. That creates another *level.* And we have identified 100 of these "levels." Sometimes we call them "logical levels" and sometimes we refer to them as our psycho-logics, that is, our psycho-logical levels.

>A *dimension,* on the other hand, describes not just levels, but many levels. It is an area of levels wherein the meta-levels within operate at a certain stage of development. So within the area there will be a whole set of new distinctions with new dynamics and processes. So while there's no hierarchy to the levels, they are totally fluid, there is a hierarchy of dimensions, i.e., developmental stages.

The hierarchical nature of the *meta-dimensions* arises from the cognitive or mental development we all go through. Piaget, the first pioneer in Developmental Psychology, mapped the *stages* of cognitive development from representational constancy, to concrete thinking, pre-formal operations, formal operations, etc. Erickson pioneered the psycho-social stages and Fowler the faith or moral stages.

Regarding terminology, I have chosen to call these *Meta-Dimensions* rather than *Meta-Domains* although my first preference would be the term "domain." The problem is that I have used the phrase *meta-domain* for some ten years to refer to some of the areas of study in NLP. When I entered the field, there were two meta-domains: the Meta-Model of Language in Therapy and Meta-Programs. I introduced Meta-States to the field in 1994 as the third meta-domain. Later I discovered that sub-modalities were not *lower* or *sub* at all, but itself another meta-domain. That gives us four "meta-domains" in the field of NLP.

The *dimensions* for navigating the landscape of the meta-levels are the following:
- Representation dimension
- Meta-State dimension
- Gestalt dimension
- Conceptual dimension

How do these domains relate to the meta-dimensions? In what follows you will see that the Meta-Model and the Meta-Modalities of the cinematic features (the sub-modalities) fit into the Representational dimension, Meta-Programs into the Gestalt dimension, Meta-States in the Meta-States dimension and the Conceptual dimension.[4]

I: The Representational Dimension

We begin with the area of representational reality because before the meta processes occur, the structure and content of consciousness consist simply of representations. We bring in the outside world that we detect through our senses and sense receptors (eyes, ears, nose, mouth, skin, inner ear, etc.). And even before awareness or words, various parts of our cortex are processing the data from the world. Our visual cortex, auditory cortex, motor cortex, etc. actively work as our cognitive unconscious gives us our first access to external reality which are expressed as our neurological maps. As we become conscious of the content of sights, sounds, and sensations in our "stream of consciousness" we have the experience of seeing, hearing, sensing, smelling, tasting, etc. a world on the inside of our mind. It is as if we have a screen on the theater of our mind and can *present to ourselves again* (re-presentation) what we have seen and heard before. (see *MovieMind*, 2002).

Regarding this domain of mind, psychologists had long been trying to bring some order to it. But it was the genius of NLP that named the internal representations as the "languages of the mind" and put them together as a communication model. Bateson noted this is his Preface to *The Structure of Magic* (1975) complimenting Bandler and Grinder on this breakthrough. They found something to be the basis of consciousness—something that could lead to practical processes for running one's own brain and managing consciousness and states of consciousness—the sensory senses.[5]

In the Representational Dimension you 'think" by using your representational systems to create snapshots and movies in your mind, and when you become elegant, you can put in a sound track with the tones, volumes, and other auditory qualities that facilitate your understanding. Then you can step in or out of the movie at choice depending on what you want to do with your inner movies. This dimension also includes the meta-representational system of language—linguistics, mathematics, and other abstract representations.

When you step back from your movies, you are able to notice the modes of thought (i.e., the modalities) that make up the movies as well as the meta-modality (i.e., the sub-modalities) distinctions in each system. This enables you to take charge of *editing* your movies. Here you are at a meta-level, the *editorial level* where you can choose how to encode the movie. So even the first level contains meta-processes. Yet because everything is focused on the Movie, the content of the Movie, and you are basically still mostly in reference to the Movie in terms of the outside world, you are mostly working with *the basic sensory and linguistic representation*s.

Relating this to the Matrix Model, the grounding matrix of State occurs in the Representational dimension. In the Mind-Lines Model, the framing, reframing, and deframing patterns occur here.[6]

II: The Meta-State Dimension

Even though self-reflexivity operates in the area of representations, when you shift your focus from the content of your thinking to your responding itself, you move fully into the Meta-State dimension. In this dimension you are more concerned about your thinking and feeling. If you feel fear about something "out there" in the world, now you might also feel *embarrassed* about your fear, *angry* at your fear, *guilty* for fearing, *proud* of the fear, *afraid* of your fear, or a hundred other responses.

Your consciousness at this first simple level of meta-stating is fluid as it is at the Representational Dimension. Thoughts, feelings, memories, and imaginations come and go like a "stream of consciousness" (William James' descriptive phrase). Here also, you experience a lot of emotion.

The Meta-State Dimension is the domain of accessing and applying other thoughts, feelings, and even physiology (physiological responses as in how you use your body, breath, move, gesture, etc.) to your previous thoughts. Structurally, this creates layers and layers of texture upon your primary states. Your *confidence* can now be textured with respect, humor, lightness, awareness of fallibility, contextual awareness, etc. Equally, it could be textured with superiority, demandingness, and irritation of others who are not as competent. The *texture* of your experiences reveals the embedded meta-states and speak about the quality and property of the state. *Calm anger* differs significantly from *intolerant anger*. *Thoughtful fear* is very different from *feared fear*.

In the Meta-State Dimension, when you bring thoughts-and-feelings of confirmation to other thoughts or feelings, you create *a first-level belief.* I discovered this structure of a "belief" more than a decade ago. A *belief,* is a dynamic meta-state, emerges by meta-stating thoughts with confirmation. Accessing the sense and feeling of a "confirmation"—that something *is,* that something is true, that that's the way the world is, that something is real—sets a frame over the thought so that you see it, perceive it, feel it, and respond to it as "real." Beliefs arise from the meta-stating of thoughts with confirmation.

As this process creates beliefs, you can now effectively distinguish *a thought* from *a belief.* As far as thoughts go, you can *think* all kinds of things. You can think, imagine, represent, and encode in multiple ways all kinds of things that you don't believe. By way of contrast, believing is more selective. That's because believing engages and commits you. When you believe something, you strongly *feel* that something is so. You feel *conviction* about it in your neurology.

First-level beliefs are much more dynamic and powerful than just thoughts. Thoughts certainly send *messages* to your body, but beliefs send *commands* to your nervous system. Such beliefs tremendously effect your health, well-being, and functioning. That's precisely why limiting and morbid beliefs are so damaging and interfering. Beliefs operate as self-organizing frames that can create self-fulfilling prophecies.[7]

In the Matrix Model, the central two process matrices of Meaning and Intention occur in the Meta-State Dimension. These matrices describe the levels of our meaning-making processes. In the Mind-Lines Model, all of the outframing patterns occur in this meta-dimension.

III: The Gestalt Dimension
While first-level beliefs are dynamic and emotional, they introduce a

new distinction about the meta-levels. The distinction is that in meta-stating *confirmation,* our thought becomes something more than just a higher level state, it becomes *a gestalt state.* The reason is that it operates as a *whole,* the confirmed-thought as a belief commanding and governing the nervous system. As you now hold this form of consciousness in mind, your consciousness becomes less fluid. As the belief further solidifies you experience it is more staid and solid. The "belief" *holds* the particular content in your mind as your "meaning."

In the Gestalt Dimension these very complex states, because they operate as a whole, now come to feel and function in a way similar to a primary state.[8] Gestalt states such as self-esteem, proactivity, responsibility, uninsultability, etc. operate as if a singular state, and not as layers upon layers of complex understandings. They have been gestalted, and because of that the variables coalesce together into a whole. Now "the sum of all the parts is greater than all those parts."

To gestalt several layers requires a certain elegance in the meta-stating. It requires the ability to hold constant the nugget of the experience while layering it with various qualities and doing so until it coalesces for the person and is felt as a *whole,* as one singular state. When that happens, *it becomes* not only a belief, but a *belief-system as a dynamic hologram.* So if you are meta-stating the experience of a "set-back in life" and wanting the meta-state of *resilience* to emerge from the process, you hold constant the set-back experience in order to ground resilience to the context. Then you layer ideas that grow into beliefs about acceptance of life, the openness to just witnessing, the self-efficacy of trusting yourself and your resources, the importance of actualizing your dreams and passions, the importance of persistence, etc.

Every gestalt state is made up of beliefs within belief systems. This means that a *belief system is a system of beliefs embedded inside of other beliefs so that there's a whole system of inter-connected beliefs supporting a single idea.* Realizing this led to the Opening Up a Belief System pattern in the Living Genius training. A belief system, represents a higher level of meta-stating, involves the creation of multiple gestalt states. And as such, it is a higher dimension of meta-levels than all of the first level of meta-levels.

The gestalting process that takes one or more variables and enables them to coalesce into a singular whole. *By this very process meta-states become meta-programs.* As perceptual filters, meta-programs are your conceptual, emotional, conative, and semantic *lens* for perceiving the world. The meta-programs you use for focusing your attention are the ones you *meta-stated* into existence.

IV: The Conceptual Dimension

Above and beyond the Gestalt Dimension is the area where beliefs and belief-systems describe things as "the way it is." So you experience them in a matter-of-fact and non-emotional way. Emotion becomes much less pronounced in the Gestalt Dimension and becomes almost entirely absent in the Conceptual Dimension. If beliefs grow up to become belief-systems, what do belief-systems grow up to become? They become Conceptual or Semantic systems.

Sometimes when I work with a person, I will ask about something important and then listen to how the person expresses a thought or a belief. After pacing the experience, I will comment, "So you believe that?" I do that to test the strength of conviction in the belief. I want to know the energy intensity of the belief. Typically, the person will say, "Yes, definitely!" But not always. Sometimes the person will say, "No. I don't believe it, I *know* it."

For the longest time I didn't know what to make of that. My first response was to counter,

> "Of course, it's a belief. Everything is a belief. It's beliefs all the way up. You are just not wanting to call it a belief because it feels more than a belief."

Eventually, however, I came to recognize that the phrase, *"I know it"* cues a level higher than just a belief and the loss of the belief emotions.

If a belief is a command to the nervous system, and a belief-system is a whole gestalt structure that commands even more neurology, governing emotions, skills, and perceptions, then when we graduate from a *belief* to a *concept*—we move up to a yet higher area where we experience our thoughts as *the very fabric of reality*— as the way it is, as unquestionable reality. You know you are getting to the highest levels of a person's mapping, or your own, because you hear more "end-of-the-map" kind of words and language: "It's *just* this." "It's *only* X." "There's nothing else." "That's it." At this level the person is engaging in identification—his or her maps *are* real to the person, and so the person feels absolutely sure and speaks as totally definite.

The Meta-Dimensions

Dimension		*Feature*	*Nature*
IV:	Concept	Concepts	Fabric of Reality
III:	Gestalt:	Belief System	Personality Structure

As I think about this now, I recognize that this has, in a way, been inside *the Meta-Yes pattern* for belief change all along, although not explicitly. We typically begin with the *emotional Yes,* and repeat that until it eventually settles down to the *matter-of-fact Yes.* We then encourage repetition until you get the neurological feeling in your body of, *"Of Course!"* And this *of-course* feeling is the strongest experience of all. "Of course, that's just the way it is." When you get to this place, your idea is not only believed, strongly believed, gestalted as a whole, *it is now part of the very fabric of reality in your mind-body system.* It now becomes your framework and assumptive reality.

What happens when you meet someone who says something at this level that conflicts with your fabric of reality? We're talking about something far above *a counter-belief.* We're talking above a gestalted meta-state like resilience or proactivity. We're talking about someone who says something against your *model of the world,* your *conceptual reality,* your *semantic understandings of life.*

At this level and in this dimension, disagreement is no longer expressed as direct disagreement. It is expressed as a smile of contempt and a laugh of nonsense. Suppose someone asserts that the human race evolved on Mars and migrated to Earth 100,000 years ago and that we are all actually Maritans? If someone said that to you with a straight face, how would you respond? Would you feel a strong urge to argue against it as a belief? Would you feel any compulsion to try to set the person straight? Wouldn't you rather just smile and perhaps inwardly laugh it off as ridiculous nonsense? You use *the laugh* of contempt to laugh off something that you consider so stupid and nonsensical that it is not even worth your time or trouble to fuss with.

Things at the Conceptual Dimension are mapped so much as "the way it is," and as what's real and unquestionable, that you don't have much emotion about it. *Instead, it just feels right and obvious and without question.* Get an idea to that level, to the area of Concepts, and it commands even more of your neurology.

I think this explains the Haitian voodoo deaths. Those who *believe* in the hexing of the dolls do so not only as a singular belief, but as a belief-system. It is not only a gestalted reality for them, it is at a higher dimension. It is their Model of the World, their Semantic Reality, their assumptive reality. Conceptually, it makes sense to them as just the way things are. So when they are cursed by a voodoo hex, there's just no question. Somewhere and somehow in their neurology, the message is sent as an inevitable command—"I've been cursed; I will die." And so they do. Non-believers do not. Heathens do not. Infidels do not. Only believers die—those who *know.* And when autopsies are conducted, the doctors cannot find any natural cause of death. So we call this the placebo effect—a self-fulfilling prophecy of a belief.

In the Meta-Programs model, the higher or semantic meta-programs are in the Conceptual Dimension. Here Self, Responsibility, Morality, Time, etc. are concepts that each of us develop and map. These concepts then guide us as we navigate our fabric of reality.[9]

In the Matrix Model, the five content matrices (self, power, others, time, and world) are in the Conceptual Dimension. We solidify and embody these content maps about specific concepts so that they then become so close to us. This explains why Emanual Kant and other philosophers assumed that they were *a priori,* prior to birth and built into consciousness. In the Mind-Lines Model, the Time framing patterns (preframing and post-framing) occur in the Conceptual Dimension.

Distinguishing the Dimensions

As you move from one meta-dimension to the next, there's development, richer complexity, and different mechanisms that operate in each.

At the Representational Dimension, you call forth sights and sounds for your internal Movie. Within the Movie there may be words. You may also have self-talk about the movie.

> "When I think about my job, I see the office building, then I start hearing my boss and some of the people I work with. It's like I'm there."

At the Meta-State Dimension, you assert things that may be difficult to see as a movie. Mental things now become more abstract. Language begins to predominate in the way you encode your beliefs.

> "I believe I'm a good person."
> "I believe in telling the truth."
> "I believe I can learn to become an excellent learner and a life-long learner."
> "I believe I can make a difference."

At the Gestalt Dimension, you create multiple beliefs and link them together into a supporting system. Here there can be layers upon layers of thoughts and feelings, states that have coalesced into a singular state or experience.

> "I believe I'm a resilient person who has the ego-strength to look at reality without falling apart and taping into my personal resources for coping and mastering, I believe I have the self-efficacy for bouncing back from any set-back."
> "I believe in being uninsultable in the face of criticism and rejection because it's not about me as a person, that's settled, I'm already a Somebody and unconditionally so and I'm open to feedback, nothing to fear in that."

At the Conceptual Dimension the energy and emotion of your beliefs fade into the background resulting in a more matter-of-fact feel as your sense of reality. Here you use your intellectual understandings to map reality and to orient yourself within what you have mapped.

> "I know the sun will rise tomorrow, that the planet dependably spins around the sun."
> "I know that I'm mortal and that I will die."

When you read the early NLP literature about beliefs and belief change, Bandler and Grinder made no distinction between these levels. For example, when Richard Bandler proposed changing beliefs with sub-modalities he used the following as an example of a belief, "Think of a strong belief like 'I believe the sun will rise tomorrow.'"

You can now see that that sentence is *not* an example of a strong belief. It is an *understanding*—it is conceptual knowledge. You *know* that, you don't believe it. After all, what would be the opposite if you didn't believe it? This is *knowledge content* about the everyday life on this planet, namely, the sun rises. It is not a belief about what you can, or cannot, do or what does, or does not, exist. So as an *understanding* or fact of *knowledge,* "I believe the sun will rise tomorrow" is an inadequate comparison. So using that to try to change a limiting or weak belief doesn't work merely using the coding devise of the cinematic features of representations.[10]

Summary

*   *Within the realm of meta, we have many, many, many levels.* We have a great many phenomena that are called by a great many terms: "logical levels" and psycho-logical levels.

*   We layer these *levels* one upon another as we think, feel, and live inside a neurology that feeds information in and energy out of our mind-body system. And because these levels describe human experience, this is what makes them so central to modeling expertise and facilitating self-actualization.

*   Via these levels, we combine, merge, and synergize all kinds of experiences, from our highest and best states to our lowest and worst states.

*   The *meta-questions* enable you to dance around the jewel of human experience. They expand your awareness of the many facets of diamond of consciousness.

*   Now we can recognize the *dimension* at which we're operating, we can detect clues indicating the different *dimensions,* develop elegant skill at working at each dimension of consciousness, discover how to move up the dimensional hierarchy, and develop our felt sense of where we are with a client and what to do next.

The Meta-Levels within the Meta-Dimensions

Dimension I: The Representational Dimension

The first dimension involves what you select to represent on the screen of your mind. You do this as you foreground some things and background others. You use your sensory representations to create your mental movie.

There are two meta-level categories in this dimension. The first meta-level above that is *the editorial level* where you develop your style of working with the cinematic features of your movies (Sub-Modalities).

The next meta-level within this dimension involves linguistically representing the movies, labeling, classifying, categorizing, and all of the things you do with words (the Meta-Model of Language).

Basic meta-level distinctions:
1. Foreground - background
2. Aware (awareness, cognizant)
3. Think, thought (notion, idea, word)
4. Feel, feeling
5. So? Yes? And?
6. Metaphor (story, poem, symbol)
7. Open up, emerges
8. Frame, framing
9. Meaning
10. See, sight, perceive
11. Hear

Dimension II: The Meta-Stating Dimension

In this dimension you layer thoughts-and-emotions upon your representations. Here you set frames, via the mental-and-emotional states that you apply to your primary states. Your first-level beliefs are here which are warm, emotional, and full of conviction.

General meta distinctions —
12. Step back, witness
13. Meta, higher level
14. Transcend
15. Impression

Mental meta distinctions —
16. Believe, belief, confirm
17. Valid, validate, approve

18. Value, count, honor
19. Appreciate, celebrate
20. Permit, permission, allow
21. Prohibit, prohibition, taboo, censor
22. Disapprove
23. Resist, refusal
24. Decide, decision, choice, will
25. Weighing Pros and cons, oscillate
26. Conclude, conclusion
27. Intend, intention, will, desires
28. Outcome, goal, agenda
29. Interest, fascination
30. Expect, expectation, anticipation
31. Consequences, imply
32. Differ, difference, comparison
33. Inspires, inspiration, moves
34. Ascribe, affix
35. Assess, assessment
36. Plan, game plan, strategy
37. Connect, connection
38. Remember, memory, historical referent
39. Imagine, imagination, fantasy
40. Speculate
41. Judge, judgment
42. To know within self, conscience: should, must, ought
43. Converse, conversation
44. Reconcile, reconciliation
45. Insight, contemplate
46. Merit
47. Refer, reference, referent

Linguistic meta distinctions:
48. Catalogue, classify, group, encompass
49. Possible: can, could, will
50. Feasible: might, could
51. Probable, probability, extent, degree: might, may
52. Rules, demand, should, authorize
53. Cause, causation
54. Define, definition, class, category, label
55. Rubricize, rubric

Dimension III: The Gestalt Dimension

In this dimension, beliefs become belief-systems. There's even less emotional affect left, if any at all. And the state has been gestalted so that it works as a whole — commanding much more of your neurology. Installing states at this level requires meta-stating elegance for holding the gestalt as a whole while grounding it.

56. Generalize, generalization, abstraction
57. Construct, computation
58. Symbolize, symbol, symbolic
59. Realize, realization
60. Theme, thematic
61. Reason, rationale, explain
62. Extrapolate
63. Reckon, recognize
64. Reputation
65. Identity, identify, self
66. Myth, archetype

Dimension IV: The Conceptual Dimension
In this dimension, the emotional quality drops out of the meta-states entirely. Here you experience your conceptual states as the sense of, *"Of course"* which represents a sense of reality as what you assume and expect. It's just "the way it is." With no emotion left, the experience seems purely "intellectual." Here you "know" what you know. Meta-states at this level are called concepts, principles, knowledge, reasons, models, paradigms, and definitions.

67. Know, knowledge, epistemology
68. Abstract, abstraction
69. Principle
70. Conceive, concept
71. Presuppose, presupposition, assumption
72. Hypothesize, hypothesis, proposal, premise
73. Mathematize, mathematics, equate, calculus, calculation
74. Understand, understanding, comprehend, comprehension
75. Paradigm, model, map, schema, schematize
76. Cultivate, culture

End Notes

1. In the Neuro-Logical Levels of Robert Dilts, his first three distinctions (behavior, capability, and environment) are not meta-levels, but primary state levels. For more, see www.neurosemantics.com Articles: Meta-States, Logical Levels.

2. See *Mind-Lines* (2005, 5th edition). This book applies the Meta-Model distinctions to the skill of framing and reframing. Because lines can change minds, the discipline of reframing in 7 directions provides thestructure of persuasion. This book updates the old outdated Sleight of Mouth patterns from NLP.

3. See the Meta-Coach Series, Volume I *Coaching Change* (2005) and Volume II *Coaching Conversations* (2006).

4. You can see this in the articles on www.neurosemantics.com that use the term "meta-domains" that refer to the 4 meta-models: Meta-Model of language, Meta-Programs, Meta-Modalities (sub-modalities), and Meta-States.

5. See *The Structure of Magic, Volume I and II,* also *User's Manual of the Brain, Volume I* which is an introduction to NLP.

6. See Appendix D.

7. This was the insightful discovery noted by Richard Bandler in *Using Your Brain — For a Change* (1985). Beliefs *command* the nervous system. Also see "The Magical Nature of Beliefs" on the website.

8. And if they operate as a primary state, then we can anchor these more complex higher states.

9. See *Figuring Out People* (2006).

10. See *Using Your Brain — For a Change* (1985) as well as Andreas' work on sub-modalities. For a deeper analysis of this, see *Sub-Modalities Going Meta.*

PART II:

SPECIFIC

META-STATES

Chapter 21

DANCING WITH

DRAGONS AND OTHER

META-MUDDLES

De-Constructing Negative Meta-States

"It is not too much to say
that anything resembling a satisfactory understanding
of personal and social adjustment is out of the question
unless it includes an adequate understanding
of the role of self-reflexiveness
in such adjustment and in maladjustment."
Wendell Johnson
People in Quandaries (1946)

As meta-states make up our most positive, empowering, and transcendent states, they can also comprise our most negative, dis-empowering, and terrifying states. The structure of a meta-state can be either a wow or a woe. Many meta-states bring out the worst in people. *All you have to do is bring negative thinking and feeling against yourself.* Structurally this sets conflicting frames against yourself putting you at odds with your own experiences.

The power of making a meta-move and setting higher frames enables you to not only create your best states, it also empowers you to set destructive frames. And, if you bring judgments, irrationality, destructive ideas, anger, fear, disgust, etc. *against yourself,* and you set higher frames of self-conflict, judgment, unsanity, and neurosis, you create some of the most ugly and hurtful states possible. *Negative and morbid meta-states* include such states as self-shaming, self-contempting, looping in a runaway mode with worries, guilts, fears, narcissism, etc.

On occasion in the previous chapters I have noted numerous negative meta-states. The time has now come to describe the marvelous art of *de-constructing morbid meta-states* or *dragon slaying*. *Slaying, taming,* or even *transforming dragon states* means pulling apart the conceptual constructions that create toxic semantic states that undermines effectiveness and diminishes you as a person.

With some of these morbid states you will sometimes simply *tame* the energy as you do with the primary emotions of fear, anger, sadness, etc. Don't reject or fight against this energy, instead tame the energy, and put it to good use. Sometimes you will *transform* the structure of the "dragon" so that it enhances your life. In these instances, you befriend the dragon and utilize its energy. And then sometimes, you will *slay* or destroy the "dragon" because it is completely sick, morbid, neurotic, and erroneous. In all of these maneuvers, you are learning to *dance with the dragon.*

If the metaphor of "dragon" is primarily a positive experience and you never use it in a negative way, then let me invite you not to take offense when I play with the metaphor of "dragon" slaying. *After all, it is just a metaphor.* And the actual referent is that of de-constructing a negative meta-state that has put you in a position of self-attack and self-abuse.

Given the nature of states-about-states constructions, meta-states not only transcend primary states, they set in force numerous systemic processes. This holistic and circular way of functioning describes how higher states set up self-reinforcing loops so that they take on "a life of their own." *As higher states set the frames,* which then permeate down through the logical levels to the primary states, *they establish circular loops.*

This creates the state dependency of *seeing, feeling, and experiencing the world in terms of that state.* If you experience a primary level fear which is appropriate and useful, and then reflect that fear onto yourself so you become *afraid of your fear,* and then *afraid* of that higher level fear, and so on, you create a meta-fear dragon. And if you're not careful, you could become disgusted with that fear, depressed about it, angry at your depression, etc. And all of that will set in motion a negative downward spiraling.

These operations of a negative meta-state describes the structure of pathology and morbidness. It explains why some patterns of consciousness (e.g., personality disorders) can seem so impossible or difficult to change.

How then do we change a frame in someone who responds *with* and *from* that very negative set of embedded frames? Obviously, the change we want to effect occurs at a level higher. So somehow we need to create a shift which will enable a person to step outside of the frame. If we can facilitate that for ourselves or another, we can get to the leverage point where change occurs.

The Fear Dragon
With the primary state of fear, you experience fearful thoughts and feelings about the object of your fear. At this level, you can reality test the object of your fear. Then you can make a decision to either get away from the danger or to develop the skills necessary to deal with the danger effectively. Accepting, welcoming, and learning from the primary level fear serves you well in terms of coping, adaptation, learning, development. This allows you to use fear appropriately and wisely.

Fear provides information as an emotional signal, energy as the somatic energy of a true *e-motion*, and an interruption to give the space and time to deal with the situation. In accepting, understanding, and managing the fear, you do not eliminate or destroy the fear, you *tame* it.

Now on to meta-level fears. How different things become at the meta-level when you *fear your fear.* When you fear your very experience of fear, a higher and very different kind of experience emerges. You will typically experience *fear-of-fear* as unrealistic fear, paranoia, self-fear, self-alienation, repression, etc.

What happens then? *Typically, you back away from yourself and your experience.* This means that you do not address your thoughts and emotions of fear, but suppress, repress, and deny them. This, in turn, then leads to developing defensive maneuvers which prevent you from actually dealing with the factors fueling the downward spiraling. *Fearing yourself* (and the very powers of your personality by which you could deal with reality) then cuts you off from the very resources you need most.

A *fear-about*-fear state amplifies the original emotion and misdirects you about the actual problem. Then you think the problem is your experience of fear. It is not. You need your fear. Your fear, as an emotion that somatically registers the difference between your map and experience of the territory, is valuable, important, and informative. And since you need your fear, then paradoxically what's required is *acceptance of your fear*—a state of welcoming, embracing, being curious so that you can learn from your fear.

So the resolution of that morbid meta-state involves doing the very thing which you do not want to do when fear comes over you—facing, embracing, accepting, entering into, and learning from the fear. Yes, it is counter-intuitive and paradoxical. Yet if you meta-state your fear with fear, all you end up achieving is setting up a forbidding frame.

What can you do to effectively handle this? First, appreciatively recognize this structure. Realize that the seeming paradox is a confusion of levels; realize that fear and fear-of-fear are two very different experiences. The first is a precious value, the second is self-conflict that undermines and diminishes you.

With this realization, use the Meta-Model as a linguistic tool to *deconstruct your meta-state framing*. Question your languaging and index the levels of your states. "What are you afraid of?" "What do you think or feel about that?" Probe around until you find the constructions of your belief frames that create the problem. This will enable you to sneak around the taboo of the forbidding fear and see the real dragon—the taboo.

When you ask *about-ness* questions, you indirectly jump meta-levels and simultaneously *access an empowering state of just witnessing the experience*. This process applies *the innocent healing state of non-judgmental observing* to the fear.

> "Now as you notice this level of fear about your state of fear, how do you know to experience it in this way? How realistic is it to *fear* your emotion of fear? Does this serve you well and enhance your ability to deal with the first level fear? Does it empower you to be more courageous?"

These questions invite you to step aside from the fear frame and reality test it. Your linguistics move you to a higher meta-state of *calm evaluation* which gives you a platform for making systemic changes.

Paranoia, as a meta-state of fear-about-fear, provides a prototype for most negative meta-states. The higher fear thoughts-feelings about the primary fearful thoughts-and-feelings amplifies the original state, creates a morbid, unsolvable problem (a runaway system). It also creates unsolvable paradoxes and double-binds and distorts the primary state into a gross exaggeration.

Dragon Slaying or *Taming*
It is your insights into the meta-level structure of meta-states that enables you to effectively work with these layered expressions of consciousness. As you now know, the *stuff* of meta-states is the sensory-based representations of sights, sounds, sensations, and words. These factors make up the "languages" of your mind and the components of your meta-states that have become monstrous.

Because language encodes higher level concepts, understandings, and ideas, your self-talk linguistically glues the layers together giving them coherent stability. Language patterns not only map out your reality, they also *reveal* and *sustain* these constructed realities.

Coalesced negative meta-states often seem to have a life and energy of their own. As they emerge from all of the systemic processes, they seem so real. No wonder that people once upon a time thought of them as literal "demons" and talked about people being "possessed" by destructive spirits. Yet in reality we are the ones who speak these human constructs into existence.

By your languaging, complex meta-states emerge. You compose them of many layers of thoughts and emotions and then glue them together by cause-effect statements, complex equivalent structures, presupposition statements, etc. By languaging you construct hypnotic inductions for your own dragon states. This is why you can also use the relanguaging tools of the Meta-Model to slay, tame, and transform the dragons. Now you can simply pull the pieces apart. You can rip off the horns and armor. Does that sound like fun? Then get out your Meta-Model sword and let's go *dragon slaying!*

If you think language is about grammar and spelling, about the right and wrong ways to put sentences together, someone has deceived you. That's not what language is about. Language is our way of mapping and framing our inner sense of reality to become our outer experiences. This explains why and how the languaging and re-languaging tools of the Meta-Model (Bandler and Grinder, 1975; Hall, 1998) puts into your hands a set of most powerful technologies for taking charge of your linguistics. And because meta-states involve linguistically driven inductions, you now can slay and tame dragons.

> *Meta-modeling the ill-formedness in the logic, structure, and meaning of your states pulls apart and unglues the coherence and stability of those meta-states.*

I illustrated this earlier with regard to the idea, and the state, of "failure" as a meta-state. The non-referencing *term* "failure" works like linguistic glue accessing and anchoring a very unresourceful state. For many, the word "failure" induces a negative state of judging, evaluating, and condemning oneself. It happens every time the person thinks or says, "I'm just a failure." Talk about a short hypnotic induction!

All you have to do is to keep repeating the words, "I am a failure." Or, more subtly, assume failure in your questions:

> "Why does failure plague me so? Why does failure follow me in everything I do? When will I ever break this failure streak?"

Use that kind of languaging often enough and it will organize and structure your inner reality. Are you a failure or is this just a sick hypnotic induction? It is a sick hypnotic induction! The problem lies in the abstract meta-term "failure" which over-generalizes some specific action or actions wherein you fail to reach some goal. The morbidness here arises from over-generalizing and inappropriately applying it to another concept, "self."

How do you de-construct the meta-state of "failure?" Begin by asking the indexing questions of the Meta-Model to create more specificity:
- What task did you fail at?
- When did you fail at it?
- Where did you fail at that thing?
- What was the standard that you used to make this evaluation of failure?
- To what degree did you fail? In what way?
- How many times have you failed at this?
- Does anything stop you from learning from the feedback and trying again?
- How long have you been interpreting non-success at that thing in a personalizing way?
- How are "you," as a person, a "failure?"
- How does failing at that activity turn you, as a human being, into a "failure?"
- What are you trying to do that's a value or benefit for you in thinking and interpreting this way?
- Does languaging yourself and this activity as a "failure" make you more resourceful? Does it empower you as a person?
- Does it enable you to feel more ready to go back to the task, to learn from what didn't go well, and try it again?
- What stops you from learning and improving your performance so that you eventually succeed?

In this meta-model questioning you simultaneously elicit the original experience from which you made the construction, and gently nudge yourself or another to re-map the experience more productively.

This questioning illustrates that a great many of the morbid meta-states arise from *an unthinking use of nominalizations* in everyday talk. Many of the mental-and-emotional "dragons" that torment people simply hide from awareness inside conceptualizations that they mentally construct using these ordinary words.

In pulling apart these conceptualizations, first take them out of the noun-form which makes them seem like a static and permanent thing and *re-language them as processes*. This makes them much less formidable and facilitates the realization,

> "Hey, they are not dragons after all! They are just *actions* — in fact, *my actions!* I created this dragon-like state with my words and interpretations."

Doing this will bring to your own awareness that it is nominalizing the behaviors that creates so-called dragons. As you develop a greater mindfulness about your mapping, you realize that creating ill-formed meaning constructions is what gives birth to negative meta-states.

Free yourself by recognizing this principle. Behind so-called dragons or demons or monsters that lurk in the back of your mind, in the dark corners of your memory, or in the labyrinths of your id, are thoughts. How about that? *There are no actual dragons or demons. There are just thoughts.* They are just ideas and meanings tied together in stupid, irrational, silly, childish, and unnecessary ways.

While you're at it, set this as your frame: *"All of my distresses arise ultimately from my thoughts."* All of the stuff out of which you create your highest level understandings, concepts, beliefs, identities, etc. are made out of the same primary level stuff: sights, sounds, sensations, and words. As you de-mystify what otherwise seems real, overwhelming, and unsolvable, you will be able to quickly undo the monstrous constructions that sabotage your well-being, optimal functioning, effective thinking, and resourceful performances.

Ultimate freedom will come to you the day you realize that *there's nothing to fear inside yourself.* No alien beings lurk within. All you have in there are ill-formed words, ideas, terms, stories, metaphors, narratives, etc. There are only pictures, images, sounds, etc. that generate disturbing states which you have framed as "real." You create your layered consciousness, conceptual states and realities as you use symbols and language. So by languaging you create internal monsters, and by re-languaging you reorder your inner world for excellence and genius.

Reactivity

There are different levels of reactivity. You can access both *primary* states of reactivity as well as *meta-levels* of reactivity. At the primary level, the kind of reactivity involves interpreting a stimulus as threatening and dangerous. When you do this, you send your body messages of survival and so you go into the emergency mode of fight/flight. This primary level activates the defense mechanisms of the body as your neurology and physiology shifts into an emergency mode.

Most critically, the lower brain withdraws blood from the cortex and stomach and sends more blood to your larger muscle groups. It releases a rush of adrenalin in the blood stream and your whole physiology goes into hyper-state. Then, you react. You don't think —you react! Your thinking at that time becomes highly colored by various fear-anger emotions.

Reactivity also occurs at meta-levels when you apply thoughts and feelings of threat to other thoughts and feelings. When you meta-state yourself with reactive thoughts and emotions you become *reactive to yourself, your emotions, your thoughts, your wants/needs, your history, your sense of time, your sense of self, etc.* You become reactive to whatever abstract state you create in response to your original thoughts and feelings. You now react with fight/flight.

And none of this is good. This creates sick and morbid meta-states. You now apply "danger" and "threat" to various conceptual states like self, time, history, consciousness, emotions, and the list goes on and on. *You then become afraid of yourself.* You fear your powers, your mind, and your functioning. You become phobic-of-self, angry-at-self, frustrated-at-self, hateful-to-self, etc. You fear your sensitivity, spirituality, greatness, possibilities. This is what gives birth to the most devastating dragons—mentally and physically.

It also creates an unsolvable situation. After all, how can you *flee* from yourself except by such morbid responses as denial, repression, regression, splitting of the mind, etc.? Or how can you *fight* yourself except by more morbid responses: damning parts of oneself as "dark," demonic, or "bad;" judging and contempting oneself, guilting, or turning it outward on others? Meta-level *reactivity* represents some of the most painful, ugly, gruesome, gloomy, and morbid experiences that we can generate. And if your mind doesn't pay the price for this, your body will in the form of illnesses and psychosomatic diseases.

Figure 21:1

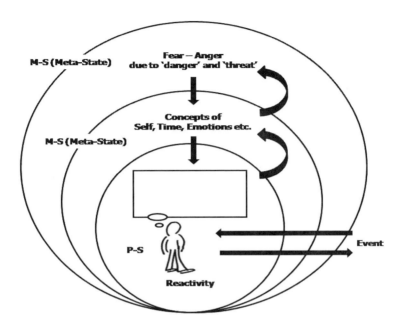

How can we address such morbid states? Is this truly unsolvable? The first and foremost solution is to become conscious of the processes that create this unsanity. Becoming conscious of your part in their creation enables you to *see* what's happening and how your responses play into the mix. And sometimes, just sometimes, that's enough to transform the whole system. When that happens, then we experience how "Insight is curative *per se*."

Self-Contempting

To construct a morbid state of self-contempt-ing, you only need to apply *contempt* to yourself.

> "I'm a nothing!" "I'll never amount to anything." "Idiot that I am, I always say the wrong thing." "I'm inferior to most people."

Typically people evoke this meta-state when things go wrong, when frustrations, set-backs, failing to reach desired goals, criticisms, insults, and other "bad" things occur. They then use these unpleasant experiences to create a negative abstraction about the self. Concluding that they "are" a nothing, a worthless, good-for-nothing, miserable

S.O.B., so they believe. As they jump to this negative judgment, they begin languaging themselves constantly with insult, contempt, put-downs, etc.

Figure 21:2

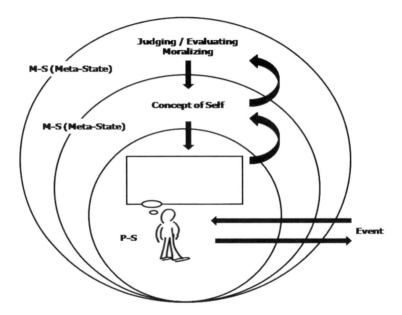

In self-contempting, you use a higher level standard to harshly judge yourself. These usually have to do with cultural or personal values and standards that you regard as conditions for your self-hood and self-esteem.

> "I can allow myself to treat myself with dignity, value and worth *if and when* I meet certain conditions. I will not recognize it as a given, as inherent as a human being. I will treat myself well, respectful, and as a valuable somebody *when* I reach a certain level of accomplish. Until then I will look upon myself with contempt."

To re-language this non-sense, use meta-model questions to index and quality control meanings:
- So you really believe that you need to think, feel, and show contempt toward your self when you mess up, fail at something, or make an error?
- Do you do the same with other selves?

- Does this motivate them to do better?
- Does this assist them in becoming better people and contributing more?
- How does this help you?
- Have you found it a useful and productive way to live your life?
- Where did you learn this?
- Could this simply be a bad habit that you received from someone else?

Guilting as Self-Condemning

When you feel guilty, the emotion of guilt refers to your awareness that you have violated a divine or universal law. Guilt functions as a moral emotion creating your "conscience." When this emotion signals, you feel that you have done something wrong, that you have violated an important value, and that you have missed the mark of correct behavior in some context.

"Guilt" is a legal or forensic emotion. In a court of law, judges and juries pronounce people "Innocent" or "Guilty." Such declarations pronounce a court judgment regarding behaviors. The job of the court is to consider whether a person has violated some law. *Guilt alludes to a judgment of right/wrong according to some law.* But what law? God's, the universe's, man's, your own, another person's? With the forensic pronouncement comes some kind of penalty, punishment and/or forgiveness.

Now violations of the various laws come in all sizes, shapes, degrees, and kinds. You can violate a principle of the universe—one of God's laws. When you do something truly wrong (murder, rage, violations of others, etc.), you should feel guilty. Feeling the wrongness of the significant wrong enables you to correct it, make amends, and/or change your behaviors. Those who can't feel and use guilt for change are sociopaths. They are without conscience about the impact of their behaviors on others.

You can also violate society's laws. If you speed at 70 mph on a 50 mph road, you have done wrong. But what should you feel? How "bad" should you feel? And what kind of badness? Should you feel embarrassed, ashamed, "bad," upset, discouraged, anger, or naughty for speeding?

Guilt / Wrongness

Guiltiness	
Self-betrayal	*Degrees of "Guilt"*
Pained Conscience	*and feeling of*
Guilt	*"Wrongness"*
Shame	
Embarrassment	
Remorse	
Disappointed	
Feeling bad	

You may violate another person's values and expectations. Perhaps you don't show up for an appointment on time. The other waits for ten minutes for you. The other feels impatient and put-out. What should you feel? Have you done something that's morally wrong? No. So guilt would be an inappropriate emotion. More appropriate emoting about such might include feeling ashamed, embarrassed, angry at yourself, disappointed, something like that.

What if you violate your own values, goals, standards, and expectations? You mess up in a project, spill paint all over the place and end up spending more time and money on it than what you consider appropriate. What should you feel? Again, not guilt. You haven't done anything morally wrong. More appropriate emoting would include feeling embarrassed, disappointed, frustrated, or upset.

As wrong-doing comes in different sizes and shapes, so should the *ability to feel bad in lesser ways*. So on the scale of "violating a value" we need the ability to distinguish different levels of "wrongness." We need the big moral feeling of "guilt" for moral wrongs. We need shame, embarrassment, frustration, etc. for facing mistakes, failings, faults, imperfections, mess-ups, etc. For these we do not need to go into a state of feeling condemned. If a "sin" is a serious and moral violation for which guilt is appropriate, then for lesser violations we need one of these lesser negative emotions.

The fact is, there is no need to guilt yourself (insulting, judging, condemning, declaring yourself good-for-nothing, worthless, inferior, etc.) over *non-moral* issues. Doing so misuses your moral conscience and will not do you any good. You'll only end up feeling guilty and over-moralizing about non-moral issues which happens to be an occupational hazard for people who care about ethical behavior and who want to live moral and upright. Yet if you become over-sensitized to "wrongs," you can guilt yourself for being a fallible human being (!).

In the place of this destructive form of guilting, learn to make distinctions about levels, kinds, and degrees of wrongs. Most issues have nothing to do with morality. They have to do with finances, emotions, communication, relational behaviors, stress, fallibility, etc. Moralizing about every problem, fault, or error creates a sin-consciousness that can then color your world in terms of "sin." And that's not an empowering, pleasant, or accurate way to live.

Even when you do commit a moral or ethical error—guilting yourself seldom makes things better. *Guilt,* like the other negative emotions of fear, anger, disgust, dread, and sadness, *functions primarily as a warning signal.* It alerts you to "stop, look, listen and make corrections" about how you think or act. Like the gauges in a car, when the lights and bells go off, they provide you information about dangers and problems. A proper response to such involves heeding, checking, understanding, and acting. So with guilt.

Figure 21:3

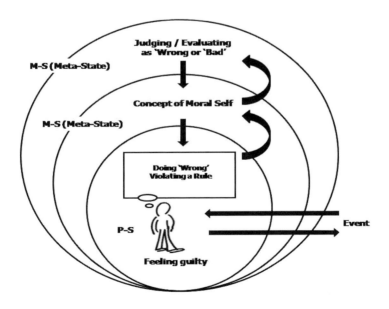

Lots of Negative Meta-States

There are far more ways to mess yourself up and induce negative, painful, destructive, and monstrous meta-states than ways to induce positive meta-states. This principle is true for every rule-governed phenomenon. When the components and syntax in a system play a critical role in generating an emergent quality that's "greater than the sum of the parts," then it is possible to mess things up in far more ways than to "get it right."

You can mess up baking a really great cake in many more ways that you can get it right. If you don't use all of the components (flour, sugar, eggs), if you toss in components not required, needed, or useful (egg shells, pepper, toilet paper), if you ignore syntax (put in oven before you add the eggs), etc., you can sabotage the desired outcome.

This is also true for *screwed-up morbid meta-states.* There are many formulas for creating "a living hell" for yourself and others. To de-construct them, shift the inappropriate pieces of consciousness, especially those comprised of erroneous thinking patterns (exaggerations, discounting, mind-reading, awfulizing, personalizing, judging, etc.). As you do so, you may have to interrupt the meta-state. Do this by making it ludicrous, ridiculous, laughable, and silly. Then meta-model the language constructions until you get to a more enhancing well-formed construction.

Evoking the Dragon of "Victimization"

To access the state of *feeling like a victim,* simply apply the thoughts and feelings of victimization to yourself. See yourself at the mercy of others, of outside forces, and unable to do anything. Believe that you *are* a helpless victim—make this your identity: "I am a victim. I can do nothing. Everything is against me." Once you set the meta-frame of a helpless and hopeless victim, you will be able to see and experience the sense of victimization in all kinds of places in life. You will not even have to have an actual experience, your frame will project it into situations.

Figure 21:4

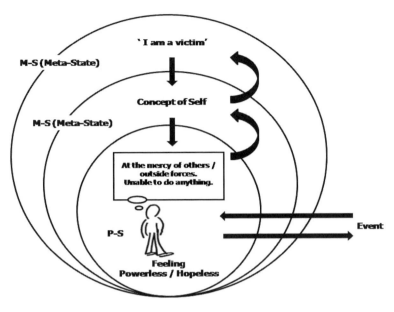

Evoking the Dragon of Despair

What about the dragon of despair? How does that one work? All you have to do is apply the feelings of *grief* to yourself, or upon your life in general. Then amplify this grief by catastrophizing the problem, the feeling, the experience, etc. To make it even worse, apply the three "**P**s" that create "learned helplessness" to this.

Figure 21:5

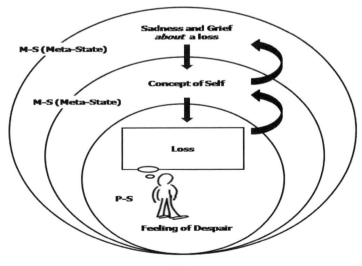

- Make it *Personal*: "Something is wrong with me!"
- Make it *Pervasive*: "This affects everything in life"
- Make it *Permanence*: "This will last forever."

Evoking the Dragon of Rigid Stubbornness

Have you ever fought with the dragon of stubbornness? This dragon is created by applying a belief of conviction to a previous belief. Let this conviction be characterized by a strong sense of rightness. "I am right." Make up your mind about this so that you *feel definite* about your rightness. "I can't be wrong about this. No way!" As you then come to believe in your belief, you will generate a fanaticism. This will build up the meta-dragon state of being righteous, dogmatic, stubborn, and proud of it.

Summary

- Your highest and most unique powers can be misused to construct morbid and sick experiences. You only have to turn them against yourself to create a living hell for yourself and others.

- As a semantic class of life, you are quite able to set negative frames and generate morbid meta-states. You can construct such neuro-linguistic states-about-states to your detriment. All you have to do is apply negative thoughts and feelings *against* yourself to undermine your happiness, contentment, effectiveness, and resourcefulness.

- There is a solution. You can use the Meta-State model to detect and slay your morbid dragon states. By using the re-languaging of the Meta-Model you can create new and more empowering meta-states. Use your *going meta* powers to quality control your states and choose those that unleash your best potentials.

Chapter 22

UNLEASHING

POTENTIALS

WITH META-STATES

By meta-stating you can unleash tremendous potentials within yourself. As you create new structures for mapping understandings, beliefs, identities, etc., you can create rich and robust frames of mind that become beliefs and belief systems which will send commands to unleash your highest and best potentials.

To illustrate this, we will probe into several specific meta-states to identify their structure of states as higher frames to create a resourceful matrix of frames. Here I will show the power of the meta-move for constructing higher states that will enrich your life so you will be able to set executive self-organizing frames that will enable you to unleash all kinds of new possibilities.

To do this, this chapter will explore four meta-states: proactivity, self-esteem, inner peace, and un-insultability. As you gain perspective about the structure of these meta-states and their content of empowering beliefs, you can begin to try them on and make them yours.

Proactivity

How mindful are you in taking effective actions? One of the problems about problems is that, more often than not, they catch us off guard. Does that happen to you? Problems knock you around because you never even imagined them. You then react, which usually makes things worse. What you need is *a proactive frame of mind* by which you anticipate possible problems and prepare for them in a positive and productive way. Wouldn't that be great?

What would a proactive state be like for you? As you access a proactive state, simply recall an experience of proactivity so fully that you step back into that experience. What is the quality of your inner movie that produces proactive thoughts and feelings? What are the ideas and beliefs in the back of your mind. *Proactivity* is much more than a primary state, it is a state with many meta-levels and multiple layers of frames.

Grounding Proactivity

The primary experience calling for proactivity is a state of problems, challenges, and distresses. In this context, *pro*-activity means thinking, feeling, valuing, and choosing *prior to* both the problematic challenge and your response. This makes proactivity an active mindfulness which distinguishes it from primary states of reactivity, impulsiveness, anxiety, and stressful tensions.

In creating this meta-state, begin with almost any state of concern about a project, program, or intended outcome. Begin with a state of trouble, worry, bother, or problems, or begin with a state of challenge, desire, passion, or commitment.

Once you have the initial state, then explore your current frames with meta-questions. The first meta-questions, *What do you think about it? What are you aware of?* What do you believe in? Once you know your current frames, ask,

> *What thoughts feelings, and actions will give me a sense of choice and resources?* What will empower me to be mindful and proactive about my options for taking effective actions?

These questions will help you decide on the resource states as frames and beliefs to meta-state yourself with. Frames that typically facilitate

proactivity are:
* A higher meta-awareness of the situation.
* The ability and willingness to take the initiative.
* Clarity of mind about your values and principles.
* Self-discipline to follow through.
* An implementation state.
* Anticipation of future needs, problems, and challenges.
* Strong sense of the power to choose.
* Knowing and appreciating the stimulus and response *gap*.
* Owning your circle of power.
* Self-definition as a proactive person.

Meta-awareness enables you to more thoroughly understand yourself and your world as you step back and reflect on your experience. As you become mindful, you develop a *presence of mind* for thinking at your best even in intense and dangerous situations.

Figure 22:1

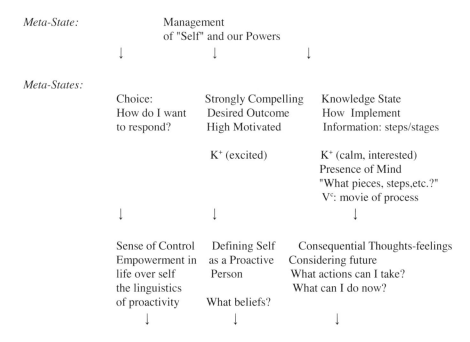

Meta-State: Management
                     of "Self" and our Powers
              ↓   ↓   ↓

Meta-States:

            Choice: Strongly Compelling   Knowledge State
            How do I want   Desired Outcome   How Implement
            to respond?   High Motivated   Information: steps/stages

                                 K⁺ (excited)   K⁺ (calm, interested)
                                                        Presence of Mind
                                                        "What pieces, steps,etc.?"
                                                        Vᶜ: movie of process
              ↓   ↓   ↓

            Sense of Control   Defining Self   Consequential Thoughts-feelings
            Empowerment in   as a Proactive   Considering future
            life over self   Person   What actions can I take?
            the linguistics   What can I do now?
            of proactivity   What beliefs?
              ↓   ↓   ↓

Primary State:

                     Problem, Setback, Distress
                     Challenge, Commitment, Desired Outcome

Meta-Stating for Proactivity

1) Anticipation of future needs and problems. Proactivity requires the ability to anticipate and prepare for future needs and problems. Proactive thinking occurs before problems arise as the preparation you make for thinking through and preparing coping strategies. Otherwise you merely react with unthinking passivity or aggression, which starts a downward spiral for feeling like a victim.

Being proactive supports resilience in the face of traumatic events. Ultimately success in life comes down to being prepared to effectively cope with whatever life throws at you. When a traumatic event occurs, a proactive person refuses to suffer the trauma passively, but takes effective action and *does something to handle it* — which brings us to the next resource.

2) Responsible choosing of responses. The proactive person assumes responsibility for him or herself, for interpreting what things will mean, and for generating the most effective and creative responses. Proactive people, having a strong sense of choice, actively choose their responses. They act with an awareness of their ability and freedom to respond as they choose. This builds a sense of self-efficacy about being able to handle any challenge.

Access your right and responsibility to choose how you will respond to problems, the attitude you will adopt, how you will interpret events, the emotions you'll choose to cultivate, and the actions you will take and those you will not take.

How well do you know how to keep your mind and heart vigorously alive? The more vigorous your thinking, emoting, speaking and behaving responses, the more robust your proactivity. To elicit this state, start with the invigorating belief, "I can always make some response." Use the inner self-talk that made Viktor Frankl proactive,

> "They cannot make me hate them. I always have a choice about how I will respond! I can always do something that will make a difference."

Viktor Frankl demonstrated incredible proactive behavior in Hitler's Death Camp by choosing his attitude. His decision? He refused to let them make him hate them. He refused to give his power away to them and allow them to determine his emotions. Claiming control of his own attitude, he decided he would choose his emotional response. Imagine learning proactivity in a concentration camp! If proactivity can be learned there, proactivity can be learned anywhere.

Frankl's captors took away every external freedom that he had. But they could not take away *his ultimate liberty — his right and freedom to choose his response.* While developing this inner freedom as a center of strength does not come easy, human beings can develop it. Access this inner sense of your personal power by setting the meta-knowledge that even in situations that limit your actions like prison, you can always choose responses that will make a difference. Use this meta-knowledge to empower your proactive posture.

Practice engaging in small acts that is solely given birth by your choice. Proactivity doesn't depend on doing big or great things, it often consists of doing the smallest of things. It is not the size of the proactive response that matters, but the fact that you are responding. So knowing that you can always do something, *do* something.

3) Own your response-abilities.
Proactivity is all about the *ability* to *respond.* This power arises from an internal "locus of control" as you acknowledge and own your powers of mind, emotion, speech, and behavior to respond. These powers create the special state of *response-ability.*

> "Whatever happens, I can always mentally respond to it through my thoughts, emotions, speech, and behaviors. It does no good to hold another person responsible for these powers. I claim and fully own my behaviors, choices, emotions, and thoughts as mine. *They belong to me.* I produce these responses since they come out of my mind and emotions."

Use this meta-frame to empower yourself to take full responsibility for yourself. Build your proactive state by accessing the ownership of your choices and responses.

Your nature is not fully determined or explained by stimulus-response patterns. There's something else. Between the stimulus and the response there is a gap wherein you are free to choose. Inside this gap you think, represent information, reason, imagine, remember, fantasize, etc. to create your inner world of meaning.

Stimulus　　　　—>　　　　Response

The Gap of Consciousness

Your self-reflexive consciousness uniquely endows you with the ability to move to a *choice point*—where you choose your responses. People who respond resiliently to set-backs express their inner power by choosing their thoughts and responses. This sense of choice and personal power is *self-efficacy*—the sense of efficacy or power as you trust yourself in choosing, strategizing, solving problems, coping, handling the challenges of life, noticing responses and flexibly adapting.

Research in job stresses and the relationship between business environments shows that unpleasant job demands in themselves (e.g., noise, heat, physical exertion and repetitive work) do not cause the stress that leads to heart disease. That kind of stress arises from combining high level job-demands with *a sense of not being in control of your own responses.* Stress increases if you believe you have little say over things like the rate of your work or ability to access supports (like using a telephone). By concluding that you are helpless, you construct a "learned helplessness" map.

A Contrastive Analysis

When you do *not* respond proactively, how do you respond? What is the opposite of proactivity? *Reactivity.* And reactivity can take several forms: passivity, aggressiveness, denial, laziness, etc.

What drives such reactivity? While lots of specific triggers can set it off, it is a sense of threat or danger that primarily evokes defensiveness. Defensiveness is activated by the fight/flight syndrome and then undermines state management. Reactivity can arise from stuffing emotions so that one becomes increasingly uninvolved with life. By concluding that they are helpless, they construct a "learned helplessness" map.

We all need to feel in control. It is an important and basic need of being human. Feeling in control of our lives reduces stress, enables us to tolerate more, and gives us a sense that we have the power to respond. A leading researcher in the field of Type-A behavior, Redford Williams, an internist and behavioral medicine specialist at Duke University Medical Center, wrote, *The Trusting Heart: Great News About Type-A Behavior*. Williams and colleagues demonstrated that cynicism and hostility actually causes bodily responses that lead to heart attacks. The editor of *Psychology Today* (1989) noted:

> "Since the 1950's scientists have been exploring the link between Type-A behavior (driven, harried actions and hostile emotions) and heart disease. Hostility and cynical mistrust are now regarded as the lethal elements of Type A behavior. Driving ambition itself is no longer viewed as dangerous" (Jan. 1989)

Owning your powers keeps your heart free from hostility and cynical mistrust. So when angry, deal with it, keep it current, and then let it go. Focus on what you can do. Focus on what you can trust in others as you adjust your expectations so they are appropriate and realistic.

4) Own your Circle of Power

To develop the feeling of being in control of your responses, it's required that you own your circle of response. Covey (1987) describes this circle as that arena within which you can make a response. If you can make a response to something, it is inside your circle of power. If it is something beyond your responses, it lies in the circle of concern. In your circle of concern you care and have best intentions and wishes, but no direct or immediate impact.

So focus on things within your circle of influence. Focusing on things beyond that arena only dis-empowers you as you give your power away to things you can do nothing about. And that is simply not a wise choice.

Figure 22:2

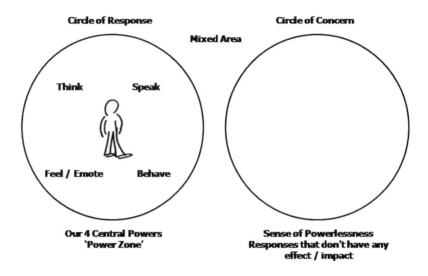

When you are reactive, your problems seem to be "out there." While it's natural to put problems outside, this often creates a second level problem because it empowers things "out there" to control you. The bottom line is to focus your actions on things within your circle of response.

5) Implementation state
What do you already know to do for actualizing your best? If implementation is what transforms knowledge into actual power, how is your ability to implement what you know? Do you daily exercise your proactive muscles by putting what you know into action?

6) Acceptance of mistakes
Develop a positive, solution-oriented approach to mistakes by treating them as friends rather than enemies. View mistakes as feedback information about what *not* to do. Proactively approach mistakes by seeking to learn all you can from them as quickly as you can. Quickly acknowledge errors, recognize them for what they are, give others permission to point them out to you, learn from them, and correct them.

7) Solution-focused probing
Get into the habit of asking solution-oriented questions.
*   What can I do as a highly constructive response?
*   What ways of thinking, speaking and behaving would empower me to cope best with this?
*   What resourceful states do I need to learn to access with greater skill and speed?
*   What one thing can I do today that will put me on track toward my desired outcomes?
*   What feedback can I gather from this setback that will improve my next attempt?

8) Identify yourself as a proactive person
Set an identity frame for yourself as a proactive person and develop the language that makes it compelling and memorable.
*   "The ultimate freedom lies in my freedom of choice, therefore I will maintain an active and thoughtful coping style. I will stay alert as I move through life and maintain my internal locus of control."
*   "I can and will make use of opportunities for purposeful action and will take the initiative whenever I can. I will use empowering questions to shift my focus to solutions."

9) Use proactive language
Counteract the language of reactivity, passivity, and victimization with the language of proactivity. Use *I* when expressing your thoughts, feelings, values, and wants to own and acknowledge them as yours. Reduce the number of *you* statements that you make. Completely eliminate the language of blame, accusation, and excuses as well as the language of explanations, projections, and blaming.

Now, Let the Meta-Stating Begin
Which of these resources will you use to create the higher frame of mind of proactivity for yourself ? How will you sequence the syntax of these states to create a robust frame of mind?

Self-Esteem
Throughout these pages I have frequently mentioned self-esteem as the ability to value yourself unconditionally. Do you absolutely feel yourself as unconditionally valuable, important, and worthwhile as a

person? This is the most enhancing resourceful state which will ground you so that you can get on with life. When you meta-state yourself with self-esteem, you can thereafter live with a sense of dignity about yourself so you never question your basic worth. Then with a center of personal value, you will have the power to live authentically, courageous, defenselessly, and lovingly. If that sounds good to you, then here's how to do it.

1) Recognize self-esteem as a process.
As a nominalization, "self-esteem" hides the process and actions of esteeming, of mentally appraising your "self" as having worth, importance, and value as a human being. As a process, rather than a thing, you do not *have* or *not have* self-esteem. You either *esteem* or *dis-esteem* yourself. Which do you do? How do you do it? What criteria do you use?

Self-esteeming is an evaluation process. If you hear yourself languaging "self-esteem" as a noun, catch it and *stop it!* Refuse to mystify yourself with such non-sense.

2) Own the esteeming process
As you put the process back into this experience, you are then able to *take ownership* of the esteeming process. When someone complains about feeling low self-esteem, I immediately ask that person confrontation questions to put the person at choice. I confront as directly as I can to put them at cause.
•   Does anything stop you from highly valuing your *self* today?
•   So *when* are *you* going to begin to *esteem* your self with a sense of dignity and worth?
•   If you were to highly esteem your *self,* how would you do that?
•   Are you ready now to esteem yourself unconditionally as having worth and value as a human being?

3) Identify your current frames.
You already use your self-reflexive consciousness to make evaluations about yourself so first, identify how you are currently esteeming yourself.
•   How do you respond to good times? To bad times?
•   What do you believe about success or failure?
•   How do you respond when you receive positive reinforcements

and rewards and when you find yourself up against lots of blocks, frustrations, and defeats?

•   What do you believe about human nature, human worth; is it conditional or unconditional?

4) Separate other-esteem from self-esteem.
Do you distinguish self-esteem and other-esteem as two different processes? After all, if your own self-esteeming *depends* upon other-esteeming, then you make yourself dependent on the liking, validating, approving, etc. of others. That creates an unhealthy vulnerability leading to fearing the possibility that others may *not* esteem you. Then, if you do not receive sufficient esteem from others, you will fail to esteem yourself or falsely conclude that you cannot esteem yourself.

5) Unconditionally esteem your self.
As a mental valuation process, self-esteeming involves *a standard.* What criteria do you use when you make this valuation? What are your expectations and rules for esteeming yourself as having unconditional value? What do you believe about human nature, is it conditionally or unconditionally valuable? Are people innately special, sacred, and loveable?

Whether you believe in the construct of self-esteem being *un*conditional or conditional, the esteeming process involves *your beliefs.* It involves beliefs about persons and about the standards you use. Most cultures impose *conditions* that people have to meet to esteem one's self. Do you wear the right name-brand clothes? Do you have money? Do you go to the right places, have friends of the in-crowd, have the right degrees from the prestigious universities? What about your looks, weight, fitness, connections, beliefs, etc.? *Conditional* self-esteeming means that you can only esteem your self *if and when* you get it all together and achieve the necessary conditions.

Unconditional self-esteeming means you believe in innate human value. You see and think of yourself as a legitimate human being who deserves to be who you are and to live your own life. When you think about yourself as *a person,* how clear are you that you are more than your brain, body, roles, labels, etc.?

6) Distinguish self-esteem from self-confidence
Do you clearly distinguish self-esteem and self-confidence? To confuse these mixes up two very distinct phenomena. If self-esteeming is mentally valuing yourself, self-confidence is feeling good about what you can *do*. It's about the faith ("fidence") that you have "with" ("con-") yourself regarding a task or skill.

Figure 22:3

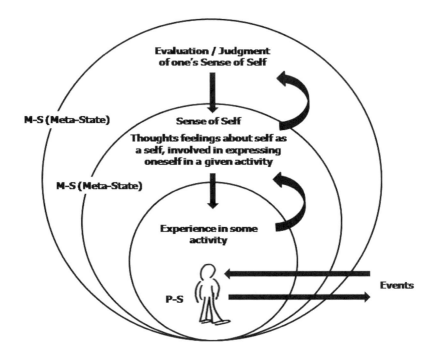

7) Distinguish your self from your functions.
When you stop *identifying* yourself with your functions, powers, ideas, or experiences, you can then unconditionally value yourself. How well do you recognize and experience your inner *self* as transcending your roles, beliefs, ideas, experiences, etc.? Which of the following lines would set this frame for you?

> I am more than the sum of my parts and functions.
> I reflect the very image and likeness of God.
> I'm a human being and nothing anybody can say or do can take that away from me.
> I think, emote, act, speak, relate, make meaning, etc.

I am more than my thoughts since my thoughts don't fully express me.

I am more than my emotions since my emotions do not express me fully either.

I am more than my behaviors, my talk, roles, skills, etc.

8) Decide to unconditionally esteem your self.
The bottom line is that it is a decision. So have you made the decision to esteem yourself? Nobody can do this for you, only you can do this valuing of your self. What supporting beliefs will strengthen this for you?

As you distinguish your person and your behavior—you can esteem yourself and step into a state of defenselessness. And what a resource this provides. Now you can endure the not-okayness of others (their attacks, criticisms, negative emotions, etc.). After all, you have nothing to defend since your worth and value is a given.

So, Let the Meta-Stating begin
Since there is no one right way to map out an empowering self-esteeming program, design it with whatever resourceful ideas, beliefs, and values that enhance your sense of self. Then your self-esteeming will offer you a powerful and authentic way for being in the world, and the resources for living with integrity in an open, defenseless, and assertive way.

Inner Peace
Do you have a core relaxed state that allows you to move through the world with a sense of inner serenity? Would you like to? Then imagine meta-stating yourself with a "peace that passes all understanding" so that you feel at peace with yourself, the world, and the universe regardless of torturous winds of misfortune. Would you like that? Would that enhance your life and give you an inner gyroscope for turbulent times? What else could you do with a state of *calm alertness*?

The paradox of meta-stating inner serenity is that you do it for times of trouble, distress, problems, frustrations—for times when things are not going well and not peaceful. You meta-state the resources to create an inner peace, which is "a state of tranquility or quiet, freedom from civil disturbance, state of security or order, state of harmony, state or period of mutual concord between parties."

1) Release the myth of external peace.
First dispense with the external myth that looks for peace by wanting "everything to go my way." Peace isn't the absence of problems. Nor is it attained by fleeing stress or by becoming a hermit. Inner peace is a tranquility of mind-and-emotion so the storms of life don't unnerve you. It's your ability to transcend unpleasantness, frustrations, and button-pushing events of everyday life with a more positive focus of mind—an optimism about life.

2) Develop a positive optimism.
The inner stability of a core relaxed peaceful state involves a positive optimism about life, self, coping, and engaging in your passions. Similar to how resilience effectively deals with setbacks and disappointments via learning from feedback, inner peace involves a passion for learning and developing to actualize your highest and best.

The Hebrews had a great word for it—*shalom*. Instead of focusing on the absence of conflict, hostility, war, disturbances, etc. (freedom from), *shalom* focuses on the positive facets. *Shalom* highlights the positive qualities of completeness, soundness, security, harmony, tranquility, wholeness, and goodness (freedom to).

Inner peace, the internal unruffledness of mind and emotion, allows you to stay centered, sane, and integrated in your sense of self (identity) and purpose. The inner quiet and solitude involves a strong sense of acceptance of reality, mastery of self, and commitment to your self-actualization.

3) Acceptance
You will probably experience acceptance as counter-intuitive to building serenity. But remember that acceptance does not mean liking, desiring, or wanting what you have, it is welcoming what *is* precisely because it *is*. It is acknowledging reality for what it is. So begin by applying acceptance to your troubled state.

Figure 22:4

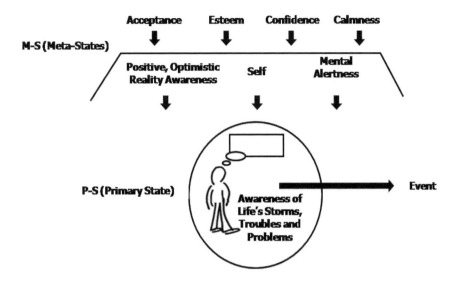

As you do this, release the need to judge events or people as good or bad. Just perceive what *is*. For discovering reality, *acceptance puts you in a search mode*. It enables you to live more consciously without deception, delusion, denial, or the use of any other mechanism to defend yourself against reality. By accepting reality for what it is, you eliminate frames of judgment, rejection, and discounting from the way you perceive things.

The principle governing this is: *There's nothing to fear from reality*. So acceptance enables you to *not* make reality your enemy. As you make yourself a friend to reality, you effectively adjust yourself to whatever you have to face. If you don't acknowledge a reality, you cannot adjust yourself to that reality, whether it is the reality of physics, of inter-personal relations, of language, of culture, etc.

Acceptance implies that you know that you are not the Creator and no longer need to play *God*. You are not all-knowing, all powerful, ever-present. As a human being you have many limitations mentally, emotionally, verbally, and behaviorally. You are perfectly fallible and that is your glory.

Because serenity comes from the wisdom of discerning what you can do and what you cannot, inner peace arises from the proactivity distinction—from recognizing the difference between your circle of response and power and distinguishing it from your circle of concern and wish.

4) Reality checks for adjustment to reality
With clients who experience lots of inner turmoil, conflict, distress, and upsetness and who want more inner peace, I invite them to 0do a *Reality-Check and Adjustment* exercise. On the top of a blank sheet of paper, they write the words,

"I can expect X to . . . "

I then ask them to identify a facet of their world in which they have lots of conflict, anger, fear, or distress. They might write a person's name for X: a spouse, boss, child, friend, parent, etc. They might write a context: work, home, school, etc. They might write a condition: their back, heart, illness, etc. Then I ask them to do a sentence completion and to *write down all of the things that come to mind* (at least ten expectations).

> "*I can expect* dad not to call, not to say 'I love you,' not to be an emotionally available person."
> "*I can expect* my coworker to act like a snob, to use condescending words, to act as if I do not exist . . . "

As you make these real world facts explicit, something magical happens. You align your expectations creating a "fit" with your experiences. In this way you experience "a cessation of hostilities" inside. You stop fighting what exists.

5) Esteem your self.
What do you think about yourself when you are in the midst of troubles? Do you ever *personalize* the troubles on the outside? To what extend do you *personalize* the external troubles and problems? Are you ready to unconditionally value yourself independently of the external conditions and become un-insultable?

6) Emotionally calm for problem solving.

For a creative problem-solving mind-set, a calm and collected perspective is required. And when you have that, then you can access situations with the mental alertness of clear thinking. The goal is to be able to look at reality without going into a panic, fearful, insecure, worry, or angry state.

Feeling inwardly at peace with yourself and your skills obviously calms your mind and emotion. Now you're free to occupy your mind with something else. Now your calming thoughts gives you the space for problem-solving or for giving yourself to your passions.

> "Whatever is true, whatever is honorable, whatever is just, whatever is pure, whatever is lovely, whatever is gracious, if there is any excellence, if there is anything worthy of praise, *think* about these things."

It's not enough to be free from fearful conflicts and problems, you also need to direct your consciousness to something positive. Then your mode of calm and collected thinking will enable you to quickly access a relaxed core state to become your neurological reality. You will breathe in a relaxed way as well as move, release muscle tension, speak, etc. in a relaxed way.[1]

Then your "peace that passes all understanding" state of mind will enable you to see distresses, frustrations and troubles without exaggerating them. With this calming power you will then be able to index the trouble (when, where, how, who, etc.) which thereby contains the trouble and that prevents it from becoming pervasive.

Next, with your long-term thinking you will view immediate challenges and upsets more appropriately. Your beliefs about long-term processes will give you the power to stay centered, collected, and sane. You will then refuse to give too much importance to immediate distresses, "This too will pass."

So, Let the Meta-Stating Begin

Creating a meta-state of inner peace offers a powerfully serene frame of mind for dealing with reality as it *is* and for responding with a calmly serene attitude to disturbances. You will then be able to experience *yourself* as a calming influence in whatever storm you may encounter.

Un-Insultable

How would you like to have an executive state for taking criticism positively? Then you could stay positive when you are criticized. Then you would hear the criticism as information, respond effectively to it by learning and using it.

How susceptible to insult do you feel by criticism, insults, hurtful remarks? How un-insultable are you? As you imagine an un-insultable state, does it excite you as a possibility for handling unpleasant situations? As a meta-state un-insultability consisting of many layers. First, there's the presence of an insult, criticism, put-down, or indignity. Then there are the meta-levels that enable you to respond with contentment, delight, appreciation, understanding, pleasure. How about that?

The layered pieces of conscious that you bring to a critique tempers, modulates, modifies, and transforms your responses. All meta-states work in this way. So as you move into the dynamic and resourceful state of *un-insultability,* your response to the critic comes from a place where you do not use the criticism to damage yourself. Un-insultability increases your effectiveness in every area of life. So what are the resource frames to meta-state for uninsultability?

1) Esteem your self.
The foundation of un-insultability is a solid sense of your own unconditional value. When you have that, you can absolutely refuse to put your self-esteem on the line due to what anyone says. Assert your basic dignity so that your value never rests on any condition. Keep meta-stating your self with unconditional esteem.

And, as with resilience, adopt an optimistic explanatory style for your inner explanations about why the "evil" of criticism, attacks, insults, etc. occur. Tell yourself things about yourself, your critic, his motives, consequences, etc. that fits an optimistic explanatory style. Explain things as non-personal, temporary, and specific. Refuse to make them personal, pervasive, and permanent.

2) Identify your current frames.
Even though it doesn't work, most of us *try to make things better by criticizing* others. We dish it out, yet we don't take it very well. Most

of us are highly sensitive to criticism—it pushes our buttons, rattles our cages, and induces us into highly defensive states. Does criticism do that to you?

Figure 22:5

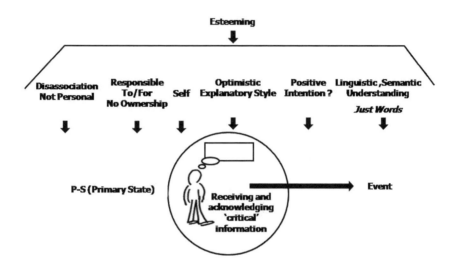

Few know the art of making good use of criticism. Do you ever *use* criticism to feel good. Do you ever make good use of the feedback information contained in criticism? Depending on your state, your overall health and well-being, the context, the one criticizing, and your frames—you may have had times when you heard it *without* immediately feeling bad. On the other side, have you had times when you felt so much "on edge," irritable, stressed, etc. that you responded negatively to even innocuous or positive comments? Most of us have.

Common frames about criticism include things like:
- "This is insulting! I don't want to hear this. I don't want them to say these things."
- "These words mean I am inadequate. This feels like an attack of my self-esteem!"
- "They don't have any right to talk this way to me!"
- "If they are right, that means I'm going to have to go through the time and trouble and pain of changing."

3) Just witnessing.

If personalizing occurs through stepping into and associating with a critique and interpreting it as "about me," then *de-personalize* it by stepping away from the sense of attack. As you step aside from the content of what is said, you can think more clearly about the information and your thoughts about it.

Step outside yourself to see *yourself* being criticized by the critic. Now see *your* responses. This psychological distance protects you from getting caught-up in the content. If you forget that "the map is not the territory," the story will hypnotize you. You will forget that words are not real, but just symbols that stand for and represent some referent. Stepping back from the content also gives you a larger perspective.

4) Draw the responsibility for and responsibility to line

Gain emotional distance by mentally drawing the sanity line, between *responsibility to and for.* Imagine behind the line, "Responsible *for* yourself and responsible *to* X." When someone comes in with some information that seems critical, imagine them standing on the other side of the line. Whatever they say is their response, not yours. They are responsible for what they say. Instead of *immediately* believing it, *just perceive it.* Perceive it as *their* thinking and believing, *their* opinions, and *their* mental maps. If it is theirs, don't make it yours.

Figure 22:6

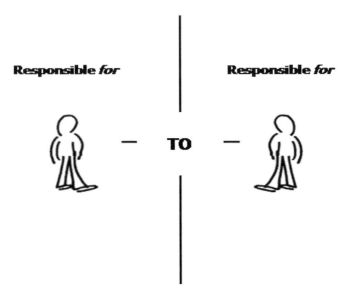

Use this distinction to stay calm, collected, and sane when under attack. Tell yourself the truth, *"Their ideas, words, and responses belong to them, not to me."* Don't be a thief who steals responsibility from them. You are *not* responsible *for* what comes out of them. At most, if you have a relationship to them, you are responsible *to* them. You may be responsible *to* treat them with respect, to affirm them, and to not hurt them, to listen, to respond, to care, to speak your truths, to reflect what you think about their responses, etc.

If they spew out hurtful words designed to push your buttons and "get" you, gain emotional distance by stepping back from it in the comforting realization that it comes from their side of the responsibility line.

Gain distance also by giving yourself permission to be *response-able*. If someone wants to act like a jerk; who are you to forbid them? It's their right. Release the need to control them. How they choose to respond is their choice. If you don't want certain responses, say so, make your request, and negotiate the relationship.

5) Re-represent the criticism and your distance from it.
Identify how you represent the insult, then shift it. Cue your brain to see the movie of the criticism by listening to it as if it comes from a mile away. Push your pictures back and put them on a movie screen a long way away. Imagine them behind a wall of clear plexiglass. Turn the movie into a black-and-white snapshot. Hear the criticism in Donald Duck's tonality. Or create a picture of yourself so you observe *you* in your internal pictures and someone criticizing you. Be a spectator and just witness it. By keeping the criticism at arm's length, you won't be so thin skinned about it.

6) Add meaningful reasons for being un-insultable.
Develop powerful reasons and compelling meanings for not responding defensively to criticism. For example, frame ignoring an insult as demonstrating a higher intelligence:

> "When a fool is annoyed, he quickly lets it be known. Smart people will ignore an insult" (Proverbs 12:16)

Solidly frame your sense of identity and dignity so you cannot become defensive. Frederick Douglas said this about insults:

> "A gentleman will *not* insult me, and no man not a gentleman

can insult me."

Meta-state yourself with that great line. Meta-state yourself with appreciation for feedback taking a more humorous and light-hearted attitude toward yourself. Over-seriousness will get you caught up into content and defensiveness. Prepare yourself to receive criticism with a thank you.

> "Thanks! I appreciate you bringing this to my attention. This could possibly benefit me. How thoughtful of you!"

If you can't thank your critic for *what* he says, thank him for his concern or for her straightforwardness.

> "So you think I'm a sorry mess for a human being? Well, I do appreciate your honesty in telling me that, not everybody can do that. I appreciate that you didn't go behind my back."

If your critic criticizes with vague statements. "You turkey, you're so clumsy." Then, without any sarcasm, ask for more information.

> "Would you tell me more? Just how do you think I exist as a turkey, or why I am clumsy? How specifically do I remind you of a turkey?"

If the comment hits its target and is right on in pinpointing a real fault, thank your critic for his or her courage, then apologize. It's just an error, nothing more. Face your errors forthrightly with courage to improve things.

7) Evaluate criticism for its value.
Evaluate criticisms for how they can help you. Use them for learnings, then, let them go. Stay true to your values, principles, relationships, and visions. Abraham Lincoln used this frame:

> "If I were to try to read, much less to answer, all the attacks made on me, this ship might as well be closed for any other business. I do the very best I know how—the very best I can; and I mean to keep on doing so until the end. If the end brings me out all right, then what is said against me won't matter. If the end brings me out wrong, then ten thousand angels swearing I was right would make no difference."

After the criticism simply *move on*. When severely criticized, Paul, an early proponent of Christianity, described his response to criticism as irrelevant. He framed human judgment as inadequate, fallible, and beside the point—irrelevant. So he just did not give criticism much weight.

> "This is how one should regard us, as servants of Christ . . . With me *it is a very small thing that I should be judged by you* or by any human court. I do not even judge myself. I am not aware of anything against myself, but I am not thereby acquitted. It is the Lord who judges me." (I Corinthians 4)

8) Refuse the push-shove dynamic.
Defuse the criticism by not pushing back when you are pushed by criticism. As you acknowledge the person's state, feelings, words, without pushing back, you interrupt the push-shove interaction. This will give you time to decide on how to respond. Often, it is the speed and surprise of a criticism that sucks you into push-shove matches, "I can't believe he said that!"

> "So you think I'm a dirty-rat; what gives you this impression?"

Curiously explore:

> "It sounds like you have some things on which you really want to set me straight. Is that your position? Do you feel that this is your best choice in accomplishing this? What do you specifically hope to accomplish by this encounter? How do you expect me to respond to you as you express yourself in this way? I would like to hear you out, would you consider expressing yourself so that I could feel that you offer this within a context of care and respect?"

Hold your critic responsible by asking him what he wants:

> "If I do this wrong, what do you suggest I ought to do? Will you help me to do it right?"

If the critic is just unloading his or her negative states, this will make that clear.

9) Discern between language and meanings.
Frame criticism itself as just words. "When people criticize, they merely say words that I don't like." I like to frame insult as a strong indication that the person really needs a nap(!).

Hear the criticism out as words, then explore its meanings knowing you don't have to accept any meaning that isn't accurate or useful. Evaluate it to determine if it is true or false, accurate or erroneous, useful or irrelevant. *Hearing* is only step one. After you do that, then you can dismiss it safely knowing that you have taken from it everything useful. If you dismiss it outright before thoughtful consideration you may miss something valuable.

So, Let the Meta-Stating Begin
Criticism is not the worst thing in the world. It is just information communicated that reflects another person's opinions. As you refuse to over-load it with too much meaning, treat it simply information from another person's model of the world.

When you meta-state yourself with all of these resources, you become an explorer of the critique. This will enhance your personal development, objectivity, and convey the sense that you're not afraid of reality. The un-insult-ability that emerges from your meta-stating gives you an empowering center out of which to live, think, relate, work, and respond. This will make life more fun and more of an adventure. It will support resilience and create an inner sense of peace—unshakable by criticism.

Summary
- The process of meta-stating resources builds up the meta-structures of beliefs, decisions, permissions, identities, etc. that unleash new potentials for living more fully and humanly.

- The four meta-states described here—proactivity, self-esteem, inner serenity, and un-insultability—are four richly layered meta-states that you can now create. As you now set the frames that establish these empowering attitudes, they will cascade downward into your daily expressions.

End Notes:
1. See the book, *Instant Relaxation* (1999) for the process of accessing your core relaxed state.

2. See *Art of Defusing* (1992) and *Defusing Hotheads and Other Cranky People training manual* (1998). Metamorphosis Journal, 1994, "*Mastering 'Verbal Abuse' and Semantic Reactions.*

Appendix A

JOURNALING STATES

Developing State Awareness Through
Monitoring States

As you think about your states, what kind of states (e.g., moods, emotions, attitudes, dispositions) have you experienced today? To discover your regular states, journal them from the time you get up and throughout the day. What state did you find yourself in when you woke up this morning? Tired? Grumpy? Alert? An excited "bring on the day" state? A hesitant and whinny "Why do I have to go to work? state? Would you call the state you first experienced an up one or a down one?

It's not uncommon to find it difficult to journal states when you first begin. Even the process of naming your states may prove challenging. At first you may struggle developing your own vocabulary of your states. "What do I call this state?"

To facilitate the ability to label on your state, use the components make up the state's internal form. Consider the quality of your *mind* (i.e., alert, curious, wondering, slow, etc.), the condition of your *emotions* (i.e., angry, stressed, upset, joyful, pleased, in love, etc.), and the state of your *body* (i.e., tired, rested, relaxed, tense, etc.). Be assured, awareness of your states and these components will grow with practice.
- How long did you stay in the first state?
- When did you shift to another?
- What would you call that state?
- What factors (events, people, words, situations) played a part in shifting your state?

Draw circles or bubbles to indicate your states. Then put the name on the bubbles that you moved in and out of throughout the day as you register your state of mind, emotion, and body.

Because we are always in some state of consciousness, recognizing and

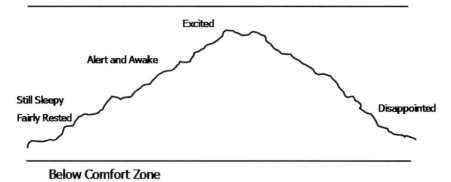

Above Comfort Zone

Excited

Alert and Awake

Still Sleepy

Fairly Rested

Disappointed

Below Comfort Zone

calibrating to these states enable us to develop more skill at managing them. This is also true for how we all constantly shift states. How much awareness do you have about the states you go in and out of throughout a day? How much awareness do you have about the constant changing and shifting of activities, stimuli, interactions, etc. that evoke different states in you?

How much pleasantness or unpleasantness do you experience from the states you visit in a day's time? How jarring or smooth do you experience the shifting of your states? Which are your favorite states (playful, energetic, excited, relaxed, curious, etc.)? Which are your most disliked states (anger, fear, dread, terror, tiredness, anxiety, etc.)? In which states do you feel the most resourceful? The least resourceful?

Detecting, identifying, and evaluating states requires that you step aside from those states to use your reflexive consciousness and choose those states that enhance your life. This will develop your state-management skills.

States may last thirty minutes, two hours, or fifteen seconds. Sometimes when you don't pay attention to your states it seems like one or two "regular" kind of states may last all day. Due to habituation, states can norm out so that you don't even notice them. Then they have little by which you can distinguish them. Because most of your states will be in the middle of your emotional comfort zone, they will be difficult to describe. Lacking either positive or negative intensity, they seem *invisible*.

States in the middle become invisible to inspection as does habituated states. Step into any state often and regular enough and, after awhile, you won't notice it. As your irritable, cynical, or sarcastic state will fade from awareness, it becomes your attitude — your frame of mind. Others will detect it long before you do. You will be tempted to confuse habituated states with "reality."

Shifting state seems to occur primarily in response to people and things in your environment. The phone rings. Someone says something. You have to go somewhere. You turn on TV. Your son or daughter comes home from school. At the phenomenal level, your states seem to have a life of their own. External stimuli seem to "cause" them. They do not *seem* to arise by the exercise of your will or the meanings that you ascribe to things.

Yet *states inevitably and inescapably reflect your consciousness.* If you shift to a fearful state, guess what will be your state of mind and the kind of thoughts you'll experience? Full of angry thoughts? No. Full of wonder and awe ideas? No. Full of thoughts of love and compassion? No. Your fearful states *always* relate to fear thoughts. Your anger states *always* relate to anger thoughts. Joyful states *always* relate to joyful thoughts.

Appendix B

THE FOUR META-DOMAINS OF NLP

Would you like four pathways for the adventure into subjective experience? Great! Then welcome to the four meta-domains. These domains give you four models to describe the same thing—*subjective experience*. You now have *four* avenues for exploring, playing, and transforming human experiences and even "personality." And these four meta-domains describe the structural genius of NLP and Neuro-Semantics.

First Meta-Domain: The Meta-Model
The Meta-Model of language identifies the form and structure of mental mapping and so provides an understanding of the linguistic magic. It provides you the structure of precision as you move from the primary representational domain of sensory-based information and language to the meta-linguistic domain of evaluative words.

Language works by eliciting sensory-based references. If you can *representationally track* the words to the theater of your mind and see the specifics, the words are sensory based. If you have to fill in because the words do not give you the specifics, then ask more questions.

Second Meta-Domain: Meta-Modalities (Cinematic Movie Features)
The qualities of the modalities of your inner movies—your sights, sounds, sensations, smells, etc. were mistakenly conceptualized as a lower or "sub" level. Because they are smaller facets of each representational system, Bandler, Andreas, and others jumped to the conclusion that they were at a lower logical level or "sub-modalities."

But the cinematic features of your mental movies are not at a lower logical level, they are a higher logical level. Even to detect the features of close/far, bright/dim, loud/soft, big/small, etc. *you have to go meta*. You have to step back to observe them or to change them by editing those features of construction. The "sub" metaphor was a mistake.

It is in moving to a higher logical level that you can now *edit* and *encode* your movies. You step back from the movie and edit in or out various cinematic features so that the movie will do different things to you. This explains why the "sub-modality" shifts, tracking over, and altering are so powerful in many NLP patterns.

So while there's no question about the power of re-editing your inner movies, there is a question with the metaphor. Because Bandler postulated them as "sub" and attempted to develop a whole new field in Design Human Engineering (DHE). I say *attempted* because after twelve years he gave up on it. It led nowhere and produced nothing new. See my critique, *Ten Years and Still no Beef,* www.neurosemantics.com.

Third Meta-Domain: Meta-Programs
Meta-Programs are your structured ways of perceiving. They govern your everyday thinking-and-feeling at a meta-level as *perceptual filters.* You create meta-programs form your meta-states. It begins with the state of your thinking style which you then over-generalize so it becomes your way of perceiving. The thoughts you reflexively apply to yourself habituate to become the way you see things. As they then coalesced into your neurology, they get into your muscles and eyes as meta-programs. When you think globally and sort for the big picture consistently and regularly, you habitually default to this state. Eventually global thinking and feeling become your *frame of mind* or meta-program.

Fourth Meta-Domain: Meta-States
The fourth meta-domain obviously is the Meta-States model that describes your self-reflexive consciousness as you create states about your states.

Originally Bob Bodenhamer and I put these together to create a Systemic NLP Model. We played with this for a year or so seeking to use the meta-domains as a way to unify everything in NLP. Then I happened upon using the Frame Games framing (*Winning the Inner Game*) and that led to the *Matrix model* which we now use as the Systemic NLP Model in Neuro-Semantics.

Today we use and describe the four meta-domains as the mechanisms within the Meaning Matrix of the Matrix Model giving us four ways to think about the creation of meaning. Use them together and you can track how you create your experiences. Use them as redundant systems (language, representation, perception, and holarchical levels), and you can follow the neuro-semantic energy of meaning through your mind-body system or another's.

Appendix C

META-STATES BOOKS

What's Your next *Meta-States* Book?
Beyond this first book there are numerous books on Meta-States. Now that you know the origin, theory, foundation, and application of Meta-States, there are other works to explore.

Winning the Inner Game (2006, originally, *Frame Games,* 2000) is a good place to begin. These meta-states are the inner games you play in your mind as your frames which lead to your outer games of performances. These user-friendly books take the levels of thought in Meta-States and views them as the frames that make up the rules for the games you play.

Dragon Slaying: Dragons to Princes (1996/ 2000) more fully develops Chapter 21 as it applies Meta-States to therapy for personal development. The book is based upon some of the first workshops using Meta-States.

Mind-Lines: Lines for Changing Minds (1997, 2006) is a book on influential language. I used Meta-States to re-model the NLP "Sleight of Mouth" patterns. This led to seven kinds of framing: deframing, reframing, counter-framing, pre-framing, post-framing, analogous framing, and outframing. Today the Mind-Lines model offers a format for conversationally meta-stating as you reframe meaning which transforms mind, emotion, and behavior.

Secrets of Personal Mastery (2000) applies Meta-States to being able to step in and out of "the zone"—the focus state of genus, at will. This is the foundational work for the APG workshop (Accessing Personal Genius).

Meta-Stating Magic (2000) is a spiral book of 40 meta-state patterns originally published in the *Meta-States Journal.*

Personality Ordering and Disordering Using NLP and Neuro-Semantics (2000, Hall, Bodenhamer, Bolstad, and Hamblett) is an academic book being used in Universities that applies Meta-States and NLP to the structure of personality and how you can order or disorder "personality" itself.

States of Equilibrium by John Burton, Ph.D. integrates Meta-States with Developmental Psychology so you can create balance and wholeness in your life.

THE MATRIX
AND MIND-LINE MODELS

In Neuro-Semantics we have two additional models that are derived from *Meta-States*.

The Matrix Model
A systemic model designed to think holistically and systemically about all of the models, processes, and patterns in NLP and Neuro-Semantics. Based on the cognitive-behavioral sciences and psychologies, the Matrix Model is comprised of three *process* matrices and five *content* matrices.

The three process matrices describe *how* we create our sense of reality through our map-making processes. We divided these into the following:
> *Meaning:* The levels of constructing "meaning" through meta-stating layers of thoughts and feelings.
> *Intention:* The thoughts in the back of the mind about our purpose, agenda, motivation, and direction.
> *State*: The embodied experience of meanings and intentions, the grounding of the matrix as we incorporate our maps.

The five content matrices identify some of the developmental content that arises over the years of our lives as we create meaning about five categories that are especially close to our sense of self.
> *Self:* The meanings, intentions, and states that we develop and create about our identity, sense of self, worth, value, "being."
> *Power:* The meanings, intentions, and states that we develop and create about our powers, abilities, talents, skills, and competencies for coping and mastering life's challenges.
> *Others:* The meanings, intentions, and states that we develop and create about our relationships, connections with others, social skills and abilities, beliefs about people and human nature.
> *Time:* The meanings, intentions, and states that we develop and create about how we measure and detect previous, current, and future events, what we call "time," thereby giving us our temporal self.
> *World:* The meanings, intentions, and states that we develop and create about all of the universes of meaning that we navigate as we move through life in our interactions with people and events.

The Matrix Model (2002) is now available as a 400 page book ($30).

The Mind-Lines Model

A model about the multiple ways that we can set frames of meaning about things resulting in seven directions for framing: reframing, deframing, counter-framing, pre-framing, post-framing, outframing, and analogous framing. Since linguistic meaning is one of the key ways that we create meaning, the *Mind-Lines Model* is a linguistic model for working with the *lines* (the sentences, statements, beliefs, explanations, reasons, etc.) that form and change our minds.

Mind-Lines, arose using the reflexivity of Meta-States to provide a model which gives structure and form to the old NLP "sleight of mouth" patterns. Considering a statement of belief, explanation, understanding, decision, excuse, objection, etc. as an "X," then we can understand the seven forms of mind-lines in the following ways:

> *Reframing:* Statement X does not mean Y, it means Z.
>
> *Deframing:* Statement X is made up of these many sensory-based components. Seen in this way, X is de-constructed.
>
> *Counter-framing:* When X is applied back to the speaker or listener, it means A or B.
>
> *Pre-framing:* The things that brought about X are these factors.
>
> *Post-framing:* As we think consequently into the future the consequences that will result from X are these.
>
> *Out-framing:* When you view X through the lens of M, N, O, etc., it now has an entirely different look.
>
> *Analogous Framing:* When you view X in terms of various metaphors, stories, examples, and other ways of how we can compare what it is like, it looks like J, K, and L.

Mind-Lines: Lines for Changing Minds (2006, fifth edition) is available ($25).

DIAMOND OF CONSCIOUSNESS

"Logical levels" are not *things* and are therefore not *externally real*. They are also *not* a hierarchy of responses to each other. Any and every "logical level" is at the same time every other "logical level." A better way to think and talk about these meta-processes and psycho-logical layering of our thoughts and feelings is to think of them as facets of the diamond of

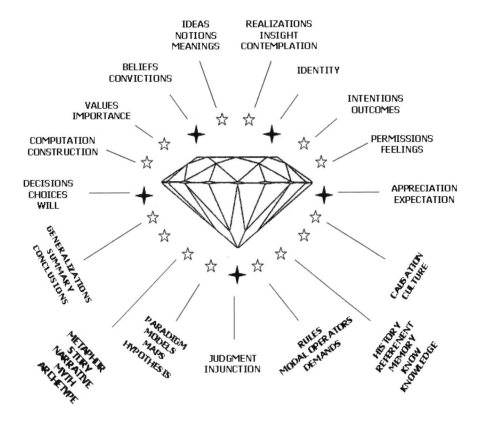

consciousness and experience.

GLOSSARY

Accessing Cues: the cues we use in tuning our bodies for specific processing patterns as we breathe, move, posture, gesture and move our eyes. Accessing cues reflect the representation systems we're using.

A$_d$: Auditory digital, the digital representations of our words, symbols, and language.

As-If Frame: Imagining something and pretending as if it is present and real, thinking "as if" a goal has already occurred, a creative problem-solving experiment that imagines beyond an obstacle.

Analogue: Continuously variable between limits, like a dimmer switch for a light, a watch with hands. An analogue varies.

Analogue Marking: using one of the senses to *mark out* and give special attention to a word or phrase. A way to simultaneously layer multiple messages. Calibrating to gestures, hand, arm and/or eye movements, tone and/or pitch shifts that a speaker uses to emphasize an idea.

Anchoring. process of linking a stimulus with a response, an user friendly form of Pavlovian conditioning, connecting an automatic unconditioned response with a conditioned one.

Association: associating into an experience, mentally seeing, hearing, and feeling from inside an experience, in contrast with dissociated (seeing a representation from the outside, as a spectator).

Backtrack: reviewing, summarizing, feeding back to another responses, words, posture, tonality, etc. The Backtrack Frame checks understanding to insure accurate hearing.

Beliefs: confirmation thoughts about thoughts, a meta-level frame of confirmation and validity about an idea, understanding, or concept, can be conscious or unconscious, a generalization or concept about causality, meaning, self, others, behaviors, identity, etc.

Calibration: tuning in to another's state of mind, emotion, and body by noticing the non-verbal signals and relating to words, expressions, etc.

Chunking: the size of a piece of information, from large to small, moving up and/or down the levels. *Chunking up:* going up to higher abstractions, inductive thinking. *Chunking down:* going down to more specificity and details, deductive thinking.

Complex Equivalence: a linguistic distinction, equating two statements as if having the same meaning, e.g. "He is late; he doesn't love me." Taking an external behavior (E.B., "late") and making that equivalent to an internal state (I.S., "doesn't love").

Congruence: a state of unity or harmony wherein our thoughts and feelings are aligned and working together, thoughts and feelings correspond. What one says corresponds with what one does, both signals match.

Content: the specifics details that answers *"what?"* Contrasts with process or structure.

Content Reframing: giving a statement another meaning, "What else could this mean?" This doesn't mean X, it means Y.

Context: the setting, frame, or process in which events occur and provides meaning for content.

Context Reframing: changing the context of a statement, "Where would this be an appropriate response?" Meaning depends on context, meaning changes with the context changes.

Criteria: values, standards, what we find important in a particular context.

Deep Structure: term from Transformational Grammar indicating the complete linguistic form from which the surface structure derives.

Deletion: the missing portion of an experience either linguistically or representationally.

Digital: varying between two states in an either/or fashion, a light switch is either on or off. A digital watch contains numbers.

Dissociation/ Dissociating: stepping apart from, and out of, an experience, seeing or hearing something as if from a spectator's point of view. An unspecified verb about a style of thinking and emoting.

Distortion: a modeling process, inaccurately representing something in neurology or linguistics, typically creates limitations, can create

resources.

Downtime: not in sensory awareness, "down" inside one's mind seeing, hearing, and feeling thoughts, memories, awarenesses, a light trance state with attention focused inward.

Ecology: the question about the overall relationship between idea, skill, response and larger environment or system. Internal ecology: the overall relationship between person and thoughts, strategies, behaviors, capabilities, values and beliefs. The dynamic balance of elements in a system. Checking to see if something fits, is useful, productive, enhancing.

Elicitation: evoking a state by word, behavior, gesture or any stimuli. Gathering information by direct observation of non-verbal signals or by asking meta-model questions.

Elicit a Meta-State: How do you feel about feeling contempt toward yourself? What do you think about these reactive thoughts and feelings? Using meta-questions to uncover higher frames and multiple levels.

Eye Accessing Cues: movements of the eyes in certain directions indicating visual, auditory or kinesthetic thinking (processing).

Epistemology: study of how we know what we know.

First Position: perceiving the world from your own point of view, associated, one of the three perceptual positions.

Frames: Frames-of-Reference, the ideas, experience, people we reference as we create meaning, conceptual contexts. A meta-level, a way of perceiving something (Outcome

Frame, "As If" Frame, Backtrack Frame, etc.).

Future Pace: mentally practicing or rehearsing an event before it happens; a key process for ensuring permanency of an outcome.

Generalization: a modeling process by which we take one specific experience and have it represent a whole class of experiences.

Gestalt: German term designating *an overall configuration,* something "more than the sum of the parts," an impression.

Incongruence: state of conflict involving incongruent messages and the lack of alignment so that one has reservations.

Installation: putting a new mental strategy inside mind-and-body so it operates automatically, we install via anchoring, leverage, metaphors, parables, reframing, future pacing, etc.

Internal Representations: internal "presenting" of information "again" which we saw, heard, felt, etc. on the outside.

Kinesthetic: sensations, feelings, tactile sensations on surface of skin, proprioceptive sensations inside the body, includes vestibular system or sense of balance.

Languaging: use of any symbol system to represent information (RS, word, mathematics, music, icons, etc.)

Linguistic cues for meta-states: about, beyond, of, concerning, regarding, transcend, class, category, in terms of, bring to bear upon, quotations, etc.

Linguistics environments: The words and linguistic environments that enable us to create, communicate, or glue together a meta-state. Language which gives stability, strength, and permanence to meta-states. As linguistically driven phenomenon, meta-states need linguistic structures.

Logical Level: a higher level, a level *about* a lower level, any meta-level which drives and modulates a lower level.

Loops/ Looping: a circle, cycle, a story, metaphor or representation that goes back to its own beginning, so that it loops back (feeds back) onto itself. *An open loop:* a story left unfinished. *A closed loop:* finishing a story. In strategies: loop refers to getting stuck in a set of procedures with no way out, the strategy fails to exit. In a closed system, the thoughts and feelings go round and round so that the state or states loop back onto themselves, repeating the same thoughts-and-emotions over and over as if caught in a non-ending loop.

Map: model of the world, representation built in brain and nervous system by abstracting from experiences; neurological and linguistic maps, internal representations.

Matching: adopting facets of another's outputs (behavior, words, etc.) to enhancing rapport.

Meta: above, beyond, about, a higher logical level.

Meta-modeling: using the linguistic distinctions and questions of the Meta-Model to specify information by indexing what, when, how, etc. to de-construct a negative morbid state.

Meta-awareness: awareness of a state about a state, self-reflective consciousness of other thoughts-and-feelings.

Meta-State: a mental or emotional state of awareness *about* another state, e.g., fear of fear, joy of anger, sadness about fear. A higher level frame-of-reference *about* another internal experience. A higher state of mind encoded by the meta-representation system of words, symbols, language, linguistics, etc. Conscious awareness *reflecting back* onto itself to create thoughts-and-feelings at a higher level. Mind attending to mind, a conceptual state.

Meta-stating: (as a verb) bringing a mind-body state to bear upon another state, applying one meta-level thought or feeling to another, accessing a higher logical level to organize, drive, & modulate a lower state.

Meta-Model: a linguistic model with distinctions identifying language patterns that obscure meaning along with challenges or questions to clarify imprecise language (ill-formedness) and reconnect to sensory experience.

Meta-Programs: the mental or conceptual programs for sorting and paying attention to stimuli, perceptual filters that govern attention.

Metaphor: indirect communication by a story, figure of speech, parable, similes, allegories, etc. implying a comparison, a "carrying (phorein) over" (meta) of a story, event, or experience to another, used primarily to bypass conscious resistance.

Milton Model: the language patterns Milton Erickson used in hypnotizing or inducing trance states in a non-authoritarian manner; using the inverse of the Meta-Model he would speak in artfully vague ways that would pace a person's experience to access unconscious resources.

Mirroring: precisely matching portions of another's behavior for the purpose of building rapport, becoming a mirror image of another's physiology, tonality and predicates.

Mismatching: offering different patterns of behavior to another, breaking rapport for the purpose of redirecting, interrupting, or terminating a conversation.

Modal Operators: *modus operandi,* mode of operation, linguistic distinctions indicating the "mode" a person uses in operating in the world: modes of necessity, impossibility, desire, possibility, etc., indicated by specific predicates (e.g., can, can't, possible, impossible, have to, must).

Model: a description of how something works, a generalized, deleted or distorted copy.

Modeling: process of observing and replicating the behaviors of others, process of discerning the sequence of representations and behaviors that enable someone to accomplish a task, the basis of accelerated learning.

Neuro-Linguistic Programming: the study of excellence, a model of how people structure their experience, the structure of subjective experience and *human programming* in thinking, emoting, and behaving in *neurology.*

Nominalization: a linguistic distinction of naming a process, a process or verb turned into an (abstract) noun, a process frozen in time.

Outframing: going outside and above all frames to create new frame-of-reference.

Pacing: method for creating rapport by joining a person's model of the world, saying what fits with and match the person's language, beliefs, values, current experience, etc.

Perceptual Positions: one's point of view, seeing, hearing, and experiencing the world from out of one's own eyes, ears, and skin, first position, associated, second position, taking a point of view from another person's perspective, third position, stepping out and away from the players in a conversation and viewing things from a neural or system perspective.

Predicates: what we "assert" or "predicate" about a subject, sensory based words indicating a particular representations (visual predicates, auditory, kinesthetic, unspecified).

Permeation of meta-states: The process of higher states of cognitive phenomena (e.g., thoughts, ideas, understandings, beliefs, values, decisions) permeating down through the levels. The transformation and pervasiveness of meta-states involve the higher frames governing the lower ones.

Presuppositions: ideas that we have to take for granted for a communication to make sense, assumptions.

Primary State: A state of mind-and-body awareness *about* some event or activity beyond the skin "out there" in the world. Corresponding to the primary emotions, primary states include fear/anger, sad/glad, relax/tense, attraction/aversion, etc.

Reframing: Changing a frame or context to give events, words, behaviors new and different meanings.

Representation: an idea, thought, "presentation" of information in some form, sensory-based (VAK) or evaluative based information (words, symbols).

Representation System: how we mentally code information using the sensory systems of sights, sounds, sensations, smells and tastes.

Resourceful State: the total neurological and physical experience when a person feels resourceful, confident, able to cope effectively.

Sensory acuity: intensely aware of the outside world, using the senses to make very finer and precise distinctions about the sensory information in the world around us.

Sensory based description: information directly observable and verifiable by the senses, see-hear-feel language that we can test empirically, in contrast to evaluative descriptions.

State: a state of mind- body hence *a mind-body state* driven by ideas and meanings. States generate an overall *feel* or gestalt, so we refer to them as *emotional states*. A holistic phenomenon of mind-body-emotions, mood, emotional condition, sum total of all neurological and physical processes within individual at any moment in time.

State Dependency: when in a state all of our learning, memory, perception, communication and behavior functions in a way dependent upon the state.

Strategy: the sequence of internal representations (VAK and words) that describe the process whereby we cognitively put our neurology (body, physiology, emotions) into a certain state. The structure of subjectivity ordered in a linear model of the Test, Operate, Test, Exit (TOTE).

Strategy analysis: The process used in NLP for tracking down the sequence of where the brain goes as it create its "programs" and "reality."

Submodality: the distinctions and features in each representation system which provides additional information about the *qualities* and *properties* of the VAK; not "sub" to the VAK, but actually meta; hence the higher frame that governs the semantics or meaning.

Surface Structure: the linguistic phrase from Transformational Grammar that describes the spoken or written communication derived from the deep structure by deletion, distortion and generalization.

Synesthesia: automatic link from one representation system to another, a V-K synesthesia involves seeing→feeling without a moment of consciousness to think about it.

Transcendental states: states that transcend the primary and common meta-states and which represent some of the highest states of mind and emotion, those often described as "spiritual" or "core states."

Technologies: The techniques, tools, procedures, and processes for working with, eliciting, altering, and handling human experiences.

Time-line: a metaphor describing how we represent the concept of "time," the sights, sounds, and sensations we use to encode our memories and imaginations.

Trance: a *transition* from the waking state to an altered state with an inward focus of attention, hypnosis.

Unconscious: everything not in conscious awareness, any representation system not attended to at the moment.

Unconscious meta-states: meta-states that operate beyond one's awareness, but whose driving and permeating presuppositions, epistemology, and paradigms powerfully effects one's primary states.

Universal quantifiers: a linguistic term for words that code things using "allness" terms (e.g., every, all, never, none), a distinction that admit no exceptions.

Uptime: state where attention and senses directed outward to immediate environment, all sensory channels open and alert.

Value: ideas, experiences, etc. which we treat as important or significant in a given context, a frame about what we believe is important and significant.

VAK: Visual, Auditory, Kinesthetic; the three primary modalities of thought.

Well-Formedness: something well structured in terms of form, e.g., outcomes, language mapping.

INDEX

BIBLIOGRAPHY

Andreas, Connirae; Andreas, Tamara (1994). *Core transformation: Reaching the wellspring within*. Moab Utah: Real People Press.

Andreas, Steve (1991). *"Virginia Satir: The patterns of her magic,"* Palo Alto, Ca.: Science and Behavior Books, Palo Alto, Ca.

Bodenhamer, Bobby G.; Hall, L. Michael. (1997). *Time-Lining: Patterns for adventuring in time*. Wales, United Kingdom: Anglo-American Books.

Bodenhamer, Bobby G.; Hall. L. Michael. (1999). *The user's manual for the brain: A comprehensive manual for neuro-linguistic programming practitioner certification*. UK: Crown House Pub.

Buscaglia. Leo F. (1982) *Living, loving, and learning*. NY: Ballatine Books.

Bandler, Richard; Grinder, John (1979). Ed. by Andreas, Steve. *Frogs into princes: NLP*. Moab, Utah: Real People Press.

Bandler, Richard. (1985). *Reframing: The transformation of meaning*. Moab, UT: Real People Press.

Bandler, Richard; Grinder, John. (1975, 1976). *The structure of magic:* Palo Alto, CA: Volumes I & II. Science and Behavior Books.

Bateson, Gregory. (1979). *Mind and nature: A necessary unity*. New York: Bantam.

Bateson, Gregory. (1972). *Steps to an ecology of mind*. New York: Ballatine.

Brandon, Nathan. (1969). *The psychology of self-esteem..* NY: Bantam Books

Bridoux, Denis; Merlevede, Patrick; Vandamme, Rudy. (1997). *Seven Steps to Emotional Intelligence*. Wales, UK: Crown House Publishing Limited.

Chong, Dennis; Chong, Jennifer. (1991). *Don't ask why*. Oakville, Ontario, Canada: C-Jade Publishing, Inc.

Covey, Stephen. (1987). *Seven habits of highly effective people*. NY: Simon and Schuster.

Csikszentmihalyi, Mahalyi. (1990). *Flow: The psychology of optimal experience*. NY: Harper Perennial, HarperCollins Publishers.

Dilts, Roberts; Grinder, John; Bandler, Richard; DeLozier, Judith; Camerion-Bandler, Leslie. (1980). *Neuro-Linguistic Programming, Volume I, The Study of the Structure of Subjective Experience*. Cupertino, Ca.: Meta Publications.

Dilts, Robert. (1983). *Applications of neuro-linguistic programming*. Cupertino CA: Meta Publications.

Dilts, Robert B. (1983). *Roots of neuro-linguistic programming*. Cupertino, CA: Meta Publications.

Dilts, Robert (1990). *Changing belief systems with NLP*. Cupertino, CA: Meta Publications.

Dobyns, Lloyd; Crawford-Mason, Clare. (1994). *Thinking about quality: Progress, wisdom, and the Deming philosophy.* NY: Random House.

Ellis, Albert and Harper, Robert A. (1976). *A new guide to rational living.* Englewood Cliffs, NJ: Prentice-Hall, Inc.

Frankl, Viktor (1953/1978). *The Unheard Cry for Meaning.* NY: Washington Square Press.

Grinder, John; Elgin, Suzanne. (1973). *Guide to transformational grammar.* NY: Holt, Rinehart and Winston, Inc.

Grinder, John; McMaster, Michael. (1983). *Precision: A new approach to communication.* Scotts Valley, CA: Grinder, Delozier & Associates.

Hall, L. Michael. (1987). *Motivation: How to be a positive force in a negative world.* Grand Jct. CO. Good News Encounters.

Hall, L. Michael. (1987). *Speak up, speak clear, speak kind: Assertive communication.* Grand Jct. CO: Encounters.

Hall, L. Michael. (1992-94). Korzybski's Neuro-Linguistic Training, *Anchor Point Associates*, May, 1992, Jan. 1993, June, 1994).

Hall, L.. Michael. (1980-1996). *Metamorphosis Journal.* Grand Jct., CO: E.T. Publications.

Hall, L. Michael. (1996/ 2000). *The Spirit of NLP: The process, meaning, and criteria for mastering NLP.* Carmarthen, Wales, England. Anglo-American Book Company Ltd.

Hall, L. Michael. (1996). *Defusing hotheads.* Grand Jct. CO: E.T. Publications.

Hall, L. Michael. (1996/2000). *Dragon slaying: Dragons to Princes.* Grand Jct. CO: E.T. Publications.

Hall, L. Michael; Bodenhamer, Bob. (1997). *Figuring out people: Design engineering using meta-programs.* Wales, UK: Anglo-American Books.

Hall, L. Michael; Bodenhamer, Bobby G. (1998, 2nd edition). *Mind-lines: Lines for changing minds.* Grand Jct. CO: E.T. Publications.

Hall, L. Michael. (1998). *The secrets of Magic: Communicational Excellence for the 21st century.* UK: Crown House Publ.

Hall, L. Michael; Belnap; Barbara. (1999). *The sourcebook of magic: A comprehensive guide to the technology of NLP.* UK: Crown House Publishers.

Hall, L. Michael; Bodenhamer, Bob. (1999). *The structure of excellence: Unmasking the meta-levels of sub-modalities.* Grand Jct. CO: E.T. Publications.

Holland, Norman N. (1988). *The brain of Robert Frost: A cognitive approach to literature.* NY: Routledge.

Horney, Karen. (1945). *Our inner conflict: A constructive theory of neurosis.* NY: W.W. Norton & Co.

Horney, Karen (1945). *Our inner conflicts: A constructive theory of neurosis.* New York: W.W. Norton Co. Inc.

Hyder, Quentin. (1971). *The Christian's handbook of psychiatry.* Old Tappan, NJ: Fleming H. Revell.

Jay, Jeffrey. (1991) "Terrible Knowledge," *The Family Therapy Networker,* Nov/Dec. 1991, pages 20-29.

Johns, E. Roy. (1975). *A model of consciousness.*

Johnson, Kenneth G. (1980). "Self-Reflexiveness in Therapy and Education," pages 95-108. *The Journal of Communication Inquirey.* Iowa City: University of Iowa.

Johnson, Wendell. (1946/ 1989). *People in quandaries: The semantics of personal adjustment.* San Francisco: International Society for General Semantics.

Korzybski, Alfred (1933/ 1994). *Science and Sanity: An Introduction to Non-Aristotelian Systems and General Semantics.* Lakeville, Conn: Institute of General Semantics.

Lakoff, George; Johnson, Mark. (1980). *Metaphors by which we live.* Chicago: Univ. of Chicago Press.

Lakoff, George. (1987). *Women, fire, and dangerous things: What categories reveal about the mind.* Chicago: Univ. of Chicago Press.

Laura M. Markowitz (1991). "After The Trauma," *The Family Therapy Networker,* Nov/Dec. 1991, (pp. 31-37).

Lederer, Debra; Hall, L. Michael. (1999). *Instant relaxation: Reducing stress at work and home.* Wales, UK: Crown House Publishers.

Lewis, Bryon A., Pucelik, R. Frank. (1982). *Magic demystified: A pragmatic guide to communication and change.* Portland, OR: Metamorphous Press, Inc.

Lewis, *C. S. (1943/ 1952) Mere Christianity. NY: Macmillan Publishing Co.*

Maltz, Maxwell. (1960/ 1974). *Psycho-cybernetics.* NY: Pocket Books

Maltz, Maxwell. (1961/1972). *The magic power of self-image psychology.* NY: Pocket Books.

Metacalfe, Janet; Shimamura, Arthur P. (1995) (Eds.). *Metacognition: Knowing about knowing.* Cambridge, MA: A Bradford Book, The MIT Press.

Maslow, Abraham. (1968). *Toward a psychology of being.* NY: Van Nostrand Co.

Markowitz, Laura M. (1991). Article. *New Family Networker.*

May, Rollo (1989). *The art of counseling.* NY: Gardner Press.

Miller, George. (1956). "The Magical Number Seven, Plus or Minus Two: Some Limits on Our Capacity to Process Information." *Psychological review, 63,* 81-97.

Miller, George; Galanter, Eugene; Pribram, Carl. (1960). *Plans and the structure of behavior.* NY: Henry Holt & Co., Inc.

O'Connor, Joseph; Seymour, John (1990). *Introducing neuro-linguistic programming: The new psychology of personal excellence.*UK: Mandala.

Overstreet, Harry and Bonaro; *"The Mind Alive,"* Norton Co. 1954.

Plutchik, Robert. (1962, 1991). *The Emotions: Facts, theories, and a new model.* Lanham, MD: University Press of America.

Poppel, Ernest (1985). *Mindworks: Time and Conscious Experience.* Translated from German by Tom Artin. Harcourt Brace Javanovich, Publishers, Boston.

Rank, Otto. (1936/1972). *Will therapy and truth and reality.* NY: Alfred A. Knopf.

Reisman, David. (1950). *The lonely crowd: A study of the changing American character.* Boston: Yale University Press.

Searle, John R. (1995). *The construction of social reality.* NY: The Free Press.

Selye, Hans, (1976). *The stress of life.* NY: McGraw-Hill Book Co.

Seligman, Martin P. (1990). *Learned Optimism.* New York: Alfred A. Knopf.

Smedes, Lewis (1983, Jan.). *Christianity Today,* "The Power To Change The Past."

Wolin, Sybil (1994). "Resilience: How Survivors of Troubled Families Keep the Past in its Place." Article in "Psychology Today" (Jan/Feb. 1992, page 36ff).

Watzlawick, Paul, Beavin, J.H., & Jackson, D.D. (1967). *Pragmatics of human communication.* New York: Norton.

Watzlawick, Paul. (1976). *How real is real?* New York: Basic Books.

Watzlawick, Paul. (1978). *The language of change.* NY: Basic.

Watzlawick, Paul. (1984). *The invented reality: How do we know what we believe we know? Contributions to Constructivism.* New York: Norton.

White, Michael; Epston, David. (1990). *Narrative means to therapeutic ends.* NY: W.W. Norton & Co.

Wilber, Ken. (1996). *A brief history of everything.* Boston MA: Shambhal.

Vailhinger, A. (1924). *The philosophy of 'as if': A system of the theoretical, practical and religious fictions of mankind.* Translated by C.K. Ogden. NY: Harcourt, Brace and Co.

AUTHOR

www.neurosemantics.com
www.meta-coaching.org
www.metacoachingfoundation.org
www.self-actualizing.org

Dr. L. Michael Hall earned his doctorate in Cognitive-Behavorial psychology from Union Institute University. He was a licensed professional counselor when he found NLP and began studying with Richard Bandler. Later he worked directly with Bandler, writing several books for him. In 1994 Dr. Hall discovered the Meta-States Model and with its acceptance by the International Association of NLP Trainers, that initiated Meta-States as a part of the NLP communication model.

Later it also launched Neuro-Semantics and the Neuro-Semantic movement. From Meta-States came numerous modeling projects: resilience, women in leadership, selling, writing, training, coaching, accelerated learning, defusing hotheads, wealth creation, and so on. And with the productiveness of the Meta-States model came numerous books, the Frame Game series, new trainings and training manuals, and the re-modeling of NLP itself.

Dr. Hall continues to model excellence and unique expertise, he is also an entrepreneur, and lives in Colorado. He is currently heading up the ISNS (International Society of Neuro-Semantics) and conducting trainings internationally. As a prolific author, and best seller in the field of NLP, he continues to write. His weekly articles appear on Neurons, the international egroup of Neuro-Semantics. Dr. Hall developer the Meta-Coach Training System with Michelle Duval and continues to train Meta-Coaching around the world.

Books by L. Michael Hall, Ph.D.

In NLP and Neuro-Semantics:
1) *Meta-States: Mastering the Higher Levels of Mind* (1995/ 2000).
2) *Dragon Slaying: Dragons to Princes* (1996 / 2000).
3) *The Spirit of NLP: The Process, Meaning and Criteria for Mastering NLP* (1996).
4) *Languaging: The Linguistics of Psychotherapy* (1996).
5) *Becoming More Ferocious as a Presenter* (1996).
6) *Patterns For Renewing the Mind* (with Bodenhamer, 1997 /2006).
7) *Time-Lining: Advance Time-Line Processes* (with Bodenhamer, 1997).
8) *NLP: Going Meta — Advance Modeling Using Meta-Levels* (1997/2001).
9) *Figuring Out People: Reading People Using Meta-Programs* (with Bodenhamer, 1997, 2005).
10) *SourceBook of Magic, Volume I* (with Belnap, 1997).

11) *Mind-Lines: Lines For Changing Minds* (with Bodenhamer, 1997/ 2005).
12) *Communication Magic* (2001). Originally, *The Secrets of Magic* (1998).
13) *Meta-State Magic: Meta-State Journal* (1997-1999).
14) *When Sub-Modalities Go Meta* (with Bodenhamer, 1999, 2005). Originally entitled, *The Structure of Excellence.*
15) *Instant Relaxation* (with Lederer, 1999).
16) *User's Manual of the Brain: Volume I* (with Bodenhamer, 1999).
17) *The Structure of Personality:* Modeling Personality Using NLP and Neuro-Semantics (with Bodenhamer, Bolstad, and Harmblett, 2001).
18) *The Secrets of Personal Mastery* (2000).
19) *Winning the Inner Game* (2007), originally *Frame Games* (2000).
20) *Games Fit and Slim People Play* (2001).

21) *Games for Mastering Fear* (with Bodenhamer, 2001).
22) *Games Business Experts Play* (2001).
23) *The Matrix Model: Neuro-Semantics and the Construction of Meaning* (2003).
24) *User's Manual of the Brain: Master Practitioner Course, Volume II* (2002).
25) *MovieMind: Directing Your Mental Cinemas* (2002).
26) *The Bateson Report* (2002).
27) *Make it So! Closing the Knowing-Doing Gap* (2002).
28) *Source Book of Magic, Volume II, Neuro-Semantic Patterns* (2003).
29) *Propulsion Systems* (2003).
30) *Games Great Lovers Play* (2004).

31) *Coaching Conversation, Meta-Coaching, Volume II* (with Michelle

Duval & Robert Dilts 2004, 2010).

32) *Coaching Change, Meta-Coaching, Volume I* (with Duval, 2004).

33) *Unleashed: How to Unleash Potentials for Peak Performances* (2007).

34) *Achieving Peak Performance* (2009).

35) *Self-Actualization Psychology* (2008).

36) *Unleashing Leadership* (2009).

37) *The Crucible and the Fires of Change* (2010).

38) *Inside-Out Wealth* (2010).

39) *Benchmarking: The Art of Measuring the Unquantifiable* (2011).

40) *Innovations in NLP: Volume I* (Edited with Shelle Rose Charvet; 2011).

41) *Neuro-Semantics: Actualizing Meaning and Performance* (2011)

Other books:

1) *Emotions: Sometimes I Have Them/ Sometimes They have Me* (1985)

2) *Motivation: How to be a Positive Influence in a Negative World* (1987)

3) *Speak Up, Speak Clear, Speak Kind* (1987)

4) *Millennial Madness* (1992), now *Apocalypse Then, Not Now* (1996).

5) *Over My Dead Body* (1996).